SELF DESIGN

First Sentient Publications edition 2006
Copyright © 2006 by Brent Cameron

Cover design by Kim Johansen
Book design by Timm Bryson

Library of Congress Cataloging-in-Publication Data

Cameron, Brent, 1947-
  SelfDesign : nurturing genius through natural learning / Brent Cameron, Barbara Meyer.-- 1st Sentient Publications ed.
    p. cm.
  ISBN 1-59181-044-2
  1. Free schools--United States. 2. Educational innovations--United States. I. Title: Self design. II. Meyer, Barbara, 1948- III. Title.

LB1029.F7C36 2005
371.04--dc22

                                                        2005025262

10 9 8 7 6 5 4 3 2 1

SENTIENT PUBLICATIONS, LLC
1113 Spruce Street
Boulder, CO 80302
www.sentientpublications.com

SELFDESIGN

Nurturing Genius Through Natural Learning

Brent Cameron

with

Barbara Meyer

SENTIENT PUBLICATIONS

I dedicate this work to
ilana and Barbara

to my daughter ilana
who inspired this work
and to Barbara
who has joined me in my life and work

and I would like to acknowledge:

the children—
ilana, now grown,
and Lia
for their enthusiasm and joy in life
and all the children and youth
in Wondertree, Virtual High, and SelfDesign
from whom I have learned so much

the parents—
Maureen, mother of ilana
and Barbara, mother of Lia
for their demonstration of nurturing
and to all the parents
who have supported us over the years

and colleagues—
Michael Maser
Kathleen Forsythe
and Renee Poindexter
for their vision and collaboration over these many years,
and to all my other colleagues,
learning consultants, and board members
for their ongoing dedication to a freedom to learn

and—
all my mentors
for their compassion and inspiration.

—Brent Cameron

To Brent
  for his constant visioning of love and possibility,
to Lia
  for her constant love,
and to my family,
  for gifting me with a love of learning
  and a deep devotion to the written word.

—Barbara Meyer

CONTENTS

PROLOGUE

Wondertree is a small learning center that has been thriving in Vancouver, British Columbia, for over twenty years and has seen hundreds of children walk into its welcoming environment. Much more than that, though, it is a grand experiment into the nature of human learning. It is a celebration of the passion and joy children experience when they are met in the positive, when they are supported in nurturing the special qualities of their being, rather than labeled for the characteristics that set them apart from others. Wondertree is about returning to children the sense of authority with which they were born, and its foundations are firmly set in honoring natural, emergent learning from a place of curiosity, enthusiasm, and community.

SelfDesign is the methodology that has been born of Wondertree, yet it is not a set methodology such as Waldorf or Montessori. Like the foundations of Wondertree, SelfDesign is created in an emergent fashion, spiraling from the center of each individual who uses it. It has been said that we never step into the same river twice, and in that manner we, as lifelong learners, bring an ever-changing set of experiences to each new learning moment. As the self evolves, the design of our lives reflects this proportional growth, and our plans and passions shift accordingly. This is the heart of the SelfDesign process.

The story of Wondertree is essentially a love story. It is about the love between father and daughter, between mentors and young people, and it is about children joyfully experiencing the very process of learning. Mostly, however, it is a rediscovery of how we can author our own lives, and it is a journey back to the self-love we must each create. If all the world's emotions can be placed within the two categories of fear and love, the former of constriction and the latter of expansion, then what better foundation than love for life's curriculum?

The doors of Wondertree are open to you in this book, and we hope you will sense the loving quality of the SelfDesign process as we demonstrate how it nurtures the unfolding of the infinite intelligence in each one of us.

—Barbara Meyer

PREFACE

When I was thirty years old, as I held my infant daughter in my arms and looked into her eyes, I sensed a deep engagement within the core of my being. In this act, I discovered the source of many years of yearning. I had found my home after three decades out in the world. In that first year, without uttering a word, my daughter communicated to me the meaning of life. I felt the bond of unconditional love.

My daughter, ilana, became my inspiration. Where Jean Piaget, the world's foremost child psychologist, had primarily studied the mental development of children, I found myself studying my daughter by intuitively connecting with her as a whole child. In our conversations and laughter, my individuality dissolved into the quality of shared experience. I rediscovered myself within the context of family. Observing my partner's mothering love, I felt encouraged to explore the nurturing domains of my own being. My daughter's joyful and enthusiastic experience of the world was the guiding principle of my newly discovered life's purpose. I was learning how to father, and I was fathering my own mentor.

Ilana's mother, Maureen, and I acknowledged our daughter as a whole human being and encouraged her to act as the author of her own life. Our willingness to consider our daughter as a legitimate representative of herself, regardless of her age, challenged the beliefs of friends and family. However, ilana's ongoing and consistent demonstration of integrity and clarity became our guiding principle. Over the years, the results of our commitment to this principle quieted even the most vocal critics.

Wondertree, our educational adventure, began because my partner and I listened to our daughter. We recognized her natural ability to make appropriate decisions about her life each and every day. From the day she was born we honored her as a competent and whole being. She clearly let us know what she wanted, and we clearly let her know what we wanted. We respected her and her needs, and she in turn learned to respect us and our needs. She modeled our style of listening and considering as we created an atmosphere of guidance and positive cooperation.

Ilana demonstrated her amazing capability as a human being, as a natural learner, and as a SelfDesigner, in the way that she learned to speak. According to psychologists, learning to talk is the most difficult neurological task we do in our lifetime. It is much harder than acquiring the skills to read or to do calculus or even to fly a plane. Yet ilana, in the first years of her life, joyfully learned to communicate sophisticated ideas and concepts to us, as do virtually all children.

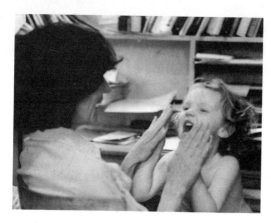

Out of the connection between ilana and her mother, I witnessed the emerging of a human being.

Ilana's comprehension of language and the world emerged naturally from her playful explorations. Because of my background as an educator, I assumed that I would be teaching my daughter about language, and yet she learned most of her words through modeling. From time to time she would ask a name for something, though even this process she directed. When she learned the name for something it was because it had some relevance to her at that moment. If a word had relevance to me and I attempted to teach it to her, she was often busy learning words that were more important to her in her world. I was so amazed at her natural way of gaining knowledge that I began to rethink everything I knew about learning. To her, learning was play. To me, her learning process became the seed for a new understanding, which some twenty years later I came to call SelfDesign.

We lived in the country for the first five years of ilana's life. When her best friend went to kindergarten, ilana decided to join her. During those first two weeks, however, I noticed that it was harder and harder for her to get out of bed in the morning. I sensed a growing reluctance about something, although ilana had no words for it yet.

One evening when I was tucking her into bed, she began describing her day. She told me that she was sitting on a swing in the school playground and it was a beautiful sunny morning. When the bell rang she realized that she did not really want to go inside. As she was swinging, she remembered her daycare, where she could sit in the sandbox and practice whistling all day long if she wanted. She remembered that having choices was really important to her, and she thought about how entering her new school made her feel as though she was giving up control of her life. "Dad," she said, "do I *have* to go to school?" I replied that she *could* go if she wanted to but that the most important thing was to listen to her heart and to do what was important to her. For the rest of that year she stayed at home with us, occasionally going to daycare when she chose.

Instead of Schooling, Wondertree

In January 1983 we moved to Vancouver, and ilana said she would be interested in going to a new daycare one day a week. We accompanied her to more than ten daycare centers before she met people who echoed her criteria of openness, choice, and trust.

In September, when I suggested to her that other children her age were going to school, she asked me, "Dad, is first grade a lot like kindergarten?" When I replied in the affirmative, she looked at me and said, "I think I already know who I would like as a teacher. Could you be my teacher? Can we keep on doing what we have been doing since I was little? Could we start a school here in our house? I will share all my toys."

Ilana and Jonathan, the second Wondertree learner, sharing their love for music. Twenty years later, she is still writing and singing her own songs.

It took my partner and me a couple of weeks to realize that we could and should support our daughter in her ongoing learning adventure. I made up posters and ilana and I went hand in hand to many businesses throughout the city to advertise our new school. When I phoned the local newspaper to ask them to do a story on our new program, the reporter was interested. He asked many questions and was finally convinced that this would make an exciting news story. Then he asked me how many students I had for this new school. When I told him, "One, my daughter," there was silence followed by a click as he hung up on me. Nobody came to the first meeting I called, and I stood in an empty meeting hall. Two weeks later at the second meeting I advertised, one man showed up, and after a lengthy conversation he agreed to bring his son to my house the next day. And so it began, a very humble start for Wondertree.

In my wildest dreams I could not have imagined what would happen in the growth of this program over the next two decades. From the foundation of the Wondertree Learning Center we developed Virtual High, a corresponding program for high schoolers. Throughout the years both programs have been open-ended, emerging from the curiosity and collective efforts of all involved in the learning community, and we have explored areas far beyond the usual educational realms. Our learners have traveled the world and accomplished some incredible things, both as individuals and in groups.

As a modest example of the notice we have received throughout the years, four of our youth went to Findhorn, Scotland, to attend the global eco-village network conference in 1995. (The work of our eco-village group is included later in the book.) There they met two writers, a husband-and-wife team, who were researching ecological and innovative projects around the world for an upcoming book. About a year later these two researchers visited the Virtual High program and chose it as the focus of their chapter on education because they felt it was the most important learning initiative in education anywhere.

Besides recognition by visitors from around the world, we have won numerous local, national, and international awards for our leading-edge projects. Over the years hundreds of people have come to visit our programs, and we have inspired many to start their own as educators or parents. In the meantime, Wondertree has kept its focus on natural learning and on enfranchising all its learners to design their own curricula from their enthusiasm to understand the world around them.

What you have in this book is the tip of the iceberg of the work, but hopefully a visible and comprehensible tip that will entice you to dive deep into the depth of the work of SelfDesign as it emerges from our websites and workshops.

As a comprehensive generalist I wanted to put everything in this book. After all, it is my life's work. For the past fourteen years I have presented a ten-day summer intensive each year. I tried to fit all of the new paradigm ideas, methodologies, and new learning technologies into the course. Although the participants were thrilled and transformed, they were exhausted. I also noticed that it took the graduates of the intensive who came to work in the Wondertree program at least another two years to integrate and really begin to understand the nature of the SelfDesign work. This book is our first attempt to simplify the ideas and spread the information out over a larger time frame.

I have learned to appreciate that it is a very difficult task to change the fundamental assumptions and beliefs upon which our lives are built. As Douglas Harding so aptly states, unless we have accurate answers to the most fundamental questions about who we are, then we can, and definitely will, get into trouble. This work has evolved through our attempts to develop and discover more accurate assumptions about who we are and how we work. While we certainly do not have all the answers, we have some good insights and maps that allow us to look deeply into the issues. Understanding that we come from a loving and open space is fundamental to this work. From this seed we grow as fulfilled human beings, with enthusiasm to engage in the world. The children have shown me this so clearly, so often. Let us come together to listen to and respect the children and to work together to model our own discoveries through living in harmony and respect. Thank you my mentors and friends.

—Brent Cameron

INTRODUCTION

Living in society is like walking a tightrope between two extremes. On one side is conservation and on the other side is innovation. Many valuable things have been irrevocably lost because of innovative changes. And likewise, many opportunities for change through innovation are lost because of the inertia of conservation. The secret lies in conserving what is worthwhile, letting go of what limits and harms our species, embracing beneficial ideas, and disallowing destructive changes. Wise decisions are not always easily made, as society is compromised between vested interest groups vying for either innovation or conservation to benefit the few rather than everyone.

The issue of balance operates as well in the realm of education. SelfDesign holds that living in alignment with our own natures creates the greatest balance. When our children are happy and fulfilled, we all benefit. When, as lifelong learners, we in the adult world are happy and fulfilled, society benefits. Social scientist Gregory Bateson has suggested that we are free to choose to work with nature or against it, but we always run into problems when we choose to work against it. Staying in alignment with nature, and especially with our own nature, gives us a significantly increased chance for harmony and life success.

SelfDesign reaches into the past, choosing living patterns that echo sustainable and traditional strategies that have historically brought forth fulfillment. It also reaches into the future through innovation, creating new and more efficient ways of living on earth through understanding deep truths about nature.

While schooling tends to condition people to live within a given situation, to cooperate with authority, and to think only within the box, the art and science of SelfDesign emerges from our creativity and our intelligence. Innovation arises out of creativity and compassion, allowing us to shift toward more natural and ecological models.

We would probably all agree that it would be absurd to glue wings onto a caterpillar and expect it to fly. Yet this is virtually what we are doing to children in school. In current culture, becoming an adult is largely focused on forgetting what it is to be a child. Our mechanical and manufactured world views growth and maturation as a production process. The factory model of schooling does not allow a natural transition from childhood into adulthood. Rather than giving children room for their gifts to uniquely unfold, the assembly-line schooling style glues wings onto caterpillars, trying to turn out a consistent "product." The curriculum is assigned grade by grade without regard for individual levels of development, and tests are used to determine whether the wings of knowledge have stuck.

The more natural way, a developmental way, is to allow our caterpillars to metamorphose into butterflies. Do we doubt that the caterpillar has what it needs to make its natural transition to the next stage? Then why doubt the child? Do we really believe that children do not have within them all that they need to unfold their inherent genius? Children are not empty vessels that need to be filled with knowledge in order to prove their ability or value. When we allow natural learning habits to flourish, our children can fly with new wings of understanding.

My Personal Evolution

At age twenty I began a ten-year quest to help me understand life questions that had not been answered, much less posed, during my formal education. Although I loved learning, coercive techniques aimed toward the competitive art of test-taking never made sense to me. My experience with sports was much the same. I loved to play, but as the focus turned more and more toward winning, I backed away from competition and turned to activities like skydiving and whitewater kayaking, where the challenge lay within myself.

In my schooling, the teachers who intimidated me daily felt like a conquering army, and the books I was made to read were filled with tales of winning and losing. As my school career extended into university years, I found that the majority of my professors were interested in playing intellectual games rather than facilitating understanding and discussion. Once again the competitive model played out in ways that necessitated my feeling "less than." I wanted out, and I wanted to regain the childhood sense of freedom that was now gone and almost forgotten.

Stepping beyond the mainstream and into the growing movement of alternative thinking, I began my personal evolution. The first book that turned my world inside out was *The Book: On the Taboo Against Knowing Who You Are*, by Alan Watts. Then I read *Summerhill School*, by A. S. Neill, which describes a free-school program in England. Neill's book ultimately influenced me to become a schoolteacher in order to change education. I began reading books from every culture and from every perspective possible, and my world changed as I looked through new eyes.

My life journey soon took on aspects of a river ride, with the current of exploration carrying me from one port to the next. Each stop along the way gave me a new way of looking at things, a shift in perspective that broadened my view. I experienced encounter groups, where I had my first opportunity to strip away my lifelong defenses and join with others in empathy and compassion. For the first time I felt heard and had the opportunity to see others step out of their societal disguises.

Yoga, meditation, tai chi, and Zen Buddhism soon followed, offering me focus and deep spaces of inner quiet. I read every esoteric book recommended by my growing network of fellow seekers. I investigated the native thinking and cultural practices with which I had felt aligned throughout my early years. Moving on, I explored the spirituality of the Baha'i and Quaker faiths, both of which exposed me to a unique political process based on contemplation and consensus.

During this period of my life, I attempted to teach in the public schools for two years. Once again I encountered the educational system's inherent limitations and controls, and although I loved working with the students, I realized that conventional teaching was not for me. The following year I was hired to teach in Calgary's first free school, which had been initiated by professors in the faculty of education at the university. The free school was a great adventure for us all, but I soon saw that I needed a deeper level of understanding before I could begin to offer a model for learning that reflected my germinating theories.

Throughout a decade of personal exploration, I found myself returning again and again to anthropologist Ruth Benedict's theories about people who worked together in "synergistic communities." Her life's research had been focused on discovering why the environments of some communities felt enriching and welcoming while others had a closed, self-protective atmosphere. Years of scientific study with societies throughout the world had helped her identify two qualities that separated these communities from one another. Put simply, she discovered that some societies were generous and others were greedy.

The generous societies were the ones where the most successful members readily gave to others. For example, in Native ceremonies on the western coast of North America, those with wealth gave their riches away each year in a ceremony called the potlach. This spirit of giving created a sense that everyone would be looked after, and it established an atmosphere of generosity throughout the community. Children experienced their world as a place of plenty. A beneficent society evolved.

In contrast, Benedict also identified cultures that were insecure, where the rich feared losing their wealth to others and social relationships were based on protection. Those with less had fewer choices and less influence in their society. There was an underlying sense of guardedness throughout these communities. Children absorbed this attitude and soon created their own pecking orders, emulating their parents from a base of fear.

Benedict's research was much on my mind as I looked at the environments we have created for our own children. Our modern school "communities" operate in the competitive atmosphere of a win/lose system, a context that diminishes the potential of the individual *and* the group, as each individual internalizes the fear of being "less than." Students are taught not to listen to their inner directives. They learn to work in isolation, being told that sharing information is "cheating." Adults in authority control the children, and the children do not trust themselves to know what is right and wrong. They are instructed to tell an authority if someone deviates from the rules. It's a small wonder that the pecking order of control remains such a focal point in our society. We train our children to follow this model for their first twelve years of school, and we do not give them the skills to make adulthood any different.

As mentioned, I had made a commitment upon my daughter's birth to create a different sort of life experience for her, one built from positive principles within a beneficent community. Because ilana's first five years were founded in self-authority and positive relational interaction, she was clear in her request for a learning experience that was aligned with her own developing values. When I said "yes" to her, I did not have the details of our coming adventure clearly in mind, but I had a sense of the form.

Wondertree's birth was founded on a question: "What are the optimum relationships and environment that will allow a child's potential to unfold naturally?" I had an intention to create an optimum learning environment for my daughter, but I did not yet have a well-crafted methodology. I was willing to do whatever was necessary to achieve the ideal, yet I was not sure of the steps toward achieving that goal.

As part of our learning experiment, I set out to see what would happen if we created not only a context for learning naturally but also a community context that would be safe and psychologically nourishing for each member. Beginning with a few simple principles from many years of research, I developed my understanding and methodology over the next twenty years.

Modern society appears to be in a profound dilemma about how to live in community and how to successfully organize the increasing complexity of society. On one hand, society is seduced by the myth of the "loner-achiever"— the high-performing individual who exemplifies the idea of winning by making those around him lose. This persona is largely created by mass media, and it is fostered by an educational system that emphasizes competition over cooperation.

On the other hand, we have the choice to look at ourselves in relational ways, coming together in community, sharing resources and knowledge, and finding excellence through group problem-solving. Segments of human history reflect this social choice, and indigenous cultures echo the harmony of cooperative living. The model of the loner-achiever is a more recent icon, contributing to the current phenomena of the isolated individual and the isolated nuclear family. Many of us today feel a deep need to find our way back to community, and we are unable due to our fractured and stratified society.

I have experienced both routes. I took the path of the loner as I was growing up, attending and then teaching in conventional schools as well as working in business. Then, fortunately, my daughter's simple request to learn from her father led me to pioneer Wondertree and then co-create Virtual High. This was the path of living in community. I observed cultural community on a larger scale as I traveled to places like Bali, where cooperative living is the norm. I now believe unequivocally that the path of living in community, and especially a learning community, offers far greater benefits to learners and society than the path of the loner–achiever.

Bali

One of the many sources from which I drew inspiration about the development of community was Ashley Montagu's *Learning Non-Aggression*. After extensive reading of anthropologists' research around the world, he noted their observations that communities tend to have a more harmonious atmosphere in cultures where children are consistently carried and touched. When I read in Gregory Bateson's work that "babies do not cry in Bali," I decided that firsthand experience of a non-Western community would help me grasp these roots of harmonious relationship. My family and I headed off to Bali for six weeks to study village life.

It is true that babies do not cry in Bali—and it is because they do not have to. People of this tiny Indonesian island are so attuned to their babies that basic needs are met before infants need to become tearful. I went to Bali thinking that I would observe the bonding and deep physical connection between mothers and infants. What I found instead was a continuous, community-wide readiness to respond to children's desires. Fathers, siblings, aunts and uncles, grandparents, and neighbors were always at hand to meet the needs of the village children.

I soon saw that taking responsibility for any child was just a small piece of a whole-community philosophy. Every villager took responsibility for holding the balance of the universe. If someone stole food, all members of the village would sit down to figure out how they had allowed this person to become so desperate. If I asked them for directions, they would put down whatever they were doing and walk me to the place I wanted to go. In this way the entire community maintained a harmonious balance.

This sense of mutual responsibility is demonstrated in their socio-politics as well. Bali maintains an elaborate system of water management for the rice crops that sustain the population. If it were a hierarchical society, the top-of-the-mountain residents with first access to the water would be allowed to use it as they desired, leaving whatever remained for those who live downstream. However, in this collaborative culture, those who are affected by the actions of others are consulted first, and they are invited to take part in the decisions that affect them. In this way, those most vulnerable have equal say to those most advantaged, and the needs of all are considered in the process.

This sense of mutual responsibility is demonstrated in their socio-politics as well. Bali maintains an elaborate system of water management for the rice crops that sustain the population. If it were a hierarchical society, the top-of-the-mountain residents with first access to the water would be allowed to use it as they desired, leaving whatever remained for those who live downstream. However, in this collaborative culture, those who are affected by the actions of others are consulted first, and they are invited to take part in the decisions that affect them. In this way, those most vulnerable have equal say to those most advantaged, and the needs of all are considered in the process.

At its base, the political context that makes people the priority in Bali is quite simple. All people have time to hold babies and attend to the needs of youngsters because all work is done in service of the community. Everyone feels cared for, and everyone cares for others. Decisions are made by consensus, with each person's needs being considered and included in the collaborative process. Residents own their own homes and land as part of the village collective, and few have debts. Work is done to feed and support the family and the village, in rhythm with the patterns of daily life. There is time to put priority on the nurturing of children, and there is time to respond to life in the moment.

My experiences in Bali profoundly affected me, as they confirmed the greater implications of our Wondertree experiment. When I got back to Vancouver, I realized that Bali had given me a living model for the fulfilling, collaborative community I was attempting to develop within our program.

Ilana with a young Balinese woman who included her in the making of sacred offerings for a village ceremony.

Wondertree: A New Learning Model

As a part of researching my master's thesis during the early Wondertree years, I studied the writings of many educational and community theorists in an attempt to conceptualize what I was observing at Wondertree. Something important, something out of the ordinary was happening in our program. I was looking at synergistic community, but I was not yet able to delineate the process.

Part of my effort went toward examining the free schools of the 1960s and '70s. I felt there were strong similarities between these programs and ours, and I wanted to closely examine the differences. The main ones, as best I could tell, lay in the fact that the free schools generally made their decisions based on majority rule, and disputes were settled through a student judiciary. This process still created winners and losers, playing into the right/wrong, either/or way of thinking that dominates many of our current social structures. While it seems appropriate to expose learners to that type of process as one of many, the Wondertree way is designed for a different outcome.

Our political process operates on a basis of wellness and balance. The process is informed by both family and individual wellness strategies drawn from the work of Virginia Satir and Milton Erickson, among others. The research I did with John Grinder and Neuro-Linguistic Programming became a fundamental basis for it. I learned basic language and process skills that had their foundation in business and therapy, and I adapted these skills to the context of a learning community. We want to create a win-win resolution from disputes, and we do so through a process of consensus which ensures that each person is heard and respected. We have modified well-known negotiation strategies used in business to allow children to achieve personal fulfillment in collaboration with others.

The second difference is in the learning process itself. In the free-school movement, children are taught when they are motivated to learn. This is clearly a different model than conventional schooling, and it is echoed in Wondertree. Yet when free-school children declare an area of interest, the approach for teaching resembles standard classroom methods.

In comparison, Wondertree works toward collaborative learning strategies and project-based experiences. As the basis of our design we have combined breakthrough theory from systems thinking, cybernetics, cognitive neuroscience, and the human-potential movement. Some of the Wondertree techniques parallel those of leading-edge businesses that are humanizing and optimizing the workplace. Visionary business consultant Peter Senge has spoken to the increased need for this type of model:

> We are so focused on our security that we don't see the price we pay: living in the bureaucratic organizations where wonder and joy have no place. Thus we are losing the spaces to dance with the ever-changing patterns of life. We need to invent a new learning model for business, education, healthcare, government and family. This invention will come from the patient, concerted efforts of communities of people invoking aspiration and wonder.

In Wondertree, we assist learners in supporting their unique designs for learning and living. Working specifically to develop self-observation skills, we help learners optimize their strengths and act as their own self-authorities. Our mission addresses wellness, balance, congruence, integrity, and fulfillment. The rights of the learner are held sacred, as is the experience of life as joyful and full of wonder. Because we hold positive relationships at the center of our program, our evolution has taken us beyond the free-school model and into a realm that more closely resembles the development of a healthy, synergistic learning community.

Virtual High: Synergistic Community Realized

After nine years of working with the children in Wondertree, several of our older learners (including my daughter, ilana) decided they wanted to see if they could succeed in high school. At about this time, I met Michael Maser, a teacher who was also disenchanted with the public educational system. In discussions together we began to form an idea for a new and unique learning experience for these students. Over the next six months, we began to tell our idea to anyone who would listen. When we were ready, we rented a four-hundred-seat theater to announce that we were starting a new learning system called Virtual High.

The night of the event, to our amazement and delight, over three hundred people came to watch and listen to our multimedia event. Even though our learning experience didn't offer a diploma, many learners still applied that night. At that point we had no building and no funding, just enthusiasm and sheer determination—plus the Wondertree experience. We began interviewing prospective learners, filling out funding proposals, and looking for a facility. By the time the program began in September, we had received a Vancouver Foundation grant and had been offered a four-story mansion in Vancouver to house our program. Virtual High was off and running. Just ten years after walking hand in hand with my daughter out into the world to start our learning adventure, we were beginning still another experiment.

The thirty teenagers who joined us had a variety of reasons for being there, but the common factor shared by all was that conventional school did not meet their needs. Some of the young people who came to Virtual High came from a home-learning background, while others had attended public school. The traditionally educated students chose Virtual High because they were bored, frustrated, or terrified by the regime of schooling. Some had been bullied by teachers or by fellow students, and some were affixed with numerous learning-disability labels. Over the next eight months the learners and their learning consultants moved toward becoming a community. The one activity we "highly recommended" that learners attend was a weekly community meeting. At first it was difficult to get attendance and attention, but as the youth learned that they had a voice and that their concerns and interests actually shaped the community, they began to participate with enthusiasm.

Early on, learners challenged me during one of our meetings, claiming that while I talked as if everyone were equal, I actually acted as if I were the authority. In response, I stood up and slowly walked around the room. I stopped in front of every second or third participant and said firmly, "I am the authority *here*." As I affirmed my authority, most of the teens winced or smirked. Finally, at the dramatic peak, I said, "Notice where I am pointing as I tell you I am the authority." As I shouted one last time, "I am the authority here!" I drew their attention to the fact that I was pointing at myself.

I reminded them that generally when people declared their authority, they pointed out toward other people. I said, "While I am the authority *here*, each and every one of you is the authority *there*, for yourself. I am the authority for Brent Cameron, so if you want to know what it is like *here* then please ask, and if I want to find out what it is like *there* where you are, then I will ask you, as *you* are the authority *there.*" We had many experiences like this one, and each incident began to shift the paradigm toward SelfDesign.

The goal of Virtual High was to create a program where everyone felt ownership, where SelfDesign and collaboration were both encouraged. Our only conditions, we told the learners, were that everyone would be included and respected and that we would use something called the consensus process to ensure this. They readily agreed, even though they had little idea what we meant. It took nearly a year for the teenagers to grasp the depth and breadth of consensus, but once they did, it became the lifeblood of the community.

Years after the unique collaboration that had become Virtual High, I read an article that discussed findings from a study by the Organization for Economic Cooperation and Development. In a survey of fifteen-year-olds in twenty-eight countries, one out of four Canadian youth and one out of five American youth stated that they regularly chose not to attend their high school classes. I found it ironic that conventional education, with all its coercive and punitive measures, could not keep learners in school. In contrast, the learners at Virtual High could not be kept away. Not only did they want to be there, but they changed the schedule from a nine-to-five, five-days-a-week program, to a twenty-four-hour, seven-days-a-week program throughout the year. This was enthusiasm in action.

This book, drawn from a lifetime of observation and thought about children and youth learning according to their enthusiasm, is an opportunity for all of us, as parents, educators, or lifelong learners, to carefully consider how we have been influenced and shaped, and to begin today to take responsibility for our lives. By stepping into the present moment and taking an inventory of our sense of wellness and satisfaction, we can begin to set the stage for SelfDesign.

SelfDesign: Patterns for Learning

When we are asked what we got out of school, we often first mention a significant relationship with an adult or with our peers, but we then move on to the subjects that we hated or loved. We are taught to focus on the subject, on the "what." No one in my schooling experience focused on the "how," the methodology by which we actually acquire understanding. SelfDesign encourages a focus not on content but on process, the process of noticing how we learn. SelfDesigners are invited to notice not just the outcome but the experience that leads to the outcome. We also invite a focus on the various mental and emotional states, or qualitative aspects, that influence learning. Shifting from "content and quantity" to "process and quality," learners begin to appreciate the importance of the meaning and the sense of purpose essential to real learning.

When I began Wondertree, I knew that I did not understand how people learn or how people heal, and I felt a compelling need to find out if there had been any educational or therapeutic breakthroughs in the past decade. Looking to education first, I found that teacher training was still predominantly focused on methods and classroom management and that most teachers graduated with few insights into the learning process. Teacher training in colleges throughout the world is geared to producing content specialists: professionals who can generate lesson plans to deliver subject curricula. Teachers graduate from most colleges with little or no knowledge about how or why people learn. They are taught very little about human development and the epistemology of being human. After years of observing the transformative experiences of children and adults when learning is suddenly relevant to their lives, I am dismayed that most teachers are denied the joy of witnessing these discoveries.

In Wondertree, teachers become learning consultants by focusing on process so that they can assist and influence learning. Learners are encouraged on their unique paths, employing their highly individualized styles. In order to promote an understanding of the journey, we start with a map, a representation that organizes and reflects the learner's processes. The SelfDesign Mandala, which follows, is a comprehensive map of learning opportunities. When using this map, it is very important to shift away from seeing it as a map of expectations. Instead, it exists as a map of opportunities.

Every human being can be thought of as a unique event in the universe. As different as fingerprints or snowflakes, we are each motivated to pursue journeys of unique desires and understandings. We become potters, dancers, computer programmers. As we develop our interests, we perfect certain skills and abilities and allow others to fall away. This is the natural way that we learn and grow. It seems absurd to require that everyone learn the same facts and skills.

Few if any people develop all twelve spokes of the mandala equally. Musicians have auditory skills that scientists might not, and mechanical engineers understand systems in ways totally foreign to family therapists. The SelfDesign Mandala supports each of us in our uniqueness as we explore the world as a personal adventure. The interconnections of the diagram keep all aspects of learning in perspective to one another and connected to the whole person, and learners tend to continue exploring new domains as their enthusiasm shifts to unexplored areas.

The mandala integrates several widely accepted learning theories with the SelfDesign philosophy. In our various programs, we offer this map to learners and their families at the beginning of each year, using it as the basis for their individual SelfDesign Learning Plan. They are free to choose and not choose any areas for learning. Parents are an integral part of the process and are invited to act as advisors and observers. We introduce mentors and resources to each learner and help them track their learning experiences throughout the year.

Several years ago I met with an eight-year-old boy and his mother as they began our program. It was the start of the learning year, and our meeting was focused on collaboratively creating a SelfDesign Learning Plan for the boy. Using the mandala as a template and knowing nothing of his abilities or interests, I asked him if he was reading yet. He replied that he was not. I asked him if he was interested in learning to read this year and he answered no. He told me that his mother read wonderful, complex books to him every day. Because his mother was obviously a better reader, it seemed silly to him to learn to read right now. Taking these ideas and desires as legitimate, I entered the information in his learning plan. As his learning consultant, it was not my job to coerce him to get busy and learn to read.

SelfDesign Mandala

SelfDesign Mandala

Ontology
PHILOSOPHY
Spirituality
Ethics
Systems Thinking
Self-Fulfillment

CREATIVITY
Self Expression
Art

SCIENCE
Ecology

TOOLS FOR LIVING
Finances
Life Skills
Info Technology

Understanding

LOGIC
Math
Analysis

Psychology

SELFDESIGN LEARNING PLAN
Annual and Seasonal Planning
Learning Committee (Circle)
Family Conversations

Holism

Spirit | Body
Mind | Heart

LEARNER/CONSULTANT CONVERSATIONS
Weekly Planning
Mentoring Relationship
Mapping, Planning, Observing and Evaluating

Biology
SELFDESIGNING
Personal Planning
Journaling
Observing and Reflecting

Self

WELLNESS
Body Awareness
Physical Activity

LANGUAGING
Communication
Intra-Personal
Reading
Media

Relationship HUMANITIES
Social Studies

COMMUNITY
Second Language
Cultural Studies
Group Process
Interpersonal
Relationships

Sociology

A year later, however, the boy's situation had changed. The mother was unable to read to him as often because there was a new baby in the family. Realizing that his mom was not always available now, the boy decided it was time to learn to read for himself. Within a month he was reading on his own, and soon he was reading those advanced and interesting books his mother had read to him. As it turned out, it was the mother who had to make the most adjustments to the boy's new skill, as the two no longer shared the richness of their reading-time conversations. At our next planning meeting, we changed the learning plan to include his new accomplishments. I used the mandala to explore the diverse subject matter of his books, encouraging him to use his portfolio to keep a record of his readings. The boy continued in our program; at age ten, in the first four months of the school year he read more than forty-five books and was deeply involved in the works of Shakespeare.

This story is typical of children who are allowed to learn when they are ready. It is quite common for them to exceed the abilities of their peers in a very short time. In the conventional educational system, where children are expected to be reading by a young age, there exists a high percentage of children who either can't read, don't like to read, or have significant reading problems. In contrast, virtually all of our SelfDesign learners become excellent readers, even those who come to us with so-called reading difficulties.

SelfDesign revolves around giving space to learners and helping them when asked. This passive yet responsive engagement is a unique way of communicating to youth that the responsibility for learning lies in their hands, as do the rewards. Because learners hold the awareness that help is nearby, their feeling of connection and support creates a willingness to engage in the learning process. They soon begin to actively seek out mentors to foster their inherent desire to learn.

As a learning consultant, I work to understand processes inside the minds of our learners, listening carefully as they describe how they are seeing, hearing, and feeling the experiences that inform their learning. My job is not to intrude in or interrupt their unique process but rather to listen, acknowledge, and perhaps enhance their explorations. Tracking and recording the learning events gives us all a perspective on the learning activities and an understanding of what is being achieved. We call this "Observing for Learning." Parents, mentors, and the learning consultant are in conversation with the learner to mutually discover what is happening in the learning experience. As learners become more capable of observing their own processes, they take over this job, often through journal writing and by developing portfolios.

As a SelfDesigning lifelong learner, I also am committed to observing my own learning every day. I have surrounded myself with friends and colleagues who collaborate with me in this effort, giving me honest feedback that I use as guidance for my life process. My personal journals track my life learning, and my achievements form the basis of my ever-growing portfolio.

The Politics of SelfDesigning

SelfDesign focuses on fully experiencing and expressing our sense of being and purpose. It allows us to live life as an amazing, sacred journey shared intimately with fellow travelers. The work holds at its base a belief in the essential goodness and worth of every individual. Its methodology is intended to develop all our inherent qualities and abilities to their fruition. At its fullest, SelfDesign is a political statement. In order for it to manifest as a world model, it would first require a subtle transformation of governmental and educational agendas which assume that children are unable and that imposed education is necessary to maintain a compliant society.

Fortunately, however, as individuals we always hold the option to live as an expression of our humanity and to nurture our children in an ecological, harmonious way. We need not ask permission from the elected leaders of our society. It would likely not be granted if we did. The existing system is tuned to a different agenda, one of gamesmanship and winning, where children and families are most often the least served.

My hope is that this learner-initiated model for living from integrity and enthusiasm catches the imagination of parents, educators, and learners of all ages. SelfDesign represents another way, a strategy for living that nurtures the spirit of learning and aligns with our intuition and integrity. This intuition resides in our hearts, and it reflects inner balance and an attunement with all of our positive influences. Only when we pursue our own uniqueness, when we become fulfilled individuals, do we finally discover the commonalities of the human experience. Reaching for true connection, we can celebrate and explore our differences with love and true compassion.

Old Paradigm/New Paradigm

Many people appreciate the idea that every child has infinite potential. Many can agree that children need both meaningful relationships and rich experiences to activate and unfold this inner potential. Yet all too often we negate these ideas by our actions. This discrepancy between our ideals and our practice indicates the place where we can learn to shift and design strategies based on new assumptions so that we relate to children in new ways that nurture their natural ability to SelfDesign.

The chart that follows illustrates the important differences between the old and new paradigms. The old is sustained by assumptions and language; the new can be reached by changing our underlying assumptions through a comprehensive commitment to new experience, new understanding, and new language.

Many theories advocate educational change, but most have come from experts in universities who propose changes within the system. These theories of change advocate shifts in the schooling model, with the intent of improving it. SelfDesign is not about change in the traditional educational system; let the schools exist for those who choose to work and learn in that model. SelfDesign offers a new information-age and global-community-based model for nurturing learning as an optimum environment for individual human development.

OLD PARADIGM: TEACHING SCHOOL	NEW PARADIGM: SELFDESIGN

MODEL

production, profit	growth, proportional
machine, mechanical	organism, biological
absolutist, Newton	relativistic, Einstein
institution, organization	community, family
focus on external world, things	context of internal world, process

EDUCATIONAL

instructional	constructionist
prescribed and tested	emerging and evaluated
authoritarian, hierarchy	democracy, consensus
culturally determined, citizenship	self-actualized, individuation
bureaucratic, management	heuristic, discovery

RELATIONSHIP FRAME

adult > child (rights)	adult = child (rights)
dominance, authority	ecological, balance
other-deferring, other-controlled	self-reliant, self-design
competitive	cooperative

PROCESS FRAME

future-oriented	present-oriented
directed outside, not including inside	directed inside, and including outside
about the world	in the world, of the world

PSYCHOLOGICAL

behavioral	relational
rational, linear	trust-based, love
reactive	positive language, remember
cause and effect	inclusive, subjective, holistic
fear-based, doubt	unconscious, ancient, holistic
negative language, don't forget	adult = child (rights)
separate, objective, fragmented	ecological, balance
conscious, colonial, dominating	self-reliant, self-design

LEARNING PROCESS

expectation-driven	nurturing context
content, facts and memorization	process, events and understanding
extrinsic motivation	intrinsic motivation
artifacts of behavior	experiential
coercive learning, reward/punishment	natural learning, enthusiasm

SelfDesign Learning Systems

Although today's society is experiencing rapid and constant change, our institutions appear to be limited by the constraints of old paradigms. Educational institutions, most notably, are unable to meet the needs of many young learners who experience failure or disenfranchisement within the outdated system. While innovative businesses are shaping social change by riding the wave of creative and scientific breakthrough, the traditional educational model continues to focus on sustaining existing social patterns, thus preventing it from adapting to change.

Writers on social evolution have observed that innovations tend to occur first in art. Artistic and creative process influences the field of science in adopting these ideas approximately a decade later. In another ten years, businesses begin to incorporate the innovations, and still a decade later, these ideas may filter into the educational system. Each field influences the next in an observable flow of social change, with education at the end of the chain.

The SelfDesign model shifts this flow of influence. It introduces strategies for lifelong learning at the initial stages of social change by combining the *art* of creative living and the *science* of human development. The flow chart that follows illustrates the thirty-year lag between innovation and traditional education. When lifelong learning enters the flow, informed by the SelfDesign process, the model drastically changes. Learning now *creates* the wave of innovation. *SelfDesign is the art and science of lifelong learning.* As such, it shifts our strategies of living to the forefront of social change and growth. Our survival and success as a species no longer depend on education but on lifelong learning as a SelfDesign process.

Although this may be viewed as a futuristic and idealistic call for change, many businesses are now looking to the natural world as a source of elegant designs and processes as well as solutions to industry-based problems like pollution. The emerging fields of biomimicry, industrial ecology, and sustainable business are all oriented to an ecology-based worldview.

Wondertree has likewise demonstrated a new paradigm as a prototype for ecological and balanced whole-system learning. The prototype has been built. The methodology has been designed, tested, and documented. It is thirty years ahead of its time and yet has already shown itself as a viable model for innovation. If Wondertree can do it, so can any committed group of individuals who incorporate the SelfDesign model into their learning community.

The Spiraling Journey

This book is a dance, a dance of ideas and insights into how to SelfDesign, into how we all learn through living. Using the same mandala that learners use to approach SelfDesign, we start at the center, zero, and then move clockwise around the circle from 1 through 12. It is the zero point that is the starting, ending, and ongoing point in our life journey. Beginning with chapter 0, the essence, we see how the center is connected to all other centers. We focus on a new and yet perennial philosophy, shifting our fundamental assumptions about who we are. We literally have nothing (no *thing*) in common, and our essential sameness stems from that truth. From this place of unity, in each successive chapter we spiral through our journey in a global celebration of variety and diversity throughout nature.

- We discover that beauty, elegance, and efficiency have a common relationship or ratio. Growing and changing throughout our lives, we remain fundamentally the same. Simultaneously, we live through time and in a timeless here and now.

- This lifelong pattern of growth is an unfolding of our infinite intelligence, whereby we realize the inherent genius of our nature. Our genius as human beings is dynamic because we are designed to model and learn our fundamental strategies from others through experience.

- We are intimately linked through conversations, out of which we emerge as human beings—as individuals and in community. The context of relationships, specifically within the family, provides us with models for creating our understanding of the world and us with an opportunity for expressing our experiences.

- Our greatest tool for understanding comes from looking into language as a formative process. We have the opportunity to create a relationship between the unconscious and the newly emerging consciousness of our understandings.

- Our essential right is freedom. We are free to choose within a context of responsibility and respect for the freedom and well-being of all. Happiness is our guiding emotion in this inclusive and evolving collaboration.

- As lifelong learners, we continually mature and move through stages of growth. The process of maturation allows us to continuously explore our potential, measuring the worth of each experience as we grow. We learn strategies which support the patterns of living that keep us in balance within ourselves and within our environment.

- Our resonance with others is optimized when, as learners and mentors, we mutually explore our fascinations. The dialogue we create in these interactions is fundamental in the unfolding of genius.

- Synergistic community represents the fruition of human achievement, affirming our sense of purpose on this planet.

- Our wholeness as individuals and as a society is achieved through patterns of living that integrate our bodies, hearts, minds, and spirits. We recognize the dimensionality of our lives that replicates our spherical home, the earth.

- The spiraling journey now brings us around to the end and the beginning, the place of an exponential leap. In this place we extrapolate the attributes of the whole person to the ecology of the whole planet. "Ecology" represents the balance of systems in relationship, and it creates a global sense of balance and harmony.

Unlike schooling, the process of SelfDesign is a *whole body/whole mind* transformation, incorporating the patterns of our living into the design of learning strategies. The SelfDesign model has nothing to do with schooling and everything to do with lifelong learning. It is a model that has emerged from real children learning together in true freedom—freedom to be curious and enthusiastic and freedom to work together in community. This model has come from the experts in learning—the children. It has also been integrated with the latest scientific insights into how we are optimally designed as human beings. This emerging methodology is the art and science of SelfDesigning.

BEING PRESENT

A Journey to Our Authentic Selves

We shall not cease from exploration
And the end of our exploring
Will be to arrive where we started
And know the place for the first time.
—*T. S. Eliot*

SelfDesign begins with a journey back to our original or true identity, allowing the rediscovery of Self, the rediscovery of our essential nature. By the time we are adults, we have all been operating on our assumptions about who we are for many years. How often, if ever, have we gone back to check whether these assumptions are accurate? How is it possible to become aware of the "story within the story," the hidden message of who we *really* are within the idea of who we *think* we are? Can we recapture a sense of "authoring" our own lives, of using our self-authority to design our world as we wish it to be? Even more importantly, can we be present with the children we love in ways that nurture the sense of authority with which *they* are born?

As babies, our children engage the world with a curiosity that enthralls us. They are happy and free in their explorations, absorbing their environments with enthusiasm and abandon. Lovingly, we cheer them on as they do what comes naturally: learning. We trust in their ability to bond and model, to toddle their way into a confident walk, to experiment with sounds and words until sophisticated speech emerges. Because they wish to, they do.

For most of us as parents, though, the day comes when we shift our belief away from our children's innate desires to be learners. We begin to shape the learning experience, thinking that without our firm encouragement, our children will "fall behind." We start thinking that without the structure and curriculum of traditional schooling methods, learning will not happen. Incredibly, we fear that our children may turn away from the very basis of their fundamental design, their desire to be learners.

Wondertree was born as a place where children could be free to explore with passion. The story of Wondertree is built of a hundred stories, each with a child as its central character. Our journey through the pages of this book will offer a sampling of how children's lives have been transformed by regaining their sense of self-authority within an environment of trust and mutual respect. Once these children have begun to author their own experience again, the passion for learning is re-ignited and the authentic self can move forward with enthusiasm for life. The following is a story that exemplifies the process of Wondertree's SelfDesign methodology.

Many years ago a family brought their ten-year-old son to our program. A local psychiatrist had recommended Wondertree to them after an in-depth evaluation of the young boy's situation, recognizing that this gifted youngster needed freedom. He needed to be in a place where he felt understood and respected, where he could explore and develop trust with others. Prior to his visit to the psychiatrist, he had been on a six-month hunger strike to resist going to school. At his public school the faculty seemed unable to adapt to his needs as a gifted learner. He challenged every teacher's authority and found his deepest satisfaction in confronting the principal. Although he was bright and defiant, he was also a deeply hurt young boy.

In the first months of our program he had the freedom to do whatever he was interested in, and he chose to play. This was obviously a significant departure from what the parents were used to in a learning environment, and they struggled with the dilemma of deciding whether to go back to the type of conventional education they had been conditioned to respect, or instead to invest in the happiness and well-being of their son by supporting him in Wondertree. They had to wrestle with deep personal beliefs, yet their compassion for their son kept him enrolled in our program.

Although the boy was enjoying the freedom and respect central to Wondertree, his anger at authority would frequently manifest in behaviors aimed at his new principal — me. Although we had an open and friendly relationship, he would often poke and hit me throughout the day. He was argumentative and would engage me in intense debates. As time went on I suggested that we form a club and that it would be called the Stubborn Club. I explained that obviously I would be the president, which immediately initiated his proclamation that no, he was the president. Now we really had something to argue about.

Three months later we held our first family meeting, and the boy refused to participate. I saw him hiding in the next room while his parents and learning consultant were starting the meeting. I went in the room and said, "Oh hi, Sam, you must be John's twin brother. Look, John couldn't make it tonight to the meeting so I was wondering if you would sit in for him and tell him what happened."

His look of confusion quickly turned to a smile, and he followed me into the meeting. I informed everyone at the table that this was Sam, who would observe and report back to his twin brother, John. Through this incident John began to understand that although I was the principal, I was primarily a caring friend.

As the months and then years went by we either argued about who was president of the Stubborn Club or about which computer operating system was superior, Windows or MacIntosh. During these conversations he would often hit me, most certainly as an expression of his frustration. His anger was just under the surface, and sometimes it exploded at the Wondertree center or at home.

It felt to me that his hitting was therapeutic for him, but obviously it wasn't comfortable for me. When we had been together for nearly three years I invited him into my office and went over our history, describing it in three stages First, I recounted how he was intimidated by me, the "principal," for the first year. The second stage had lasted for almost two years, during which we debated our presidency. Throughout this time he had also enjoyed hitting me and challenging me as a playful nemesis. Then, with a shift in tone and attitude, I suggested that we had known each other for quite a while now and had had a chance to develop trust in each other. I requested that we move into the third stage of our relationship, one of gentleness and respect. I asked him if this could be possible. He paused in thought, nodded, and left my office.

The next day he came into my office and gave me a hug. Every day for the entire next year, he came in and gave me a hug. Upon leaving Wondertree to go to a computer-based program in a local high school, he unequivocally won our ongoing argument when he gave me a mug engraved VICE PRESIDENT OF THE STUBBORN CLUB. We committed to a lifelong relationship, honoring the friendship that allowed him to unfold his wings and to become the permanent president of his own life.

I find it interesting that what it took to allow this frustrated and desperate child to become a successful and self-assured high school student had nothing to do with remedial help for his learning disabilities. We allowed him the freedom to focus on his exceptional abilities, to take responsibility for his own life, and to experience meaningful egalitarian relationships with adults. Although he did no real "schoolwork" while in our program, he was able to become a successful high school student mostly because of his sense of confidence and well-being. He told me recently that after his first month back in school, he realized that none of his classmates had been paying any attention to schooling for the past five years either. The story of this young boy, while not focusing on gifted qualities he may have had, establishes instead a context for the sort of work that is at the heart of the SelfDesign philosophy. The boy's need for trust and freedom far outweighed his need for reading or math facts, and once he developed these elements in his life he was able to successfully go forward.

Some Theory Behind the Process

While creating and experimenting with the Wondertree process to nurture natural learning, I drew inspiration from certain areas of research and several key people whom I have come to regard as mentors in my exploration.

One of the first areas of research that intrigued me is from the field known as epistemology, which examines the nature of human understanding and experience. In *A Sacred Unity: Further Steps to an Ecology of Mind*, the brilliant American researcher Gregory Bateson defines *epistemology* as follows:

> If you want to know—to understand—what's the matter with contemporary education ... parent-child relations ... you will do well to study biology, and especially that branch of biology which is called epistemology. Epistemology is that science whose subject matter is itself. It is the name of a species of scientific study and talk. We set out to study the nature of study itself, the process of the acquisition of

information and its storage. The conventional definitions of epistemology would place it in philosophy . . .

The study of physics and how physics is done and the study of the language of physics . . . The study of art and poetry and of how these things are done and how history is done—all these are epistemology, along with the study of how epistemology is done. It follows that epistemology is the great bridge between all branches of the world of experience—intellectual, emotional, observational, theoretical, verbal and wordless. We stand off from all these disciplines to study them and yet stand in the very center of each.

Epistemology is inductive and experimental and, like any true science, it is deductive and, above all abductive, seeking to put side-by-side similar chunks of phenomena . . . our human machinery for perceiving— our sense organs—can receive news only of difference.

So, epistemology insists that the stuff of knowledge is always made of the news of difference. Well, the next step from news of differences is to the building up of patterns or configurations. If we have wrong ideas of how our abstractions are built—if, in a word, we have poor epistemological habits—we shall be in trouble—and we are.

Epistemology, as applied to SelfDesign, is a process that investigates the very process of learning, of what it is to learn, how we learn, and what in fact it is to be a learning individual. Indeed, epistemology does not put the learner aside as the process is studied. Instead it includes the learner in the learning and focuses on the very biological, psychological, ecological, and ontological processes a learner experiences while learning. In an epistemological sense, we can therefore question the very nature of our assumptions and question the underlying understanding of the beliefs held in our culture. We can discover the meaning in our own story, and we can examine the premises upon which we live. The worldviews upon which our extensive identities and our elaborate social systems are based can be rethought. Although often considered a daunting task, rediscovering foundational assumptions is relatively easy once you understand how to do it—and it's essential. When we are living true to ourselves and in harmony with our human nature, we step into a new kind of intelligence and realize a new kind of efficiency and elegance that emerges from integrity and congruence.

The Work of Douglas Harding

Children are born totally present, and healthy relationships are based on full engagement in the present. Thus, it follows that anyone working and living with children needs to create genuine connections with them by accessing the same state of present being. I was fortunate enough to learn this truth through trial and error in my own life, but it was not until I met the British visionary Douglas Harding that I learned the tools necessary to share this important discovery with others.

Harding has used his methodologies over the past six decades to show thousands of people how to discover who they "really, *really*" are. His work unravels and decodes many of our philosophical and religious teachings into simple experiments that everyone can experience. He begins by helping people look more closely at how the conscious mind can limit the perceptual world.

Spiritual traditions often refer to the return to a childlike worldview, and many devise elaborate sets of practices to assist the conscious mind in getting beyond—or, more accurately, underneath—our normal conventions of thinking. The cultures in which we grow up define our common identity, influencing our conscious model of the world and of ourselves in it. This identity becomes so inflexible that it can be virtually impossible to get beyond it. The techniques designed to transcend consciousness often become another fixation for the mind, and we are no closer to appreciating our spiritual, essential worldview. Harding designed ingenious perceptual tricks to provide direct insights into the original mind, into the child's worldview, by creating mental paradoxes. By experiencing the paradox, participants could see their own limitations and move beyond them.

In our SelfDesign workshops and intensives with youth, parents, educators, and business people, we introduce Harding's experiments as a primary way to access one's original worldview, giving access to true presence. Experiencing life as a sacred event brings depth and quality to everything we do and allows us to create genuine relationships. There is an exquisite pleasure in noticing the sacredness of each mundane moment in a day, and there is a special pleasure in witnessing this quality in our children.

How, then, do we break through the mundane to find the sacred in our daily lives? As adults, we discover the sacred in those rare moments when we become fascinated and absorbed in a task, when we disappear into our enthusiasm and lose our identities. Yet too often we attribute the quality to the activity rather than to the state, proclaiming that we love gardening, pottery, golf or dancing. Harding's experiments provide simple and clear opportunities to experience such spiritual awareness and to begin to understand how fundamental it is to our very being. The Wondertree program has used these techniques with children and families for the past twenty years to develop new psychological and philosophical models for understanding human development. We have found this work to be fundamental in establishing a new ethic for equality in relationships between adults and children.

I would like to introduce you to Harding's views on the four stages of life as they inform the SelfDesign process, followed by one of his experiments. In this way you can directly experience the simple yet profound implications of this work. (Further experiments can be found online in the SelfDesign Webcourse.)

The Four Stages of Human Development: Zero to Awareness of Zero

SelfDesign occurs in the patterns of awareness of Self and of our relationship with the world. We are born first into the world only as awareness. Our unconscious, all-aware process is gradually controlled and managed by our developing consciousness. This consciousness sets us apart as human beings. What truly makes us unique, however, is our ability to rediscover our unconscious process and get beyond our thoughts. This is generally referred to as enlightenment.

The process of enlightenment has been explored in hundreds of myths and stories throughout the ages. Heroes embark on dangerous journeys into the world, on quests to achieve a predetermined goal, hoping for an outcome that will allow them to live peacefully ever after. Ironically, they must leave the comfort and safety of home (in other words, their original awareness) in order to be able to find it again. Our separation from total awareness, occurring through the development of consciousness, is essential in our development as human beings. We seem to be designed to become conscious and separate. In today's world, though, we do this far too well. We focus so much on consciousness that few of us find our way back home to the state of simple awareness and total presence. Most of us confuse our Selves with the journey itself, which then becomes our social treadmill. Our journey becomes a series of tasks imposed upon us by society for success, as defined by society's standards. We lose ourselves to these tasks. We seek a goal that becomes an end point in itself. We spend our time looking for the right path rather than focusing on the path we are already on, because we have forgotten what it is to be present in this moment. Our true ability to bond with children is in direct proportion to our ability to stop thinking, to stop looking at the next task or the "right" path and join them in the moment.

Wondertree began as an experiment to see if I could design a way of living that would allow people to return home more easily. SelfDesign, the concept borne of Wondertree, is a journey during which we lose our original awareness but know, as a part of the journey, how to find our way back.

Although it is essential to leave home, to leave the garden, in the process of human development, it is important to have an understanding of the whole story. Harding has depicted this process of leaving home and returning home in four stages:

- Stage 1. Infancy, during which the baby is in the present moment and does not know it.

- Stage 2. Childhood and adolescence, during which the individual constructs an identity and experiments in the world in the present tense, shifting to the perspective of others and the role of one's identity. We often notice children role-playing as a way of trying on life roles, preparing for adulthood by pretending in the past, present, and future, thereby creating a sense of time.

- Stage 3. Adulthood, during which the individual is totally committed to living in the role of one's identity. We become "things" in a world of things, often separate and cut off from others and ourselves.

- Stage 4. The return and rediscovery of the original perspective of the child, truly knowing it for the first time. This stage is achieved by a relatively few people, as the vast majority spend their entire adult lives in Stage 3. The door to Stage 4 is available anytime to adults, once they again learn to be present and can then recognize the layering of their experience.

The Four Stages of Being Human
0, 1, 1, 2…*

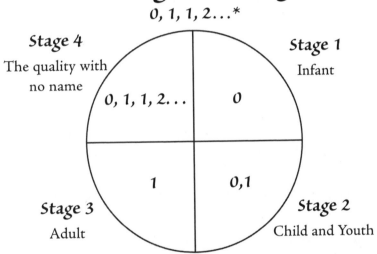

Stage 4
The quality with no name

0, 1, 1, 2…

Stage 1
Infant

0

1

0,1

Stage 3
Adult

Stage 2
Child and Youth

Harding's final stage, as developed in SelfDesign, is essential for one's freedom and for the role of parenting and mentoring. This ego-less state makes people fully available to one another. Unlike adults, who struggle with attaining this state, children are more easily able to create it according to their relative proximity to the pre-ego existence. Once connected, individuals are able to realize who they are and to develop as whole people, living in a truly congruent state.

In Wondertree's parenting course, "Transparency," I discovered that parents spend much of their energy trying to prove that their deepest fears about themselves are not true. For example, one father who focused only on his child's success was operating from a hidden fear that he himself was not successful. The mother who worked to feel

*See page 44 for information about these Fibonacci numbers.

valuable in the eyes of others was actually trying to disprove her suspicion that she was worthless. Learned beliefs such as these often shape our life activities. When we go deeper and discover our original identity, these limiting assumptions take on a new perspective.

Our sense of separateness and the external identity we take on as adults is what we make available for our children to model, which is what they are busy doing while we are attempting to teach them. Many of us live our Stage 3 lives by filling our time and homes with activities and acquisitions that make us feel content and busy. The essential quality of *no thing* feels like nothing to us, and we tend to experience it as emptiness rather than as fulfillment. Our lives are about filling up the sense of emptiness with the things of the world.

The unique aspect of Stage 4 is that it cannot necessarily be understood within the logic of Stage 3. Consistent with the obvious truth that something cannot be found until it has been taken away, lost, or forgotten, Stage 3 is a prerequisite for Stage 4. Stage 4 can only be achieved through the double-bind (or dilemma) technique that creates a paradox between the conscious and the unconscious worldviews. Once an individual becomes aware of the conscious story as a story, then it is possible to notice again the underlying and forgotten awareness, one's ground of being. Stage 4 is consistent with inclusive and holistic models in that nothing is taken away, and another choice is added.

Am I Central or Peripheral to the Universe?

To illustrate the significance of this epistemological shift, we begin with a photograph of the earth. The creation of this image, and the experience of this image, was one of the most important events of the last century. For the first time in human history we were able to glimpse our home in its entirety. That beautiful image showed us the interconnectedness of living systems and the dynamic flow of influences in this unique place in the universe. Because science made this photograph possible and science plays such a central role in our increase in knowledge and understanding, we have been able, in so many ways, to improve our condition as human beings.

Scientific research has shown that the right side of the body is informed by the left hemisphere of the brain. The left brain is logical, linear, and scientific. Consider the image shown above of the right hand pointing outward as an icon of scientific thinking, of our ability to make distinctions. We are a right-hand-dominant culture. Ironically, in the same century that we have accomplished so much through science—left-brain thinking—we are in the process of destroying our home, the very planet upon which we live. The elimination of species and cultures has put our own existence at risk. Something is tragically out of balance.

To introduce a sense of balance, we have the left hand pointing back toward ourselves. The left hand, representing the right side of the brain, is a symbol for intuitive, relational, and holistic thinking. When we do not include our sense of who we are as human beings, we live out of balance. This has been the result of our tendency to live exclusively rather than inclusively. Collectively and individually, we need to think with our whole minds, but our training has perpetuated exclusivity, and this has taken a toll. A quick history of science can give us perspective on the issue. If science has contributed to both our progress and our difficulties, it is imperative to understand the "story within the story" of science.

Shall we explore the story to see if we can find the storyteller? One of philosophy's fundamental and ongoing questions asks, "Does the universe exist only because of our experience of it, or are we peripheral and the world exists whether anyone is available to experience it or not?" The theory that the world was here a long time before humans emerged on the scene is one story—but not a story of human experience. By beginning first with the assumptions underneath the story, we can get inside it. The history of our assumptions about the universe's origin is a discovery of the still place from which everything begins. As assumptions have changed and thinking has expanded, new models have created yet another shift in our point of view.

At the beginning of Western civilization we were geocentric thinkers, imagining that the earth was a still point and that all the people and animals scrambled about on its flat surface. The planets, the stars, and the sun all circled the earth, which was at the center of the universe.

From the fifteenth century through the seventeenth century, Europe experienced a renaissance in thinking. Scientists such as Galileo, Copernicus, and Newton began to calculate that the earth was a planet moving about the sun, which they speculated was the center of the universe. The flat earth became a sphere, a model that gained acceptance with the voyage of Columbus. With the sun as the still point in the solar system, we became a heliocentric universe and the still point moved 93 million miles away from where we lived.

Several hundred years later, as scientists made more astute observations and comprehensive calculations, they discovered that the sun circles a gaseous center along with all the stars we see in the sky. Suddenly the sun became a rather insignificant star amidst millions of others. The new still place was the center of a giant galaxy called the Milky Way. The center of the universe was even more distant, about 50,000 light years from the earth, and our point of view shifted yet again.

It was soon discovered that there are millions of other galaxies in the universe, that our galaxy is just one galaxy of many swirling through space. Scientists mapped the paths of these numerous galaxies back to an ancient and distant central point of stillness or origin called the Big Bang. The center of the universe is now considered to be fifteen billion light years away from earth. The Big Bang, at the furthest reaches of the universe, has left us with a sense of ourselves as insignificant human beings, spiraling about on an insignificant planet, dancing around an insignificant star in an insignificant galaxy.

Then, at the turn of this century, one significant insignificant human being, Albert Einstein, turned scientific thinking inside out. A new way of understanding our place in the universe emerged from the mathematics within the statement "Time and space are relative to the point of view of the observer."

In other words, the universe, or any event in time and space, is centered in each human experience. Einstein was postulating a human-centered (anthropocentric) universe or possibly an experience-centered (ontocentric*) universe. This statement profoundly affected religious, mystical, philosophical, and scientific thinking, and it also holds deep meaning for the ways children perceive the world.

The Science of a Child's Worldview

In my attempts to reconcile the shift in perspectives from the child's worldview to the adult's, I studied Einstein's work. His lifelong attempt to understand his own childhood curiosity mapped out a way of understanding the development of genius—as the unfolding of curiosity throughout one's entire lifetime.

The more I studied the theory of relativity, the more I understood the paradigm shift, yet I did not experience it as relevant to how I was living my life. This connection came clear to me when I was introduced to the work of linguist Benjamin Whorf.

As I read Whorf's book on his studies of North American indigenous languages, I discovered his belief that Hopi parents unconsciously teach the theory of relativity to their children. He explored how relativity is communicated through the linguistic structure of the Hopi culture. The Hopi language has only a present tense. Future events are created and stated in the present tense. In this way they are brought *toward* the present individual through volition, through conscious choice, as opposed to a framework where individuals are walking *toward* the future.

With Einstein's work and Whorf's insights into Hopi language, I began thinking about how I could shift my own perspective. I saw a connection between being present and being at the still point, and I integrated these ideas into the perspectives and experiments that Harding had shown me. I was thus enabled to work with children in a new way, a way that allowed me to meet them within their developmental process and help them discover and construct new ways of understanding themselves and the world.

Experiment: Drawing the "Other and Self" Relationship

In order to share a little of this perspective-shifting work with you, I would like to introduce you to one of Harding's simple and profoundly life-changing experiments. It is important to actually do the exercise, because this work is not an intellectual exercise in "learning about" a new definition of who we are. This new model must be experienced in order to discover our own authenticity for ourselves. By doing this, parents and educators add to their repertoire of tools to get themselves into the present. By experiencing the perspective shift that occurs, it becomes easier to grasp the fundamental difference between SelfDesign and traditional schooling.

---

*A word I coined.

I invite you and a friend to do this twenty-minute experiment. To prepare you will need two chairs, a few sheets of paper and a pencil for each of you, and a hard surface upon which to draw. Take the two chairs and place them about six feet apart facing each other. It is better to do this in an open room rather than at a table, so that you can see one another head to toe.

Please read all of the instructions before you start drawing.

Instructions

First, take about ten minutes for each of you to draw the other person in the top one-third of the page. Leave the bottom two-thirds for your self-portrait. Draw the other person's outline and a few of their details, and then draw yourself in the bottom of the page. Sketch your relationship to the other person from your own perspective. Details are not important; the point is to get an outline of general shapes and features. *Draw only what you can actually see.* Stay in the *present moment* and draw what is before you, what you are *experiencing*, rather than using your memory to draw what you have seen in the past. Once your sketch of the other person is complete, stay exactly where you are perceptually and draw yourself as you perceive yourself in this moment. If you realize that you have drawn yourself from the point of view of another person, set the paper aside and begin again.

Remember to draw the other person as you see that person, and *draw yourself as you see yourself in this present moment. Here. Now.*

Remember to let go of conscious thought. Go for it, take a risk, and draw what you see even though it makes no sense.

Now begin drawing, and when you have finished the exercise, continue reading.

Some of you will have drawn two heads, some will have drawn one, and some will have drawn a number of heads. Which of the pictures on page 32 is more like yours, the one on the left or the one on the right?

The picture on the left is an image of someone who has moved away from the state of being present. Those who draw this way create a picture of who they think they are rather than who they really are, traveling mentally to see themselves as others see them, just as you see yourself in the mirror. Images like this are drawn from the outside, six feet away from where the person drawing them actually lives. This is the typical drawing for an adult as well as for a child who is learning to be an adult. Staying present in the present moment and seeing the world as it looks *within* one's experience is a difficult task for most. Yet again, it is the easiest thing to do, because we are all doing it, naturally and unconsciously, in every moment.

Compare your pictures and notice that, for those who drew an image like the one on the right, the self-portrait is not of a person at all. A person, by definition, is a closed system with a head at the top, two arms, two legs, and a body. What is the creature with the feet at the top, arms at the sides, and a body that ends in an open space at the bottom, a space where no head seems to exist? To this day I have no name for this creature, the upside-down one, the one with no head. Harding playfully introduces this perspective as being "headless." I am more and more certain that this being is not a person but is instead "our true but hidden identity," our story within the story of who we think we are. Our relationships are not symmetrical "face-to-face" events but asymmetrical "face-to-space" experiences.

In workshops where I have asked hundreds of people to do this drawing exercise, many people start out drawing themselves from someone else's point of view. The "learned" self-portrait is what we remember from experiences with mirrors and photographs of ourselves. We are so influenced by those images that we tend to adopt this perspective of ourselves. We describe ourselves from another's point of view, and from their perspective we look like a complete person, head and all. However, from our inner point of view, here and now, we are more the space in which the world can happen, the "headless person," and therefore our experience is the world with our own experience at the center.

Our construction of our own identity is most often a compilation of the comments from others: "You are so pretty" or "The creases in your forehead make you look stern." We incorporate these comments into a conscious "story" of our identity. There is nothing wrong with this; in fact, the whole process is essential for survival and for membership in this culture. However, what we have forgotten and lost is at issue here. As adults we ignore our unconscious reality, virtually every second of every day, when we think we *are* our conscious identity.

From the work of Neuro-Linguistic Programming these two states are called *associated*, looking out from one's own eyes, and *disassociated*, looking back at oneself from an "other" position using imagination. Children are able to slip back and forth freely from one position to another. Because of this ability, and because parents have forgotten their own childlike perspective, children are often told by adults that some of their ideas are nonsense.

To look at this idea another way, the words *person* and *personality* come from the Greek *persona*, meaning "mask." Our own faces become masks by which we no longer recognize our original selves. Through experiments like the one above, we can begin to recapture the true vision of Self, and we can use our new understanding as we begin to SelfDesign.

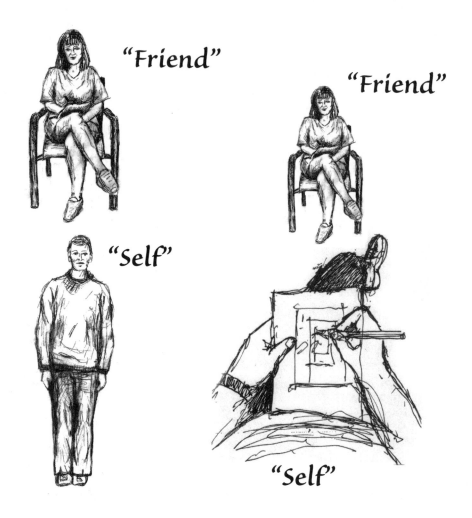

"Friend"

"Friend"

"Self"

"Self"

CHAPTER 1

BEAUTIFUL BY DESIGN

Industrialism and the capitalistic system have transformed our pre-industrial lifestyles, both for better and for worse. People in the industrialized world's top, middle, and bottom social strata have benefited proportionally from improved lifestyles and material wealth. The devastating environmental consequences of these achievements and the disruption to cultures around the world, colonized and marginalized as supply nations, are the exterior shadow of industrialism. The interior shadow is that many of us now live in a personal and interpersonal wasteland. We are out of touch and out of balance with ourselves, and our relationships are disengaged and disconnected. This is our children's legacy.

Our accumulated material wealth has been paralleled by a corresponding increase in the quantity of information in the world. The irony is that while the quantity of information doubles every few months, people generally seem to be less informed and increasingly apathetic and disenchanted. Never before have we had such amazing ways of delivering information through television, books, photographs, graphics, computers, video, multimedia, and the internet. Yet so many children are bored and have become less and less motivated to learn about and understand the world around them.

Children are increasingly expected to learn more at a younger age in order to keep up, let alone get ahead. Parents are afraid that their children will "fall behind," and schooling success is considered essential in order to get a good job. These expectations only make sense within the illusion that we live in a competitive world, that the human race is, in fact, a *race*. It is an illusion fed by an attitude of scarcity, artificially sustained by competition. It holds our children within the belief that their success is measured only through their relative position to others.

By contrast, in the grand scheme of our history, it is our moments of cooperation rather than competition that have actually enriched the quality of our living. Artists, scientists, innovators, and leaders have historically collaborated in ideas that not only hold the integrity of a culture together but move it to new levels of achievement and understanding. When we cut ourselves off from our own natures, we live in a competitive world where success is more about quantity than quality.

The ongoing tragedy is that we impose a belief system of winning and losing on our children. In response to such overwhelming expectations, students have turned schooling into a battleground. It is not a war between two equal enemies but rather a battle stemming from the domination of one group over another. Dominated groups, as exemplified by France during its occupation by the Nazis in World War II, historically resort to sabotage as a way of fighting back. Because children have no rights or power they must also resort to sabotage as a way of undermining the existing power structure with subversive activities. The violence we currently see in school and the epidemic of learning disabilities are both symptoms of sabotage, one turned outward and the other turned inward. Consciously or unconsciously, both are ways of coping with the punishing environment of imposed expectations and of having our choices taken away. When our lives are determined from the outside by the expectations and demands of others, we live more and more like victims.

Wondertree's SelfDesign process addresses this issue as it applies to both the nurturing of our children and to lifelong learning relationships. The solution arises not as a quantitative answer but a qualitative one. SelfDesign does not expect children to do more, to learn more, or to learn more efficiently as a measure of their success. As Einstein said, no problem can be solved from the same level of consciousness that created it. The solution to handling too much information is not to increase the speed at which we assimilate ideas, nor does it come from spending more time at our studies or starting at a younger age. The solution comes when we shift from "out there" to "in here," from constant stimulation and change to an internal and essential stillness. It comes when we work in harmony with the natural learning ability of each child. Fifty years ago, people could easily be knowledgeable about everything in their field. Today, on the other hand, it is virtually impossible to keep up with the research and breakthroughs in any specialty. Living in the Information Age means living with an overwhelming, daily proliferation of new facts and ideas.

It has become imperative to reclaim stillness, to find a resting place from the furious pace at which everything is traveling, flowing, and changing. We can travel on the earth more quickly than ever before, and we can send and receive information around the earth in seconds. We deal with a million times more data when we shift to light rather than voice for communication. Trying to speed up, trying to be more efficient, working harder and longer can all be helpful, yet futile if we are caught up in the process.

The faster the world moves "out there," the more important it is for us to go slower "in here." The still place at the center is our essential Self, is the "I" of the storm. Once we are here, now, present in the stillness, we can begin to comprehend the swirling energies about us while staying firmly connected to our true and authentic selves.

Nurturing that quiet, observing place within ourselves is an ongoing challenge for most of us. We are often so distracted by our own thoughts that we have forgotten how to just *be*. Even children are so caught up in their efforts to meet expectations that they forget to notice where they are, how they are, and who they are. I find it interesting to stop children in mid-sentence or action and just ask them how they are feeling or ask a question about the process of what they are doing. My sense from so many children is that they do not pay any attention to their own processes. When I first ask children to notice what is happening inside them at a given moment, I get the most confusing expressions. If I persist over time, however, they eventually find that this inner noticing of their own process leads to a deeper, more joyful way of living and learning.

Shifting from Industrial to Ecological Thinking

Most of us in this culture have been influenced to think in terms of production of goods. We talk about our lives and relationships in terms that imply the importance of outcome: "We did not have a very productive day." "Nothing substantial came of that discussion." "That was a waste of our time." These are all examples of the industrialization of our relationships. Schools are comprehensively modeled after the assembly line, with production as outcome. The assembly line is an efficient way to produce inanimate goods, but it is a completely inappropriate way to deal with living and growing organisms.

Even the explanations and understandings of our own humanity carry the language of the machine. For example, Descartes and his colleagues saw humans as similar to finely tuned clocks. Later, after motors had been invented, we began to hear expressions like "I need to rev up my energy for this meeting." Nowadays we often describe our own our functioning in computer and programming terms: "She's a talented multi-tasker."

As our scientific thinking evolves, we are able to make finer and more accurate distinctions incorporating deeper insights into the way nature works. We can model the very intelligence of natural systems. Our scientific models of nature are getting closer and closer to mimicking actual patterns and systems of natural design.

While these innovations are helpful as models to understand ourselves, we have reduced the most amazing bio-organism ever created to the workings of a few gears, switches, and computations. To do this is to extract the sacred, the joy, and the mystery out of each breath we take.

Although the majority of us in the Western world no longer participate in an industrial lifestyle, our idioms and ideas remain those of production. Because we have access to so many goods and services, we forget that we are acting as managers for the industrialization of the rest of the world. The fact that the "have" nations are extensively disrupting the global ecological balance demands that we move into the Ecological Age, one of ecological sensitivity to lessen the effect of our production. The necessary move into this next Age will be accomplished by focusing on integrated systems, on increasing global awareness of the interactions of human and environmental systems. The more we use universal and natural metaphors to understand our place and our function on earth, the more accurate will be our models to guide and balance our actions. Not only do we need living metaphors, we need to understand the fundamental design of nature and to appreciate the importance of balance in natural relationships.

Nature's Pattern: The Logarithmic Spiral

In the years since I began Wondertree, I have worked closely with hundreds of children and youth, and I have observed that they are naturally intelligent, naturally wise, and naturally loving. This is not learned or taught; it's the natural human condition.

Just as any biological system needs nourishing conditions to grow and develop, human beings need love as the fundamental nutrient for unfolding our human intelligence. It is only when our natural balance and development are interfered with that we begin to wither. Only when we are not living in a condition of love do we learn the opposite.

The ratio of the logarithmic spiral, as shown in this nautilus shell, is integral to our design, to our movements and sense of balance. This geometry of beauty and balance forms a fundamental metaphor and model for SelfDesign.

In chapter 0 we discovered the importance of being present, of rediscovering our original point of view. Now it's time to explore the importance of understanding how to allow a natural unfolding of our true design rather than manufacturing our intelligence from the outside. The metaphors we use and how we construct our sense of ourselves are critical elements. We can choose either to align with our own nature or to conflict with and confound our own developmental process.

For perhaps the past four or five hundred years, the Western world has defined humans as separate from nature. This perspective is the crux of scientific thinking, and as mentioned earlier it has created amazing technical advances as well as devastating problems connected to these same breakthroughs. Seeing ourselves as separate disconnects us from a positive and meaningful engagement with the natural world and leads to insecurity and fear of our own environment. This perspective ignores the fact that we are inextricably woven into the very fabric of nature. Our sense of separateness, which on the one hand has fostered objective thinking and brought us the benefits of scientific breakthroughs, has also deeply affected our own understanding of ourselves as part of nature's interconnected system.

Poets, artists, psychologists, philosophers, and environmental activists are, each in the way of their own medium, calling for a return to and re-integration with nature. Their call is for harmony with nature, for a visual, auditory, and kinesthetic balance that tunes us to a state of well-being and inner harmony.

In my own search for a more integrated relationship between nature and humans, I was attracted to a unique geometric shape—the logarithmic spiral. Within this elegant pattern hides a common mathematical and geometric relationship that illustrates the living structure and harmony of the natural world. The unique design ratio of the spiral influences everything we consider beautiful in nature, art, and science. Its design is found in the architecture of virtually every culture throughout the world. In fact, this pattern is constantly experienced on an unconscious level, though it often goes unknown. Its pervasive design, found throughout a diversity of animals, plants, and human cultures, holds an important clue to the underlying nature of human development.

The term *SelfDesign* implies both a quality and a process. The word *Self* suggests the quality, reflecting the essence of an individual in holistic and universal terms. *Design* is the process, a creative act of seeking growth through learning and understanding. This process continues to deepen and guide lifelong development. To design one's Self is to work with one's natural patterns and to bring these forth in a uniquely expressive way.

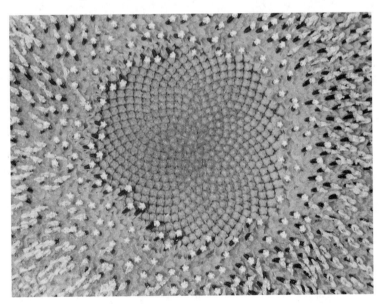

The center of the daisy radiates outward in complex logarithmic spirals in both directions. Pine cones, corn kernels, and pineapples all grow in logarithmic spirals as the parts organize themselves in patterns for growth.

Spirals in Nature

Spirals occur throughout nature, from the smallest micro-organisms to the macro-whirl of the galaxy. Let us first consider spirals at the macro level. Although we tend to appreciate the spiral nature of our galaxy, we often consider the path of the earth around the sun to be an ellipse. This is true if we imagine the sun as a still center. However, realizing that the moon is following a twirling earth and that the earth is following a sun orbiting around the center of the Milky Way galaxy, we have a more accurate map of the earth's and moon's movements as spirals. The paths of the earth around the sun and the moon around the earth are spiraling orbits. Because the center of the galaxy is also in motion, the path of the sun also assumes the form of a spiral.

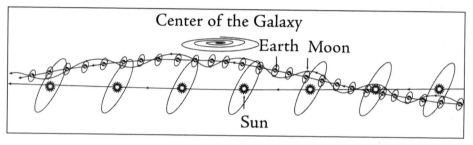

The earth, moon and sun move in ellipses only if the object that they are orbiting is still, which it never is. Therefore ellipses turn into spirals as each orbiting body follows along in the spiraling orbit of the central influence.

On the micro scale, the DNA molecule follows a double helix, two interconnected spirals that map the genetic structure of each life form. The very structure of life at the microscopic level, at the cellular level—our informational foundation—uses the spiral as its design.

Between these two extremes, the vast majority of plants and animals grow according to the mathematical integrity of the logarithmic spiral. A biological system has two fundamental tasks that are both complimentary and contradictory: it must increase in size and complexity in order to grow to maturity, and at the same time it must respect and maintain its own integrity of shape and function. The organism's ability to grow, yet maintain its original design form and proportion, requires a unique balance. This balance of growth and change with ongoing integrity of form is referred to as the logarithmic spiral, or the Golden Rectangle. The following illustration is from György Doczi's book *The Power of Limits*, and it beautifully illustrates how the mathematical ratio of the butterfly wing is proportional to the logarithmic ratio.

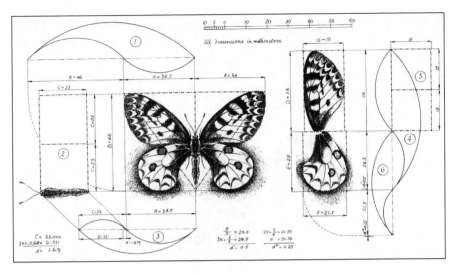

The logarithmic proportions give both beauty and balance to the shape of the butterfly.

The mathematics of the spiral can begin to be understood by observing the series of rectangles in the illustration that follows. First, notice that all of the rectangles have an identical proportion regardless of size. The smallest rectangle becomes larger through the addition of a square placed on the longer side of the rectangle, thus creating a new rectangle of equal proportion. The equiangular or logarithmic spiral is a map of exponential growth. However, this growth is in proportion to an organism's essential design, and the ratio is maintained throughout the organism's life.

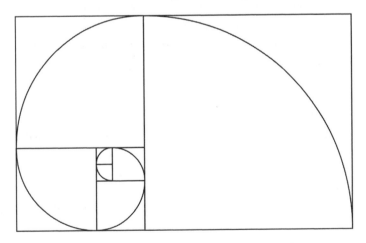

Logarithmic Spiral or Golden Rectangle

The balance between growth and proportion is also apparent in athletic forms that awaken the body's intelligence. In tai chi, for example, the distribution of weight on the feet is never equal, except for the beginning and ending postures. Throughout the movement meditation, the weight is shifted from one foot to the other in an approximate 2:3 ratio. I suspect that the ratio is optimally 89:144, which replicates that of the Golden Rectangle. This ratio is experienced during every movement in tai chi, with joints acting as markers for the adjacent sections of the body.

Because the human body is proportional to the ratio 1.618 to 1 or .618 to 1, our movements are expressions of this ratio.

There are many more examples of the spiral-ratio in nature. Over the years, I have also used the Golden Rectangle to gauge the influence people have within their relationships. For example, in some families the parents dominate and push into the domain of the child. There are also families in which the child is the boss and the parent is continually off balance. The following story illustrates how a dynamic balance can be found within the family and used to achieve both personal boundaries and collaborative space.

Several years ago I worked with a ten-year-old boy who threw the most intense temper tantrums I had ever seen. My observations suggested that the tantrums were perhaps the boy's only method of responding to his mother's overwhelming need to control and over-nurture him.

One day the mother phoned and asked if I would do some counseling with her son. Her main concern at the time was that he was lying. I told her that I would help, but only if he wanted me to and only if he determined what we would be doing together.

She was curious and said that she would set up a phone call between us. In the conversation with the boy, I discovered that he was doing poorly in spelling and wanted help in that area. When I offered to show him a technique for spelling perfectly that took just an hour to learn, he was excited. We met at the end of the week and worked together on my spelling method. His spelling success soon reached 100 percent on tests, and he was justifiably proud of himself.

Meanwhile, the mother phoned me again, requesting a session for herself. I agreed, and when we met she confessed that she had just hit her son during one of his tantrums. It was the first time this had happened, but she was terrified she would do it again. As we explored her fear, she told me that as a child she had been beaten by her mother for years. As an adult she had tried to be a model parent in order to cover up her own history and her fear that she would become like her own mother. But her over-nurturing had in fact become a form of abuse. She violated her son's space so completely that he went into rages to create some distance for himself.

I agreed to help this mother transform her hitting impulse. We began to discover that when she felt anger, the first thing she would do was to form a fist. I asked her to remember a series of happy and peaceful experiences in her life and at the same time to squeeze her fist. In this way she was able to connect clenching her hand with a calm, peaceful feeling. This "anchoring" technique shifted her so that when she next got angry and made the fist, it automatically triggered feelings that mitigated her anger and prevented the abuse that she feared.

Once this significant aspect of the problem was handled, I asked her if she did anything for herself. She said that from the day her children were born she had devoted all of her energy to them. I asked her to start taking thirty minutes a day for herself for one week. She did so, and at the end of the week she reported that this had been such a breakthrough for her that she was now taking two thirty-minute breaks each day. She added that she was feeling much more balanced as a mother and as a person.

Relating this story back to the logarithmic spiral or to the balance of tai chi postures, the learning is about the need to stay in our own bodies and not extend ourselves into other people's domains, violating their boundaries. If we stay two-thirds in our own space and share a consensual space of one-third each, we can keep our relationships in balance.

In the online course for SelfDesign we develop a complete set of strategies to help families and individuals create both personal boundaries and a collaborative space within relationships. Our focus is on designing new, simple language patterns to create a reciprocal balance of interaction that mirrors the Golden Rectangle, ensuring that everyone in a relationship is respectfully influencing one another.

Essence and Change

The ability of an organism to grow, while keeping its integrity of form and function, indicates the second paradigm of SelfDesign. The body and the conscious mind are ever-changing and growing with ever-increasing distinctions, while at the same time the unconscious mind and the spirit remain still and unchanging as the center of one's being. If you think about it, you probably have an inner and an outer sense of time that reflects this paradigm. You notice the passage of hours and days, and yet you are, at some level, aware of inner stillness of the infinite now, particularly when you are deeply immersed in something. In the natural world and in most cultures, the constant recurrence of the Golden Rectangle and the logarithmic spiral indicates the universal nature of a living quality as a mirror of our own inner beauty and harmony.

In the world of mathematics, the numbers that generate the Golden Rectangle are called the Fibonacci series, after the 13th century Italian who discovered this sequence. As you look at the series of numbers below, notice that each number in the series (with the exception of the first two numbers) is created by adding together the two previous numbers:

$$0, 1, 1, 2, 3, 5, 8, 13, 21, 34, 55, 89, 144 \ldots$$

To extend the basic understanding of the mathematical relationship of the spiral's equiangular qualities to an experiential interpretation, it is important to imagine this model's metaphoric qualities in order to incorporate the principles of growth and harmony into the patterns of our own living.

The Golden Rectangle in Art and Architecture

Humanity's unconscious awareness of the logarithmic ratio is clearly found in cultures that do not practice a theoretical study of mathematics yet consistently represent this ratio throughout their arts and crafts. In any indigenous culture living in harmony with nature, it is obvious that an appreciation for and integration with these natural harmonies exists in the artifacts of the society. As just one example, from Doczi's *The Power of Limits*, we see the spiral integrated into the curved shape of a Northwest Coast Haida hat.

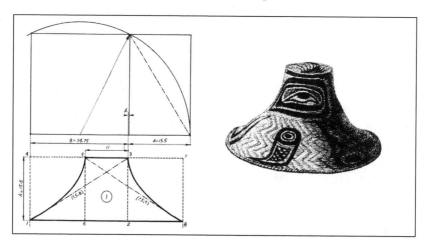

This Haida hat was made in a culture that did not have a mathematical understanding of the Golden Rectangle, yet their unconscious awareness of it in nature was consistently expressed in their work.

The fact that this shape was intuitively seen as a measure of beauty and balance is an important clue to its integral aspect in subconscious human awareness. A sense of geometric or spatial intelligence is universal among cultures that never met or communicated, yet consistently represented the exact mathematical ratio throughout their work.

In further investigations, we find that the more mathematically sophisticated cultures, such as the Greeks and Egyptians, wrote about the Golden Rectangle and integrated its proportions into their artifacts and buildings. The following picture of the Parthenon is just one example of how the building is proportioned to the Golden Rectangle.

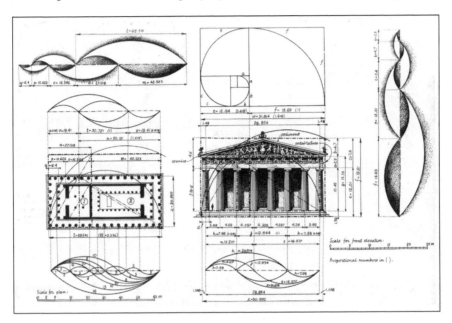

The Parthenon was built by a culture that knew the 1.618 to 1 ratio and expressed it in their art and architecture with amazing precision.

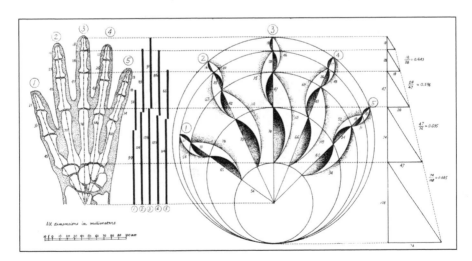

Gyorgy Doczi researched and drew amazing representations of the spiral throughout nature. This analysis of the human hand is one of his most beautiful. Each joint in relation to the joint next to is represented by the ratio 1.618 to 1.

The Plant as a Metaphor for Learning

As stated earlier, a bio-organism's growth demonstrates an increase in complexity while maintaining a balance of form and energy. Living things grow and mature toward a form that, at some point, fosters the creation of the organism's next generation. The life cycle returns to the beginning: acorn to seed, seed to shoot, shoot to tree, tree to acorn.

If we are looking for the deeper meanings of human development and lifelong learning, we need to understand that the processes of biological growth and psychological development draw from deep and mysterious realms. When are we the designers, and when are we designed? How do these influences weave together to create the fabric of our being?

One of the mysteries of the biological sciences is this ability of living things to "know" how to grow toward a mature state. Pierre Teilhard de Chardin referred to this essential genius as *entelechy*. The intelligence for a kitten to become a cat or an acorn to become an oak tree are just two examples of the principle. Perhaps our intelligence does not reside only within our minds. Perhaps it is our body-mind that converts a signal of the collective unconsciousness into our design and our thoughts. It is certainly beyond the scope of this work to ascertain an answer, except to appreciate the beauty and mystery of life. It is interesting to note that the etymology of the word *genius*, from its Sanskrit origins, is connected to such words as *generation, genuine, genitals, genie,* and *guardian spirit of a person or place*. The genius within our body-minds moves us through the cycle of life, ensuring that we will grow according to our own unique design and that life will continue.

The following diagram uses the stages of plant development as a fundamental metaphor for SelfDesign and the lifelong learning and developmental process. It is an appropriate parallel, because human beings go through the same maturational stages as any other bio-organism. These stages can be determined by genetic, entelechic, and morphogenic influences as well as the will of the SelfDesigner.

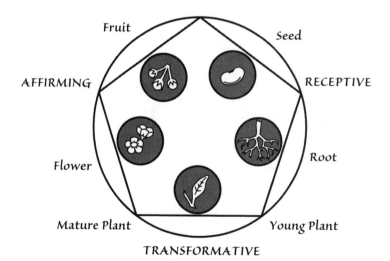

The five phases of plant development are: Stage 1-Seed. Stage 2-Rooting. Stage 3-Sexual transformation and maturity. Stage 4-Flowering. Stage 5-Fruit.

The metaphor of the plant is useful in understanding the entire journey around the wheel of life. We can think about life as beginning with a seed (a sense of purpose and quality of being) and ending with a fruit (a sense of realization and accomplishment of one's life purpose), thereby setting the stage for the next generation and finishing the purpose of this one.

On the macro-level, the five stages of a plant's life translate to human life in the following way: Stage 1 and 2 occur in childhood, Stage 3 takes us through the transition years of puberty, Stage 4 is our adult life, and Stage 5 is our elderhood.

On the micro-level, it is important to see the larger patterns in the small or simple processes. If we look at learning a relatively simple skill, like throwing a bowl on a potter's wheel or learning to drive a car, we can see the beginning and ending in the same way we view the cycle of the plant, starting with the seed and ending with the fruit. Using the plant as a metaphor for human development allows us to move from the seed of an idea or discovery, through a process of grounding the idea in our unconscious, to the "ah-ha" of mastering the task for the first time. Just before the breakthrough of understanding and ability we usually experience the struggle and difficulty inherent in learning. We move from the immature beginning of an idea to its comprehensive understanding. With practice and focus, the idea blossoms and finally comes to fruition as a fully developed skill or understanding that contributes to the individual and the world.

A Three-Dimensional Model for SelfDesign

Let us briefly examine a transition from linear to circular thinking and from circular to spherical thinking. If we take the Golden Rectangle and put it into the three planes of x, y, and z, we can create an interesting shape. The following image illustrates the integration of three Golden Rectangles into the three planes. The next illustration shows how these joined rectangles can form the basis for a three-dimensional figure called the "icosahedron," which has twenty sides.

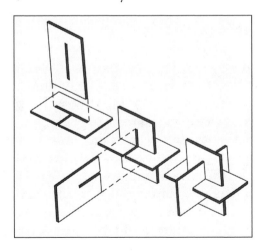

If you place three golden rectangles in relation to each other on the x, y, and z axis you get the interesting configuration above. If you then connect all the corners, you have one of the five Platonic solids, the icosahedron, which follows.

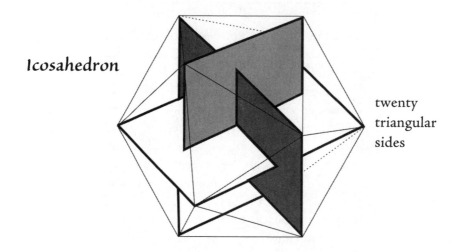

Icosahedron

twenty
triangular
sides

This sets the stage for the next chapter, which takes us on a journey to our inner architecture and the domain of experience. The logarithmic spiral informs us with its fundamental qualities of growth, change, and increase in understanding combined with orientation to the unchanging center of balance and stillness.

I am convinced that our adventure of learning is far more comprehensive when our experience in the world is a reflection of our inner integrity, when our outward and inward experiences resonate with one another. When we are respected and loved, we unfold our humanity as an expression of our own love. The duality of the world finds a balance point at the heart of our experience. We are the integration of both the mother's and the father's genetic information within one body. We can best grow and change as comprehensive learning organisms when we remain oriented to our essence, to our essential nature. Only then is our growth and change in balance so that we maintain our true identity. Our life enthusiasm is a sacred place for us all, and it stems from the etymological root of *enthusiasm*, *en theos*, or the experience of the god within.

The following illustration superimposes a drawing of the human body onto the integration of the three Golden Rectangles. It provides a beginning map for understanding our patterns of living as human beings. The three sets of pairs of body orientation are front and back, left and right, and top and bottom. Our front and back provide a sense of past and future around a present. Our left and right provide a sense of our masculine and feminine influences. The top and bottom represent our mind and body, and, in an evolutionary sense through the development of the species, our unique place in the universe. We have a map that begins to inform us about the territory in which we live and to help us learn about who we are as human beings.

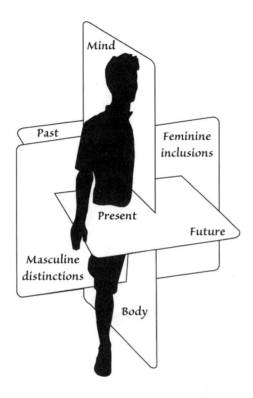

We are standing in a cube of up and down, front and back, and left and right. This cube can also be represented by three sets of opposites in three golden rectangles. The up and down plane is mind and body, front and back is future and past, and left and right is male and female.

Conclusion

The concept of spiral growth and development is inherent in SelfDesign. If we limit ourselves to linear thinking, it is true that we can be efficient in getting a task accomplished, but this kind of single-mindedness tends to disconnect the task from the rest of our lives. On the other hand, circular thinking, while it does include the natural patterns of development into our tasks and life plans, can sometimes cause us to feel like we are only "going in circles." We have a sense of making no progress. It is the spiral metaphor—using the language of nature rather than of industry or information—that offers a map for our natural processes of learning and living. Just as we can never step into the same river twice, the context in which we are moving is always evolving, and we never come around to quite the same place. We are changed in each moment, with every experience we have. Each spring we return to the same season of the year, but we bring to this new season all that we have learned in the past year. If we stay in harmony with nature and with ourselves, our spiraling becomes our dance.

CHAPTER 2

Unfolding the Infinite Interior

From wonder into wonder existence opens.
—*Lao Tse*

Adults marvel at the joyful enthusiasm for the love of learning, as well as the constant unfolding of new and complex skills evident in virtually every baby. It is as the years go by that we often see the joy diminish and sometimes disappear.

"Unfolding the infinite interior," a phrase coming out of the field of cybernetics, has been adopted within SelfDesign as a definition for genius. In his book *Cosmography*, Buckminster Fuller wrote

> All children are born geniuses, but are swiftly de-geniused by their elder's harsh or dull dismissal of the child's intuitive sense of what could be relevant. Children spontaneously weigh all information from their immediate experience and try to relate it to other experiences of some time before. The incipient geniuses must somehow weather, year after year, the barrage of admonitions to ignore what they spontaneously think, instead of only paying attention to what others think and are trying to teach.

What would happen if as adults we designed our relationships with children in such a way that they would not lose their enthusiasm?

At birth we experience ourselves at the center of the universe. We have no distinctions, we have determined no relationships or causal events. We are awash in a sea of colors and sounds, textures, temperatures, and sensations, each indistinguishable from the other. Every child is born without a culture, without identity, without language. Every child is born aware and fully present. This is the state that we must respect and trust as a legitimate worldview. It holds curiosity and enthusiasm at its center.

Using the techniques of SelfDesign, the vast majority of the graduates of Wondertree and Virtual High have achieved quite remarkable results through the rediscovery of their original enthusiasm. As adults they are living proof that the joyful enthusiasm and curiosity of childhood, extended lifelong, are the secret ingredients in becoming a genius. Therefore it is important to learn the intra- and interpersonal technologies that nurture joyfulness of learning in children as well as to learn what specifically interferes with the unfolding of each child's natural intelligence. It becomes more important to understand children and to learn to enter into a respectful conversation with them than to force them to think like us.

A new paradigm of intelligence, based on loving relationships rather than IQ testing, can increase the chances of bringing forth a more respectful and collaborative world. Our very definition of ourselves as thinking beings—*homo sapiens*, self-conscious beings—is transformed by a new definition of ourselves as loving beings—*homo amans*, a term coined by Humberto Maturano and Pille Bunnell. By living in this realm, our creativity is nurtured to come to full blossom, and the genius within each of us begins to unfold.

Schooling Folds Along the Dotted Line

As part of making public education more efficient, our society has focused on the quantifiable aspects of learning rather than focusing on children's genuine learning needs. Traditional education today is often more in service of its own bureaucratic and financial needs than it is about creating an optimum learning environment. Classrooms and grades serve the system, not the child, and testing and measurement serve the needs for efficiency and accountability of government.

School educators are taught to equate learning with schooling, and when asked what they do for a living they usually say, "I teach school." A pervasive myth within the culture of schooling is that children cannot learn, or at least cannot learn well, unless they are professionally taught. I appreciate the many dedicated, well-intentioned teachers who do their best to help children learn, yet I sense that the system of schooling itself negates much of their effort. For years I have listened to hundreds of stories of children and parents who are unhappy with traditional schooling. These anecdotal stories can be backed up with a number of studies in which the real stakeholders in education—the learners—have been asked if their education is meaningful and relevant to their lives. Approximately 80 percent of students interviewed in a survey conducted in a typical North American school system and referenced in chapter 6 of this book stated that they felt their schooling process was not meaningful or worthwhile.

Though instruction is not all that happens in a classroom, it is the dominant process, as demonstrated in the following diagram. It is a reductionist model of human interaction that is structured to ignore everything except how much information is remembered as a result of what is taught.

The Teaching Compared to The Learning Dynamic

This type of educational model measures the externals, the behavioral results focused on meeting external expectations, while excluding human experience and emotions. Educators become focused on content and curriculum, not realizing that true, relevant learning is primarily about people and experiences. In interviews I have conducted with teachers over the years, they consistently report that their teacher training focused on delivering content and managing classrooms, virtually ignoring the human learning condition.

Schooling as Learning

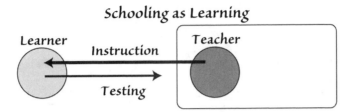

In school we think of learning as a result of teaching; we have forgotten that learning exists on its own. Teachers and parents often think that if we don't teach, children will not learn. However, teaching is only one of many dynamics for learning.

Let us turn our attention, then, to what learning really looks like as a process integral to understanding ourselves and our world. Take a moment to compare the previous "teaching dynamic" diagram with the SelfDesign Paragon on the following page, a model aimed toward excellence, integrity and fulfillment.

As you can see, the SelfDesign model unfolds as a much more comprehensive process than does the model for traditional education. It is aligned with our authentic human nature and it evolves from the richness and rhythms of real life experience. While traditional schooling generally focuses on only one approach to learning (learning mode 3 of the paragon), SelfDesign provides eight interactive dynamics, illustrating the multi-dimensionality and the complex tapestry of learning. Several other innovative and progressive educational programs do include a number of the "living as learning" ideas within the classroom. SelfDesign extends this idea considerably further, taking the processes out into the real world and into the depths of human experience. With the paragon model, learners can be validated for the kinds of learning that emerge from natural curiosity and valuable human interaction.

Using the SelfDesign Paragon, we can examine five different developmental elements within the eight types, or modes, of learning:

+ Learning as state
+ Learning as process
+ Learning as strategy
+ Learning as pattern
+ Learning as conversation

Learning as state starts in the center of the paragon at zero, illustrating that our emotional state and fundamental attitudes, beliefs, and assumptions about who we are and how we act as the central conditions for learning. A human being in balance is pre-disposed to newness, to learning as a dynamic of creatively interacting with the world.

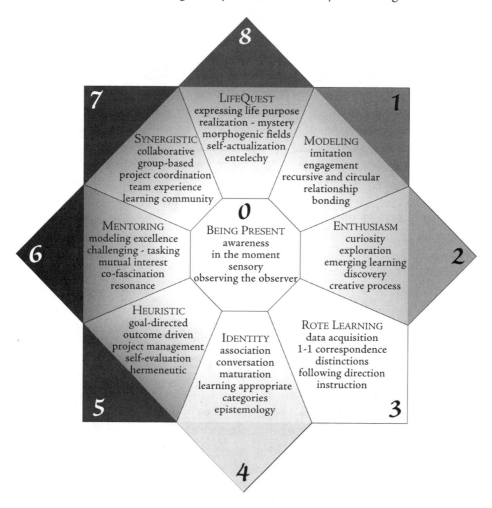

The SelfDesign Paragon illustrates eight kinds of human learning, only one of which (3) is common in schooling. The other seven emerge out of our curiosity and presence in the moment; through our engagement in the world we learn and discover.

Learning as process involves the first three modes of learning. Learning as process refers to the way we are designed as learners and to how our neurology is predisposed to creating relationships and making distinctions and associations. In learning mode 1, our early experience of bonding sets the tone and ground for our sense of ourselves and others. It is the basis for modeling and for relationship. It establishes our individuality and our connection with the world. Learning mode 2 is based on our natural enthusiasm and curiosity. Our fascination with newness allows for the growth and expansion of our intelligence. Our explorations become creative play, and we start to understand the dynamics of relationships throughout our experience. Learning mode 3 explores the mapping of name to process, fundamental in language acquisition. Memorization of facts and figures through direct instruction resides in this mode, and it is the heart of traditional schooling methods. The acquisition of such knowledge is certainly an important learning process, yet it is only one-eighth of the entire complex.

Learning as strategy is represented by learning modes 4 and 5 as we develop a conscious perspective on learning and begin to design and modify the learning process. Setting goals and developing a sense of identity and character are second-level modifications, whereby we reflect on our process and begin to make choices according to evolving criteria. This is where SelfDesign begins to really take shape in that we can create better and more comprehensive strategies to get results more eloquently.

Learning as pattern and learning as conversation are intimately involved in learning modes 6 and 7, mentoring and synergistic community. Our patterns of living can be modeled to perfection by working with mentors—those individuals already engaged in the praxis, or practice, of excellence. And working on group projects creates a synergistic energy that transforms the learner through the process itself.

Learning mode 8, LifeQuest, is an integration of all learning modes in alignment with a learner's unique sense of purpose. Being in touch with why we are here and how our deepest meaning arises is an expression our humanity and our sense of fulfillment.

While the schooling model tends to be restrictive and reductionistic, and the SelfDesign Paragon is designed to be holistic and comprehensive, an additional and important political factor should be noted in the comparison of these two situations. Most often teachers and students in traditional schools have little or no choice about the content of curricula and about whether or not to work together. SelfDesign, on the other hand, is founded on choice and on mutual agreements, with learners and mentors agreeing to support one another and work together. Changing this precept alone would address one of the current educational system's most fundamental problems: the issue of learners who are disinterested and disenfranchised and who therefore are apathetic and inattentive. If the learners were to influence and create the learning path, many discipline problems would disappear. The balance of power would shift to a more equal place, one conducive to self-authority and mutual respect, rich with opportunity for mutual growth.

Throughout the remainder of the book, we will continue to compare the "schooling as learning" and "living as learning" models to demonstrate how the genuine learning needs of children are met by the SelfDesign process.

Unfolding Our Natural Genius

How do we avoid limiting ourselves and our children, encouraging instead the full unfolding of human intelligence? How can we create honoring, open, and gentle relationships with children so that their natural genius comes forth? In one sense, the art of helping children within SelfDesign comes in getting out of their way, in making sure that their unfolding is not limited. Because we can't help influence and be part of the process, we need to understand how it is that we may inadvertently diminish the natural development of our children. Although this is equivalent in some ways to a fish becoming aware of the water in which it swims, we must become aware of the context of our thinking in order to understand how we actually influence our children. It becomes critical to develop an understanding of the hidden limiting beliefs in our cultural and family language patterns if we are to enhance our relationships. Similarly, if we can begin to notice and observe inner activities and become aware of the relationships among the players on the stage of our inner drama, we can begin to play the role of director in our own lives. We can influence, by design, the direction of the unfolding of our infinite interior into its interplay with the infinite exterior.

In John Briggs's book on genius, *Fire in the Crucible*, he considers that "thinking, which has such a high premium in our society, may not be as significant as other activities of the mind." He suggests that "genius doesn't depend on any one contingency" but has much more to do with "the sense of being instantaneously in touch with the mystery and truth of existence." "Everyone," he states, "has such moments when they are outside of the categories of consensual reality and into a rich, hidden realm." Children tend to live in these mysterious and rich realms, losing access to them as they mature. Genius may therefore be more about sustaining the qualities of early childhood than learning any specific methodology. In fact, the imposition of a methodology on comprehensive thinkers may in fact be a cause of many learning problems we see in children today. When intelligence is defined only as ability within academics, the majority of a learner's actual assets are ignored.

If a child does not conform to our expectations, society is often quick to judge and to label. Once children are diagnosed with dyslexia or ADHD, the focus is on treating the symptoms, thereby treating the children as though they indeed *are* their label.

Many children unable to cope within the school system have come to Wondertree with labels of learning disabilities. Because I have never accepted a diagnosis as anything more than a story, I have begun conversations with these children to find out from them what their inner worlds are actually like. Through observation and questioning, I elicit descriptions from them of their own experience, holding the assumption that children have legitimate authority for their own points of view and for their own processes.

It must be profoundly intimidating for a parent, with only intuition as a guide, to challenge the experts with their scientific tests and diagnoses. Recently, however, a consultant who is collecting the diagnostic histories of a number of Wondertree's learners noticed a surprising number of multiple, contradictory diagnoses from a variety of independent experts for several of the children. Even when the experts agree, most learners and their families are left without a reliable and meaningful path for change and healing. The number of failures through treatment seems to be more predominant than the successes, and even if my sample tends to put me more in contact with the failures, the stories are consistent enough to cause me to question the entire process.

Unfolding Wondertree into Virtual High

In the introduction I described the evolution of Wondertree into Virtual High, which furthered my opportunity to work with youth who wanted to learn yet could not and who most often came to us with a multitude of problems. Our group included children burdened with every learning disability imaginable, as well as a range from straight-A students who found school meaningless all the way to angry, wild-eyed, rebellious youth—and our experiment in the integrity and well-being of every learner continued. It was a natural progression that gained momentum from giving attention to the needs of the learners and truly listening to the children, who were wanting something entirely different from what the conventional educational system had to offer.

The unfolding continued as the program evolved. Each learner at Virtual High experienced dramatic shifts as the year progressed, and I offer the following story of a young man named Josh as an example of how focusing on integrity and freedom allows learners to blossom.

In the summer of 1993, Michael Maser and I met with all our high-school-age learners and their families. During these interviews we established a set of agreements with each learner. In our first meeting with Josh and his mother, we heard an extensive history of his learning problems. Josh had been diagnosed with just about every disorder in the book, including Tourette's syndrome, and he was also considerably overweight and suffering from allergies. After years of working on my own health problems with natural foods, vitamins, and herbs, and then using my experience in the natural-foods industry to counsel others, I felt confident that nutrition was a primary cause of Josh's learning problems. Toward the end of our meeting, we told Josh that we would take him into our program if he would make two agreements. The first was that he would go on a diet that I would specify at some point in the program. I kept it vague and well in the future, and he readily agreed. His mother was willing to support him in Virtual High if he would complete one school course, English 10, during the year. Again, he readily agreed, because he was willing to do just about anything to avoid public school. As Josh settled into his new program, he began to discover what freedom and responsibility felt like. I knew that Josh would not stick to a diet plan at this point, as I had no leverage with him yet. I did, however, build rapport with him over the next eight months. Josh enjoyed freedom with no expectations, and he had many opportunities to share his enthusiasm with other young people. Each day he and the other students were becoming more alive. I saw that he was beginning to love this place, a place that honored his deep and previously unmet need for fulfillment. Josh's English course had arrived as a shrink-wrapped package of books. Occasionally when Josh's mother was at the center she would ask him how it was going, and he would assure her he was making progress. Every now and then, unbeknownst to Josh, I would go up to his office and look under the couch to see that the English books were still lying there, shrink-wrapped and untouched. I never challenged Josh in his deception; I saw it as an act of being true to himself, if not to his mother.

Toward the end of the first school year, I requested a meeting with Josh and his mother. Josh looked nervous as we all sat down in my office. After a short check-in, I asked Josh how he was really doing. He said that he was afraid he might get kicked out of the program. I suggested that living in fear was no way to live one's life and that, as his mentor, I could not support this. The only help I could offer, I said, was to withdraw my support for him remaining in the program. Josh knew that in our consensus community, membership was sustained by everyone agreeing that each person should be in the community. The withdrawal of support started a process that could end with asking the person to leave.

I said, "Josh, let's make it simple. Let me show you the door, and then you are finished here." I got up, invited Josh over to the door, opened the door, and encouraged him to step out onto the porch. I closed the door, leaving him standing there looking devastated and his mother sitting in my office in bewilderment. I winked and suggested that this should be enough time, and I went back to open the door.

"How are you feeling, Josh?" I asked.

"Awful."

"Would you like back into the program?"

He nodded, looking confused but excited, and he quickly came back into the office. When we sat down I asked him again, "Josh, how are you doing now?"

"I am still worried about being kicked out."

"OK, my friend," I responded, "you are out of the program again. Let me show you to the door."

I got up and gestured to him to go out the front door, and once again he went out onto the porch. This time I waited a bit longer before inviting him in again. As we sat down in the office, I asked, "Josh, would you like to be back in the program?"

This time he leaned back in his chair, and his puzzled look began to turn to a smile. I said, "How many times would you like me to kick you out of the program before you are no longer afraid?"

He looked at me for a long moment and replied, "Brent, I am starting to get it. Twice should be enough."

"Good," I said. "I don't want you to live in fear. I want you to live in fulfillment. I am glad to work with you from a sense of well-being and cooperation." After a long pause that allowed the whole process to sink in, I said, "That reminds me, Josh what about your agreement with your mother to do that English course?"

He began an elaborate story about his progress with the course, and I quickly interrupted him to suggest that he bring his course books down from his room. He looked cornered, but I told him to hurry and to trust me. When he returned with his shrink-wrapped books, I ceremoniously put the package in the middle of the floor. A look of shock came over his mother's face.

I explained how proud I was of Josh for being true to himself by not doing something he didn't really want to do. I suggested that in this act he had achieved the first level of integrity, a fundamental part of our program. Being true to himself was more important than doing an English course, I suggested. Looking at his mother, I said, "While I did not want to be a partner in Josh's lie, I did feel that it was a minor crime compared to his actual accomplishment of being true to himself." Josh's mother ultimately agreed to release Josh from his English course agreement, and he was decidedly pleased with the miracle he felt I had worked. I chose this moment to remind him of his initial agreement with me to go on a three-month diet. The time had come, I said, for him to honor his agreement. Since he had just been "kicked out" twice, I had the leverage I wanted, and I knew he knew I was serious. Virtual High had become a vital part of his life by now. Josh would do anything to stay, and he agreed to begin his diet the next day.

The next morning we met again in my office. Once we got into the details of this new program I discovered the full extent of his diet for the first fifteen years of his life. He had rarely eaten a vegetable, except French-fried potatoes. His diet was primarily pasta and cheese, candy, and pop, and he was fifty pounds overweight. Running and climbing stairs were difficult tasks for him, and his overall energy was low. In the scores of times he had been interviewed by doctors and psychologists, he had apparently never been asked about his diet. It seemed very likely to me that his many diagnoses for neurological and learning disorders were connected with the lack of vital nutrients in his body. I told him that I wanted him to eat nothing but brown rice and vegetables for three months. His look of horror accompanied us as we headed out the door to go shopping together.

First we bought organic brown rice, and then we began to explore the varieties of vegetables in the produce section. Buying several foods Josh had never seen or tasted, we returned home and began to prepare our meal. As the aromatic rice began to cook, Josh and I examined the colors, textures, and features of each vegetable we chopped. We made cooking a journey of exploration, and eventually we sat down to eat our stir-fried meal. Josh tasted his first bite of broccoli and gagged. It took over an hour of coaching Josh for him to chew and swallow the first piece of broccoli and then another hour to finish the first meal. I helped Josh learn that he could enjoy the texture and taste of each bite, and he stuck to his diet, cooking and eating three meals of rice and vegetables every day. During those first three months Josh's life transformed. He lost weight and began to feel stronger each day. Everyone around him witnessed Josh's metamorphosis, and he himself marveled at his emerging energy and clarity of mind. Before starting the diet it was difficult for Josh to even hold a pen and write without his muscles cramping painfully. Within the first month of his diet, however, he went out and bought himself a journal and began writing, and three months later he had filled up several journals with ideas for making movies. His confidence and his willingness to join with fellow students in Virtual High activities soared, and soon he was performing in our monthly "coffee house."

Josh was so pleased with his weight loss and his health gain that at the end of three months he decided to remain on the diet for another six months, eventually losing fifty pounds. He began taking on challenges that had before limited his world at every turn. We worked on handshakes and conversations so that he could successfully apply for a job he wanted at a video store. By the end of our program, Josh had made his first short film of about ten minutes and had worked at several movie-related jobs. He focused most of his day on movie-making, and at one point he even jumped on a plane to New York to go and meet his favorite movie director in person.

Josh (l) and Alex (r) perform during one of our monthly talent nights. Stepping into their Blues Brothers routine they discovered—like nearly every learner at Virtual High—previously untapped depths of self and creativity.

Over the next few years, Josh traveled in Europe on his own, managed a team of workers at a local cinema, and produced and premiered his first half-hour documentary. He decided to go to a local college with an excellent film school, passing the three-hour exam that allowed him entrance without a high school diploma. Soon after, he met with me to toast what he considered was about the shortest high school equivalent possible, and we celebrated the life skills that enabled Josh to pursue his dream.

This is just one example of how focusing on the heart of each learner's experience so that they live in fulfillment and health is far more important than focusing on subjects or courses. Letting learners determine their own experience is the simple, profound, and essential core of SelfDesign.

"Stop Sucking Your Thumb"

Over and over, I've seen joyous results when people are encouraged to listen to their inner voice. When we are trying to extinguish an unwanted behavior, we often do so by imposing an externally defined ideal and expecting ourselves to simply stop the negative habit. Until we are able to understand that the behavior is serving a fundamental need at some deep level, it is extremely difficult to change our pattern. Once the inner need is made visible to us, we are then able to choose a more positive habit that both meets our need and resolves the conflict.

The following story is another example of some work I did in the context of a casual relationship with a young person. One summer, my daughter's friend Barb came to stay with us for three weeks. The girls had been friends for many years, but when they were both six years old Barb's family had moved away. Holiday visits and letters helped maintain the friendship. Over the years, Barb had retained the habit of sucking her thumb. When she was younger we paid no attention to it, but now she was twelve and obviously becoming a young woman, and we noticed that she still frequently sucked her thumb.

I decided to ask her what was happening in her life around her thumb sucking. I asked her if it was an issue for her or her family or friends.

> Barb: "Yes, my parents hate it and the kids at school make fun of me. My parents have taken me to doctors for help, but I can't stop. There's nothing I can do that works. I hate it!"

> Brent: "Barb, I think I could help if you're interested. I do want to say I think you are sucking your thumb for a very important reason. I think it's no one else's business but yours. Personally, I don't think you should stop."

> Barb: "Huh?"

> Brent: "In fact, now that I think about it, I missed out because I never did suck my thumb. You seem to be an expert, so I'd like to ask you something. Do you think you could coach me in thumb sucking so that I could find out what it feels like?"

> Barb: "You've got to be kidding."

> Brent: "No, the thing is that I'm a professional educator. I'm in the business of learning, and I am an expert at learning. I travel all over the place looking for opportunities to learn, and I don't know much about thumb sucking. Your demonstration of excellence as a thumb sucker has got me curious."

Barb took her thumb out of her mouth, laughed, and repeated: "You've *got* to be kidding."

Brent: "Look, I'll make you a deal. If you show me how to suck my thumb as well as you do, I'll show you how to get people to stop bugging you."

Barb replied in a shy and disbelieving way: "OK."

Brent: "Let's start tomorrow. We've talked about it enough for today, and besides, it's going to be easy for you. Let's go swimming."

The next day I approached Barb with exaggerated curiosity.

Brent: "You know, Barb, I was thinking all through the evening that there must be something really rewarding about thumb sucking, and I want to find out what that is for myself."

Barb: "I don't know why I do it. I keep imagining how it looks to others, so I am really self-conscious and nervous."

Brent: "Well, I'm ready to learn. Are you ready to teach me the fine art of thumb sucking?"

Barb: "You're not really serious. You're just trying to fool me, aren't you? It's a trick, and you really just want me to stop."

Brent: "Actually, I want you to keep sucking your thumb, at least long enough to teach me how to suck mine. You're right that there is a trick. The secret is that you get to be the magician, because I'm going to show you how to do a magic trick. Have you ever learned a magic trick before?"

Barb: "Yeah, I learned a neat card trick. Should I show you?"

Brent: "Sure!" After Barb's demonstration I said, "Ah, what seemed impossible at first was easy once you let me in on the secret. Let's see if we can discover the secret to thumb sucking. I'm ready, and first I want to get the hand position." We practiced a bit, and then I said, "OK, good, now what do I do with my tongue? And what about the rest of my hand? OK, this finger goes up beside my nose, ah yes, that is much less awkward. Now, how do I hold my body?"

Barb: "I don't understand, what does my body have to do with it?"

Brent: "Well, I've noticed that whenever you are sucking your thumb, you change your body posture and you stand in a very special way."

Barb: "I do?"

Brent: "Yes, watch me for a minute. If 100 percent of my weight is on my right foot, then I'm standing only on that foot. If it's 50/50, then I'm standing evenly on both feet. What do you sense the percentage of weight is on each foot when you suck your thumb?"

We played around with this for about fifteen minutes, shifting weight from side to side and trying body postures. We discovered there is a particular posture for thumb sucking. Barb's typical stance had one hip skewed over, with about 85 percent of weight shifted to the left foot. When we both matched that posture exactly, Barb mentioned that she was going to a chiropractor because she was developing serious back problems.

After a bit more practice I said, "OK, Barb, let me practice this for the rest of the day. Before we stop, can we suck thumbs together one more time? And let me try that card trick on you to make sure I've got it as well." Barb looked at me in disbelief mixed with a tinge of pleasure and agreed.

The next day I worked with Barb about ten times, refining my technique and elaborating on the art of thumb sucking. I noticed that our rapport was deepening and we were having fun.

Brent: "All right, now I really understand why you like sucking your thumb. It feels wonderful, and deep down inside I get a sense of calm, a deep sense of security and comfort. Wow!"

I got a look out of the corner of her eye, and no comment.

That afternoon while I was standing looking out over the lake and sucking my thumb, Barb came up to me and said, "There *is* a nice feeling deep inside, and I hate it when everyone gets on my case. The feelings are all mixed up now, and I am very confused."

Brent: "I can appreciate that, and I've been noticing that there is something very familiar about the warm and secure feeling I get from it. Do you want to join me? The feeling seems really appropriate here beside the lake with no one around to watch us."

We stood together, unabashedly sucking our thumbs as an osprey flew overhead.

The next day I shared a discovery with Barb. "Hey, I think I know why the feeling is so familiar. It feels like the feeling I used to get when I meditated regularly many years ago."

Barb: "Really?"

Brent: "Yeah, and now that I think about it, I had a very particular posture that I used to sit in to create that feeling. I used to sit in the lotus posture, and I remember that there were even different hand postures, holding fingers together in different patterns like this, or this."

Barb: "And thumb sucking feels the same?"

Brent: "It's very similar, and now I see why you suck your thumb so much, because it takes you instantly to this wonderful meditative space. No wonder you wouldn't stop. I wouldn't stop either if I were you."

Barb: "So what am I going to do?"

Brent: "Well, I have an idea. What if we could find a meditation posture that nobody would notice you doing? We know it could give you the same feeling as sucking your thumb, but this way you wouldn't get hassled."

Barb: "I don't really understand what you mean."

Brent: "OK, what if we stood perfectly balanced, like I mean totally 50/50. What if we kept our bodies perfectly symmetrical, and what if we invented a hand posture for both hands that no one else would notice? What if we trained ourselves to move the meditative feeling from thumb sucking to this new posture? Let's give it a try."

Barb and I worked for the next half hour shifting the meditative state of thumb sucking to our new symmetrical posture. We chose an arm posture that worked for us and a hand position with our fingers out of sight.

Brent: "So, Barb, how does it feel? Can you get the same state with our new posture?"

Barb: "Sure, wow, this is neat!"

Brent: "And if you were standing with a group of your friends or with your parents, would any of them tease you for standing like this?"

Barb: "Ah, now I get it. That's the trick, isn't it? I can have my feeling and no one will hassle me to stop."

Brent: "Right, I think you really understand it now. Let's practice it for our last three days here at the lake, so we can keep talking about our new technique."

By the end of our vacation time, Barb was no longer sucking her thumb habitually. She now chose to create the state with her new posture. We said good-bye to Barb and headed home for the year.

Two months later I got an excited phone call from Barb's father, exclaiming that he and his wife had just noticed that Barb was no longer sucking her thumb. In fact, they realized they hadn't seen her suck her thumb since our lake holiday. He asked, "How in the world did you get her to stop?"

I responded, "I didn't really notice that she was sucking her thumb. I guess she must have stopped on her own."

Nine years later, when I asked Barb if I could use her story in this book, I was amazed to hear she had only a vague memory of how much trouble her thumb sucking had caused her. She could remember that people had tried to stop her, but the process she and I shared had been forgotten. My daughter remembered it, however, and shared that she had learned many techniques like this from me by observing my work with other learners.

The Architecture of the Interior

As we have discussed, the move toward giving value to our interior experience can only occur as we step away from valuing how others perceive and define us. In a larger context, we need to step beyond the scientific paradigm begun by Galileo, Newton, Descartes, and their contemporaries before we find access to a new and more comprehensive understanding of universe and self. In this place, self-experience informs us as an authority, versus the currently accepted notion that information comes toward us from outside, based on the authority and expertise of others.

The paradigm shift during the Renaissance, discussed in chapter 0, changed our model from seeing the world as flat to seeing our planet as three-dimensional and spherical. While we have now lived for several hundred years with that understanding and view of our outer world, the inner realms of our lives have remained flat. It requires another shift to recognize the true dimension of our lives, a shift that will align our outer scientific models with our inner experience.

Each year that I have worked with learners I have also studied with or extensively read mentors who have given me deep insights and new models for expanding my work. Through my integration of their remarkable theories, I have come to understand that the power of SelfDesign lies in its comprehensive blend of practical real-life experiences with the latest scientific insights into human development.

Reading the works of Carl Jung, I found graphic images from his cross-cultural studies into representations of the psyche. Each contained a combination of concentric circles and quadrants in varying and complex patterns. He called these images *mandalas*, a Sanskrit term. As I studied these mandalas and played with reducing them to their most basic elements, I realized that our common representation of the qualities of body, heart, mind, and spirit could be graphically demonstrated within the mandala. By applying the four qualities of humanness to the four quadrants of the psyche, I arrived at the following image.

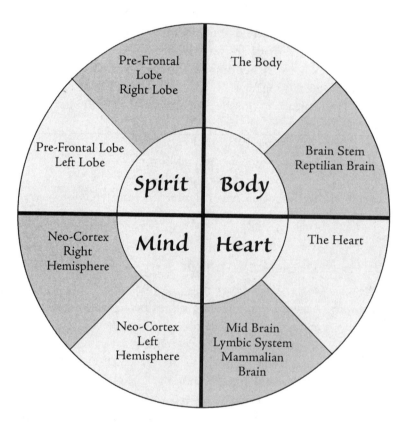

The common understanding of physical (body), relational (heart), intellect (mind), and spiritual (spirit) can be expanded to match the new evolutionary and developmental model of the mind as a fourfold structure. The duality of each stage of development and the dynamic relationships emerging between the pairs, as wells as between the other aspects of body/mind, represent a new and comprehensive model of the individual as a collaborative "we."

These qualities are not separate and exclusive but are aspects of our whole. This kind of map or graph, however, is a flat representation of experiential realms. In the same way that a globe is a far more accurate representation of the earth than is a two-dimensional map, we need to accurately demonstrate the dimensionality of our experience. The question can be asked, "What three-dimensional shape meets the requirements of four-ness and concentricity?"

The tetrahedron shape that follows is the central shape used by Buckminster Fuller in his comprehensive rethinking of the principles and processes in the universe. By applying the four quadrants of humanness to the tetrahedron shape, we begin to see a three-dimensional topography of the human experience.

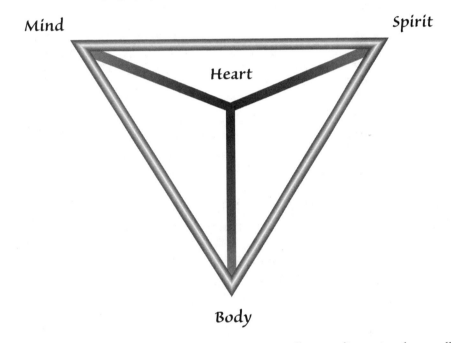

Our maps of three-dimensional territory are usually two-dimensional, as well as third-person representations of the "other." This is an example of a three-dimensional map that we can "stand inside" as an associated and integrated experience.

This three-dimensional image also corresponds with our latest scientific insights into how the brain/body nervous system is organized. In his work, Dr. Paul McLean discovered that the human brain is not one comprehensive organism but is rather more like a house with three floors. The third floor is divided into front and rear, creating a total of four areas in the house. Each area is distinct and is evolutionarily different.

Fourfold Brain

The fourfold brain in three stages: The oldest aspect is the reptilian brain, which I pair with the body. The second stage of brain development is the mid or mammalian brain, which Joseph Pearce pairs with the heart. The third stage includes the right and left hemispheres of the neo-cortex, and the fourth stage includes the right and left pre-frontal lobes of the neo-cortex.

The basement of the house is called the reptilian brain and is equivalent to the brain stem. The brain stem and the body functions are intimately connected and are represented in our "tetrahedronal mandala" as the body.

The second floor of McLean's structure is the midbrain, or mammalian brain, and is intimately connected to the heart and the emotional information system. New research on the heart suggests that it contains a significant percentage of neural cells and is far more than just a muscle. Its electromagnetic influence has been scientifically verified, and there is an intelligence of the heart. The heart and the midbrain are represented in our tetrahedronal mandala as the heart.

The third floor of our conceptual house has two sections. The back section represents the third stage of evolutionary development and is shared with other primates and cetaceans. It is divided into left and right chambers. Each mirrors the other in shape yet has quite distinct functions. For our purposes, I am going to refer to the left and right hemispheres as the domain of mind. Following is a map of the differential functions of the bilateral hemispheres, commonly thought of as left- and right-brain activities.

The front section of the third floor is called the prefrontal lobe section, and when combined with the left and right hemispheres it creates the neo-ortex of the brain. The prefrontal lobes show the most recent stage of evolutionary development and seem to be the seat of higher consciousness, which I will call spirit.

The four areas of the quadrant drawings, or the conceptual house, do not operate in isolation. Who we are is a composite of the four areas. With that in mind we can guide relational "conversations" among the aspects that assist in the designing of Self, such as the conversation I had with Barb about her thumb sucking. While Barb was unaware of the process because it simply unfolded as an outcome of play and conversation, it presents a good example of how a limiting habit can be altered by aligning it organically with our own nature. Living in a territory is one thing, and having a conceptual map of that territory while you are living in it provides a unique perspective and understanding that slightly shifts the quality of how we are living in that very same territory. The fourfold tetrahedronal map is the starting place for an evolving map of our experiential architecture.

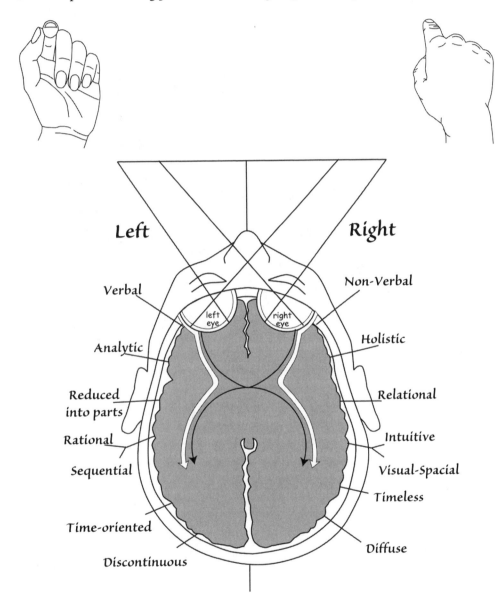

An associated representation of the third fold of the fourfold brain. The different ways the left and right hemispheres work have been well established in neuroscience. I translate these into patterns of behavior that are differentially represented, crossed over onto the left- and right-hand sides of the body.

CHAPTER 3

NATURAL LEARNING, HOLISTIC LEARNING

We are born to learn and we are designed as learning beings. Although, as discussed in chapter 0, we learn naturally, our learning is most profound when we become conscious of the very process. This order of complexity allows us to be aware of ourselves as individuals, but it is only when we rediscover our original point of view, our "child within," that we actually appreciate our abilities within the context of who we are. This rediscovery allows for a new order of learning—holistic learning. The child within is the lifelong learner, and the natural, holistic learner is the SelfDesigner.

We are also designed to connect, because we are designed for and by relationships. We acquire our strategies for survival from those with whom we have significant relationships. At an unconscious level, children constantly model the hidden agenda of our relationships far more profoundly than we realize. If we as adults hold an awareness of the intentions behind our actions, and if we integrate our patterns of living into a harmonious whole, we can provide excellent models for our children. The onus is on us.

As most parents deeply understand, and as numerous scientific studies have demonstrated, an authentic, nurturing relationship with a baby or child requires close physical contact. This includes skin-to-skin, face-to-face, eye-to-eye, and mind-to-mind connections. In Dr. Allan Schore's extensive research, he has unequivocally demonstrated that while neural development in the right frontal lobe occurs naturally in a bonded child, it is significantly diminished in unbonded children. Their ability to fully understand self and others is negatively impacted until such time that this connection is made. When children experience a connection to another human being, they feel recognized, acknowledged, and contented. The purpose of relationship is connection, and the quality of the connection establishes the condition for the full development of the individual. This involves the information communicated by the body, the feeling of touch, the postures and gestures, the tone and tempo of the words inclusively as a comprehensive language of relationship.

The following two images illustrate potential situations for bonding. In the first picture, the father is sharing the same mental and physical space with the child. There is significant opportunity for bonding between the two individuals. Human babies need this type of connection in order to realize that "I am a human being in relationship with another human being."

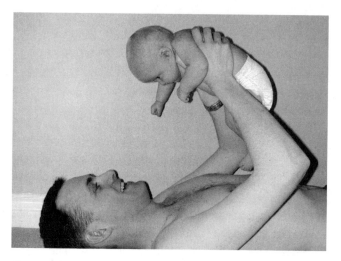

Extensive studies of bonding and attachment show that recursive and engaged communication between an infant and a caregiver are essential for the discovery of self and other to unfold.

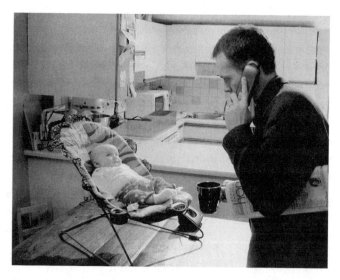

Recursive communication begins with a shared or common mental state, which isn't the case here due to the father's divided attention.

In the second picture, the father, although attentive to his child, is not sharing the same mental state as the infant. He is talking on the phone and making pictures in his mind that are related to his telephone conversation. The infant is not able to join the father in this state, and although they are in close proximity, there is much less potential for connection and therefore for bonding.

In our busy lives, how many parents are too distracted to stop and be present, to bond with the open-mind state of the infant? Unfortunately, it is often true that we live as part of a society more focused on the efficiencies and expediencies of our roles than on our experience of being human. Our speed of life has pushed aside our innate knowledge of the importance of connection. Most of us live forgotten and unseen behind masks, having been taught to pretend that what we do and what we have is who we are. We are cut off from others, and this sets in motion being cut off from ourselves.

Part of SelfDesign's work is to help us strengthen our connections. For those who work with children, strong connections enhance rather than diminish the inherent creative intelligence in each child. Shifting our way of talking and connecting with children also shifts our influence. By joining children and getting close to their worldview, we are able to appreciate the legitimacy of their perspective. The kind of conversation that emerges from this recursive, shared place allows us to gain significant insights into how to support children in maintaining their integrity and unfolding their infinite potential.

*Thank you for trusting me,
and understanding
that I am a whole person.
Not an empty outline
that needs to be filled.
Thank you
for being my father.
I love you dad.
Ilana*

Through achieving a deep understanding of how we are each designed as human beings, we can be more successful at designing our lives in resonance with others. This type of insight and "co-design" process helps us more regularly experience a sense of well-being, fulfillment, and harmony with those around us. My observations of children and adults over the past two decades have shown me a wide variety of relationship patterns, some of which are highly successful and some not. Using these patterns, I have created a set of assumptions, and these have led me to encouraging learners to be able to design their own optimum strategies for learning.

Nurturing children through the early years of development is likely the single most important human role on the planet. Developing healthy bodies and healthy relationships has been demonstrated to affect children's learning capabilities, social behaviors, self-concept, and motivation. In our culture, however, we consistently marginalize the nurturer's role. (In fact, we devalue nearly everything related to the feminine, whether in nature or in the human realm.) Child-rearing is most often driven by expectations, as is education, and nurturing takes a back seat. Yet new research points to the essential role that nurturing plays in the unfolding of our human qualities.

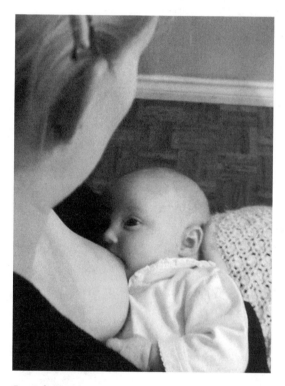

Joseph Pearce proposes that mother's breast milk is thin so as to encourage the infant to feed often. This creates the opportunity for connection and relationship which is nutrition for the mind, while the milk is nutrition for the body.

Bonding between parent and child is the foundational building block for a healthy relationship. Nature provides a simple method, breastfeeding, for initiating human bonding, and it is only in recent years that we have come to fully appreciate the complexity within its simple design. When infants feed, they are cradled close to the caregiver, and in this way relational information is passed between them. Relational information through human connection is the lifeblood of our human nature, and it nurtures the infant while the milk nurtures the body. We are nursing the integrity of what it is to be human—to be a loved, and loving, being.

We share the need for bonding with many other social mammals, using it to develop our strategies for survival. Yet we seem to be the only species with verbal communication patterns that construct a mental process allowing us to become aware of ourselves as conscious entities. Our view of ourselves comes primarily through relationships, which are either enhancing or limiting. Because our history focuses so much on control and domination, our interpersonal politics tend to be colored in this way. The creation of social order, especially with respect to parenting and educating children, has been based on limiting choices, controlling others, and on saying "no." From fighting cancer or stopping racism, to telling children that they can't play with something, or to quitting smoking, we assume that gaining control is the most appropriate method of social management. It is my belief, however, that nurturing and enhancing relationships are most responsible for the achievement of a positive sense of self, of health, and of others. When we work from a place of expressing harmony with our essential nature and the nature of others, life can be lived more successfully and profoundly and learning challenges are more easily overcome. Harmony is created through relationships arising in the domain of "yes" — the positive and affirmative.

Language and choice play critical roles in how our lives are lived. For example, let's look at a limiting habit like smoking. We have no word in the English language to describe someone who chooses not to smoke other than "nonsmoker." This label only defines the negative habit and our resistance to it. I have counseled many adults who request my help in quitting smoking. I tell them, "I will not help you 'quit,' as I am not interested in taking away any choices or behaviors that you have. I *will* help you realize you have more choices in your life, one of them being to consistently breathe clean, fresh air." I explain that I can choose to have a cigarette anytime I want to, and I choose to live beyond a definition of myself as a smoker or a nonsmoker. What I *do* is not who I *am*. There might even be appropriate times to smoke tobacco. For example, I once had the honor to participate in a sacred pipe ceremony with a native elder who came to our learning center. I smoked the pipe as part of the ceremony, and I also continue to choose to breathe fresh air rather than smoke as an ongoing strategy of living life as a sacred event. When we believe we have the power to make the choice, rather than giving power to the substance, we create a positive strategy for living beyond limiting behaviors that are defined by addiction.

If we think about intelligence as an ability that allows people to do more and better things in the world, it would follow that having more choices increases intelligence.

In the same manner, taking choices away through authoritative control limits the development of experience and therefore limits intelligence. It is the aim of SelfDesign to increase people's choices in every situation and to help them experience which choices seem appropriate, given an exposure to various consequences. Making appropriate choices in a given situation is a nonlimiting measure of intelligence, based on natural wisdom and understanding.

Balancing the Conscious and Unconscious Dance

Our educational system focuses on conscious intelligence—the rational linear and sequential kind of thinking that is associated with the left-hemisphere process. Whole-brain thinking, on the other hand, also involves the right hemisphere, the midbrain, the reptilian brain, and the prefrontal lobes. It is the left hemisphere that tends to isolate itself and, through the very act of using the left-brain function of language to name, calls the rest of the brain functions the unconscious processes. The "un-" part of "unconscious" suggests a "not," a "less than," and an exclusiveness that reduces the importance of all the remaining sections and functions of the brain. In SelfDesign, we choose to balance the conscious and unconscious processes and to integrate all the different areas of the brain in a kind of orchestration of thinking and understanding.

For example, when we first hear a new sound like the ring of a bell, we bring the sound into our conscious mind and focus our thoughts on its source and meaning. If it is a bell signaling lunch, prayer, or warning, we respond appropriately. However, if we discover that the sound has no consequence, we attach no meaning and over time come to ignore the bell. When it rings, we might focus our attention for a moment and then let it fade. If it rings on a regular basis for no discernible purpose, we will unconsciously hear the bell each time yet never let it rise to consciousness. Our unconscious state contains the background of sounds and images that wash through us each day but do not receive the focus of our conscious mind.

We process information from our eyes in two different parts of the brain. The image focused directly on our retina is processed consciously, while the peripheral vision is processed deep in the unconscious mind. The Eastern terms for these two states are "hard eyes" and "soft eyes." You can quite literally shift your mental state by shifting how you use your eyes. This shift can even aid in changing the kind of thinking needed for different situations or processes.

The following map is an exploration of the dance between the conscious and unconscious mind in learning a skill or gaining a new understanding.

We see four quadrants in this drawing, the top half representing the unconscious process and the bottom half the conscious process. The right side of the model represents lack of competence in a skill, while the left represents competence. Competence increases during the journey through that half, while lack of competence decreases. The four quadrants represent the four stages in learning anything, moving from ignorance to a state of excellence.

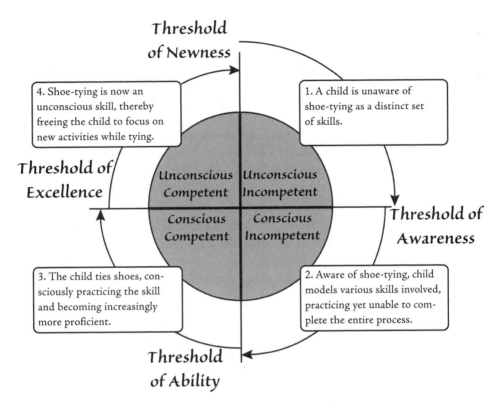

The dynamic process of learning is an interplay between our conscious and unconscious processes as well as our transference from incompetence to competence. Each quadrant characterizes a threshold of transformation, and like our other circular maps includes a spiraling return to a beginning that is different from the start.

Let us consider learning to tie shoes as a simple example to illustrate this model. In the first quadrant, an infant is unaware of shoes or shoelaces. She experiences her mother doing something down at her feet several times each day, but she pays little attention to this activity. She is unaware of her own lack of competence. As the child matures, her attention begins to focus on her mother tying the shoes. She becomes conscious of the process, though she remains incompetent; she is simply an observer of the process, but she has passed the threshold of awareness. Over time she begins to mimic the shoe tying but is unable to accomplish the task. At some point her mother likely breaks down the activity into smaller chunks, and the child begins to master aspects of this quite complicated process. With focus and attention, the child is eventually able to tie her shoes. Moving through the threshold of ability, she enters the third quadrant, conscious competence. She consciously ties her shoes regularly, and with each attempt her ability improves. One day the girl ties her shoes without paying any attention to what she is doing. Her mind is on something of greater importance. This is possible because her ability is now so practiced that it has moved from consciousness to the unconscious part of her brain. She has passed through the threshold of excellence into unconscious competence.

This phenomenon allows us to develop and expand our repertoire of abilities, with each new ability acting as a foundation for more. The model provides a collaborative, spiraling context in which we can notice our own development as experience moves us in and out of the conscious and unconscious process of our ongoing learning. Once again the spiral emerges. When we end up back at the top of the wheel, we are not the same; we have incorporated an activity into our neurological bodies in a way that allows us to move on to new, higher levels of mastery. We move through the four learning quadrants, and the end of the process signals the beginning of a more complex one if we so choose. Learning spirals us from one beginning to the next. The following image illustrates this process as a circle implying a whole.

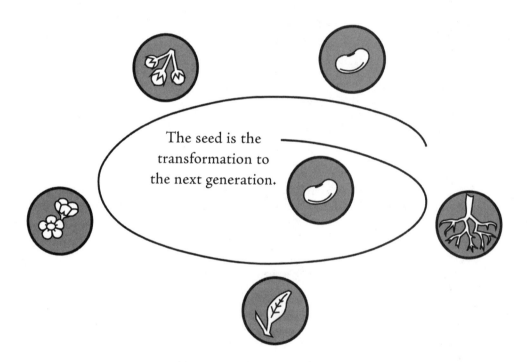

The seed is the transformation to the next generation.

Instead of returning to the beginning, we are at a new place in the circle because the center has been in motion. This new point is the seed of the next generation, the context for new learning based on what we now understand.

When learning is integrated into understanding how we accomplish life tasks, we begin to see the relevance of learning as a tool to enhance our quality of life. Self-awareness and self-design allow each one of us to unfold our infinite intelligence.

SelfDesign: The Art and Science of Holistic Learning

In my search for tools to support natural learning, I found the field of Neuro-Linguistics, built on the insights of Dr. John Grinder and his associates in the 1970s. Grinder had studied Dr. Milton Erickson, a hypnotist, and Virginia Satir, a family therapist, both of whom worked with clients to help them shift from unresourceful to resourceful states. In the context of their work, the term *resourceful* refers to our fundamental harmonious state and implies that our integrity, or wholeness, is our most essential resource. An unresourceful person, on the other hand, is out of balance, blocked, or disempowered and therefore is unable to access these natural inner resources. I studied Grinder's Neuro-Linguistic Programming (NLP) for the next several years and used it to develop my own strategies for influencing learning and for personal excellence.

In Wondertree I was no longer just a spectator. I worked with children to support their optimal learning processes. I now had the conversational tools and an understanding of learning strategies to help learners discover their conscious and unconscious thoughts. I found I could help children alter their habits, assumptions, beliefs, fears, and learning blocks. They learned to observe their own excellence and to extend their abilities into other areas.

As a learning consultant, I developed new maps and models for understanding how the mind works and discovered I could easily pass these tools and insights on to learners. For example, some of the children I worked with were naturally gifted spellers, and some of them were very poor spellers. Using my new techniques, I soon discovered that this ability is not an indication of intelligence as much as it is an artifact of strategy. The excellent spellers were unaware of exactly how they spelled well (see "unconscious competence" in the previous diagram). Yet by carefully observing behavior and asking questions, I could uncover what an excellent speller was actually doing internally to remember and spell perfectly. Once I deconstructed this strategy it was relatively easy to design or construct its elements for a learner who had previously not had a strategy. Over the years I have shared these strategies with hundreds of learners who can now spell exceptionally well.

In NLP, practitioners are encouraged to recognize that the insights may lead to the creation of a personal strategy that can be represented by a "map," or interpretation of individual experience. However, it is important to understand that this map is only a representation of the real "territory" of human experience. It is important to map the territory, yet it is inappropriate to make the territory fit the map. "The map is not the territory" is one of NLP's basic tenets from the work of Korzibsky. In other words, the map can help in understanding the territory of human experience, but it is human behavior that is real. This is totally different from public education, where human experience is made to fit the map, or the mold, as it is commonly called. Traditionally, the map is considered real, the mold is "one size fits all," and human experience must fit in or fail.

SelfDesign turns these processes inside out by using maps and models to understand territory. Territory is a pattern of behaviors and strategies that are fundamental to human intelligence as a dynamic learnable process. The following example of work derived from NLP illustrates how insights into thinking strategies offer us opportunities to design our own learning process.

Visual, Auditory, and Kinesthetic Modalities of Thought

One of the more significant discoveries attributed to NLP is the assertion that eye movements give clues to how a person is thinking. Through years of observation, John Grinder and his associates discovered that people most often look up when they access pictures in their imaginations, sideways when they are listening to inner voices, and down when they are accessing their feelings. The following is the basic NLP model of six places that people tend to look when they are accessing information in their thinking processes. There is a seventh place, straight ahead, where some people look when they visualize.

From studying NLP, I learned to view auditory messages, visual images, and kinesthetic feelings as aspects of our thinking. Each day we make pictures (Vc - visual created, Vr - visual remembered), hear voices (Ac - auditory created, Ar - Auditory remembered, Id - internal dialogue), and have feelings (Ki - kinesthetic internal), without being aware that these three processes are components of our mental activity. By learning how to observe eye movements accompanied by other behaviors, by listening for language cues, and by asking direct process questions, we are able to gather clues to how learners actually think. Once we understand the thought patterns of others, we can begin to help them design strategies for optimum learning. Several of the strategies appear throughout this book as they relate to the various chapter themes.

Schooling measures learning in an exterior way through testing behavioral abilities. SelfDesign works with learners in interior ways by designing strategies, managing thinking processes, and optimizing beliefs, understanding, perspectives, and habits so that learners can achieve a personal, subjectively-sensed quality of being.

An example of the importance of this difference in the kinds of results possible is illustrated in the following story of one young boy. His learning difficulties were so extreme that he was to be sent to a special school. Instead, his parents brought him to Wondertree, and over the next nine years I worked to help him access his own natural abilities. When he left Wondertree he entered the business world, where he easily made the transition from our learning center to a successful career as a graphic artist.

A Place to Blossom: Donnie's Story

When Donnie was in the third grade his parents found him hiding in the bushes because he didn't want to go to school. They knew something was seriously wrong. In addition to Donnie's obvious emotional distress, he could not read or do basic math. He could barely answer a question from his teacher. Donnie had been tested and diagnosed by many experts, and remedial education had only made matters worse.

His parents heard me speak at a local convention. They were desperate to find help for their son, and in spite of the fact that my ideas were contrary to those of most experts, they decided to bring Donnie to Wondertree.

To the parents' surprise, I did not test Donnie. I got down on the floor and played with him. After about an hour, I pronounced that there was absolutely nothing wrong with him. This "diagnosis" came from my choice to see all children as geniuses; first, because it is probably true, but primarily because this assumption gets better results. This idea shifts adults' focus to respectfully and appropriately see the essential integrity of every child and to respond accordingly.

While playing with Donnie, I noticed that he predominately used his visual imagination to compose information. When I asked him a question, he would roll his eyes back and spend as much as ten minutes looking at the incredible detail of his inner pictures before he would come back with a response. The reason it had seemed as though he couldn't answer questions was because no one had known to wait while Donnie did his inner work.

Can you imagine a classroom teacher with thirty restless children waiting ten minutes for Donnie to give the answer to three plus four? Imagine, also, how Donnie felt, never having his inner world acknowledged or validated and unable to communicate his thoughts because no one was there any longer when he came back with his answer. Consider his parents as well, cut off from Donnie's inner world and left to witness the physical symptoms of Donnie's frustration.

All of Donnie's learning problems and symptoms gradually disappeared as he worked with us in Wondertree. His learning needs were legitimized, and he was allowed to design his own learning adventure.

In Donnie's first year in Wondertree, we gave him all the space he needed to do what he loved doing. He and "Hopper," his rabbit hand puppet, spent about half of the year sitting up in the magnolia tree in the backyard. Often I would go outside, climb the tree, and sit with Donnie as he stared at the clouds. As I began to match his state, I could sense his loneliness and his innocent, independent spirit.

One day, the children all wanted me to give them math questions. "Give them like they do in school," they said. I made up questions and handed them out to each child. Donnie looked down, saw the math papers, and burst into tears. I rushed over and dramatically tore the papers into shreds. I told Donnie that his happiness was the most important thing in the world to me, far more important than any math questions. In that moment we became friends.

Trusting in me, he began to trust in others, building clay models with them and engaging in games. Each morning we would all sit at our round table to plan the day, and after several months Donnie began participating in the group by talking through his hand puppet.

One day I showed the children how to do video animation, beginning by putting a rock in the middle of the floor. I filmed it for a few frames, moved it, filmed it, moved it, and filmed it again. Donnie got the idea immediately, built a small movie set, painted faces on a couple of rocks, and began shooting his first movie.

Several of my learners made films that year, and I entered them in the annual provincial student film festival. That first year we won two awards, with Donnie taking first prize. Over the next four or five years, Donnie won either first or second prize every year for his videos starring Hopper, his hand puppet.

Our learners continued to create Wondertree as the greatest learning adventure of their lives. We moved from filmmaking to computer graphics when we discovered HyperCard, a computer program that allowed us to begin designing our own software.

Six months later, after one of the most exciting collaborative learning experiences in which I have ever participated, we had created a computer program that won the Canadian Northern Telecom Award for Excellence in Education. Donnie played a significant role as our graphic artist and mentor to the other children's artwork. We were all learners, tackling problems and creating solutions together.

The following year we were approached by the British Columbia electric utility company. They were looking for a software design group to create a computer game teaching children how to conserve energy. After several months of negotiation, we got the contract. My group of twelve kids, ages ten to thirteen, along with a couple of mentors and me, began to design the game with the first payment of our $75,000 contract.

We learned how to run a business, and the children billed for their hours and formed work teams to complete the project. When the project was completed a year later, we won two national Canadian awards for it. Needless to say, we invested the $10,000 prize money in new computer equipment! The computer program that we created was sent to every school in the province, and children learned how to save energy in their homes by playing our game.

The software development team studying one of their breakthrough learning discoveries. Donnie (not shown here) was the main graphic artist for our numerous software projects.

Throughout all of Donnie's positive experiences, I was aware that he was still virtually unable to read. Staying true to my approach of supporting learning that emerges from enthusiasm, however, I continued to focus on what he loved doing. He had demonstrated a strong ability in design, and so when he was eleven I arranged for him to apprentice with one of Canada's most famous architects. Over the next several years, while looking through amazing architectural-design books, Donnie became interested in learning about the history of this field. Frustrated with only being able to look at pictures and drawings, he decided he needed to learn to read. Driven by his own desire for knowledge and by the relevance of his need, and given space and support, Donnie learned to read by himself, just as he had learned how to do computer graphics.

Thus Donnie, by age fourteen, had become an award-winning video artist and an international award-winning computer graphics designer. He was the youngest winner of a MacWorld and Apple Computer contest in California, and he could now read.

Donnie was soon an excellent reader, but his lack of focus on the words themselves made him a terrible speller. He had an incredible memory for visual detail, however, and he could draw in detail anything he saw. Aware of this, I began to work with him on a guided method for spelling. We chose Donnie's last name as his first spelling goal, and I had him imagine his father's workshop filled with pieces of soapstone. One by one the letters of his last name were carved into the imaginary soapstone and placed on a shelf for display. For years afterward, when filling out his name, Donnie would stop for a second, look up into the memory of his father's imaginary workshop, and copy the soapstone letters onto the paper. Donnie had developed a successful learning strategy for spelling.

Donnie, now twenty-seven, has had a remarkable ten-year career as a graphic artist. At twenty-three he was the senior graphic artist at a top international consulting firm in Vancouver. He has designed work for clients in countries around the world, including Japan, Saudi Arabia, Germany, and Australia, as well as across the United States and Canada. Currently he works as a graphics animator for an Australian company. He is earning a great living doing what he loves. Donnie never officially graduated from third grade, and he has never looked back. We focused on what Donnie could do rather than on trying to fix what he couldn't.

Donnie learned to live each day of his life out of his enthusiasm and fascination with the world. He grew to trust himself and to work cooperatively with others. He learned the value of his gifts and how to earn a living sharing them. From his ability to design, he became a true SelfDesigner.

A Challenge to Be-Know-Do-Have Assumptions

Donnie's story exemplifies the importance of gaining insight into each of our strengths, needs, and personal styles in order to truly support our learning. I read and understood Donnie's behavior and saw what was positive in his thinking, rather than seeing his behavior through a perspective of pathology shared by other educators and counselors. In my communication with Donnie and the other learners I made use of the fundamental principles of Neuro-Linguistic Programming, one of which is to not label a child by what the child does. To develop these distinctions further I offer here a model for seeing and sorting human activity in a new way.

It is our language that makes the aspects of spirit, mind, heart, and body separate and distinct. There are four specific verbs we consistently use to organize and define how we unfold our patterns of living as individuals: *be, know, do,* and *have.* These four words describe our activities and ourselves. Our state of *be-*ing is related to spirit and thus to our true identity. What we *know* is what we create through our thinking, and what we *do* is behavioral and relational. And of course we *have* a body as well as objects and relationships that we classify with ownership. The problem with this type of languaging comes when we begin to blur the boundaries of "being," "knowing," "doing," and "having."

Since our being or spirit is essentially empty by its very definition, we tend to fill this space with descriptions of ourselves, as was discussed in chapter 0. As an example within the *be/do* realm, if I *do* carpentry I am likely to say, "I *am* a carpenter." When we link the *be* and *have* distinctions together in a causal way, we invite further difficulties. For example, "I *am* rich because I *have* a lot of money." If I have a lot of money, I might also say, "I *am* happy because I *have* a lot of money." Keeping life simple is largely about keeping these distinctions separate. We do what we do, we have what we have, and who we are exists on its own, regardless of what we do or have. We constantly confuse what we "think" and "know" with what "is," including our own identity. We become what we think, we become the story that we tell ourselves and others, rather than just being the space for the story to exist. "I think, therefore I am" is a fundamental conundrum of this modern age. This is another example of one of our culture's difficulties; we allow our thoughts to limit our experience by believing negative and destructive thoughts that have nothing to do with reality.

The implications of the blurred boundaries of language become even more significant when we make statements like "I *am* a diabetic," rather than simply saying that we have diabetes due to a dysfunctional organ. Suddenly we have become our disease. "I smoke" turns into "I *am* a smoker," and the behavior becomes the self, a much more difficult arena in which to make changes. We require a deeper level of intervention when we call up identity rather than action. In parenting classes, a fundamental example of a language shift is demonstrated by helping parents move from "You *are* a bad boy" to "What you just *did* was inappropriate."

I work with families that introduce their children with this type of statement: "My son is dyslexic." In the weeks, months, or years that it takes to turn this around, 95 percent of my efforts are spent in dispelling the beliefs around the idea that there *is* something wrong with someone. When I can shift parents to saying, "When my son tries to read, he mixes up some of his letters and finds the process frustrating," we are all much, much closer to a solution.

The problem of blending "be, know, do, have" processes in a cause-and-effect way suggests connections between domains of living that are in fact not connected. That a quantity of money can cause happiness is an absurd concept when you look at it as a logical reality. However, if we continue to explore how the mind works in terms of sensing and organizing our experience of the universe, we discover a new way of organizing experience based on relationships and similarities rather than hierarchies of cause and effect.

In our left-hemisphere/right-hand-dominant culture, we tend to project linear and hierarchical models onto the world. To achieve a better balance in our lives, it is important to develop our right-hemisphere/left-hand sense of contexts and relatedness. A context that shares common elements and systems of logic is called a set. For example, a small child may be familiar with the set of experiences in the house and in the yard but has not yet explored the larger community. As this child matures, the new set of expanded experiences becomes the community. The house is now relegated to being a subset, and the surrounding countryside becomes the meta-set to the community.

We can organize our four levels of human functioning as micro-set, subset, set, and meta-set. I have come to believe that this kind of thinking is a more accurate model of the natural world than our more typical way of thinking in levels or hierarchies. The world is more about connection than it is about separation. It is more determined by association than by distinction or difference. Distinction may indeed allow us to gather knowledge about the world, but it is association that allows us to participate in the world.

When we organize experience into the "be," "know," "do," and "have" domains we must ask the question, "Which one is inside of which? Which is the micro-set, the subset, the set, or the meta-set?" The old way of organizing them is to relate them to our biological and materialistic way of seeing the world. In that model our bodies determine our selves, and this is our set. Because our brains are inside our bodies, we think of them as a subset to our bodies. Our minds, which we think of as inside the brain, then become yet a further subset. Using this system we naturally tend to call up metaphors of biology to explain our brains or the functions of our minds. We are alcoholic (identity, be) because of a genetic cause (biology, have).

On the other hand, turning this inside out and using our being as the meta-set lets us determine new ways of thinking about ourselves. If I can't read and I believe the reason is genetic, I have little hope for change. My possibilities for success as a reader are dramatically improved when I believe that reading is simply a skill for which I need a strategy. In helping children learn to believe that they simply "have" a problem or challenge, rather than that they "are" the problem, I have been able to create significant change where others have failed.

The models that follow evolve from set theory and the idea that the larger, context set contains aspects that can not be understood from the smaller subset. The model on the left represents an old paradigm imposed on us by our culture and by scientific thinking. It suggests that we are run primarily by our biology, the *have* of our bodies and our accumulated goods. The model on the right shows us the possibility of a new paradigm, a new way of mapping the patterns of our living. In this model we place our *being* as our meta-set. Our spirit is now the largest, most all-encompassing arena for living. Our thoughts then are a subset, less complicated and complex than the domain of our being. Activities and behaviors, the *doing* part of us, becomes a further subset, and the *having* part, our bodies and our goods, is yet a further subset. We have thus turned our model of how we think about ourselves inside out. If we now try to explain our mind, heart, and being through the logic of the body subset, we can begin to appreciate that the subset operates in too small and simple an environment to truly understand the set or meta-set. The context of our *being* is suddenly established as more comprehensive, mysterious, and perhaps more intriguing than our behavior, and much more so than the context of our bodies. Our biology can no longer predict our behaviors or our thinking, and neither of these can predict or understand the context of our mind or its meta-set, spirit. In this new and probably more accurate nesting of contexts, we open up whole new realms of possibilities for creativity, for the process of SelfDesigning.

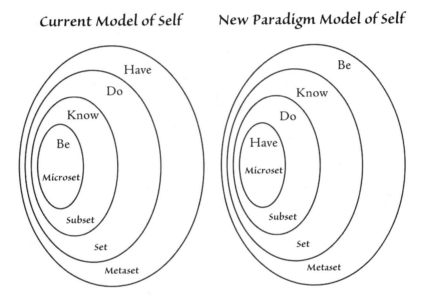

Current Model of Self   New Paradigm Model of Self

CHAPTER 4

THE ECOLOGY OF FAMILY

We commonly think that an individual is the smallest unit of humanity, a living system designed and sustained by its relationships. It may be closer to the truth, however, to consider the family as the smallest unit of humanity. I propose this definition of *self* as "family member" because we are psychologically affected throughout our lives by the experiences and influences of family. Just as a mother nourishes a growing fetus in her womb, the family acts as a second womb, responsible for the psychological nourishment of the individual. Our sense of ourselves, learned in family relationship, significantly determines who we are throughout our lives.

Children are a barometer of family dynamics and family health. They are sensitive instruments reflecting the climate of family relationships. In my role as a learning consultant I have worked with many children who came to us with learning difficulties. Over the years, I have learned that one of the best ways to resolve these problems is to identify and heal the cause, often rooted in family dynamics.

This chapter explores nurturing holistic learning by subtly shifting dynamics within the family. Just as few educators receive training in the actual learning process, fewer still are given skills to work with families. Although everyone expects to take training and certification in the profession or skilled trade of our choice, none of us receive any training whatsoever in how to parent or in how to be a meaningful and responsible family member. Regardless of the lack of specific training, however, it is important that we learn to value our children's happiness as a fundamental indicator of their wellness. Because most of us have been taught to sacrifice happiness in the present for a potential gain in the future, we tend not to pay attention to pleas from our unhappy children, especially in the educational realm. However, sacrificing happiness along the way can negatively affect the family as a whole. As a fundamental principle in SelfDesign, we start with a state of wellness and happiness, a condition of fulfillment not as a goal or future desired state but as our present state, a place to begin.

This chapter also looks at the politics of family relationships and the role of communication in contributing to harmony in the family. Most parents attempt to nurture and instruct their children to the best of their ability, understanding the importance of their influence. Children develop self-perception primarily from their parents, internalizing the emotional context and making it their own, a form of what we call "modeling." Because children model our unconscious assumptions and internalize them as unconscious attitudes about themselves, it becomes imperative that we speak in positive ways when we refer to their identity, or be-ing, reserving critical comments only for their behaviors, or do-ings.

It is my belief that we would need far fewer formal therapeutic interventions if our interpersonal relationships were based in respect, positive thinking, and a nurturing style with others. To create this base of wellness and respect would require healing throughout society to make up for past injuries. It is reassuring to note, though, that both the literature and my own counseling experiences point to the fact that we can recover our initial state of wellness. We can even bond with a significant person at any time in our lives. Carefully constructed therapeutic strategies can help in re-imprinting our root experiences and in establishing an ongoing sense of fulfillment as our fundamental condition.

Influencing a Family Ecology

Some years ago I worked with a boy named Sam who was labeled as severely dyslexic. His mother and father continually tried to find specialists who could help their son. Sam experienced so much embarrassment when anyone focused on his reading that he found relief by distracting everyone with his disruptive behavior. His acting-out had become so negative that he was suspended from every school he attended. Although the attention he got for his actions was not very satisfying, Sam at least felt he had some control, and it was certainly more comfortable than struggling with reading.

When Sam came to Wondertree he was thirteen years old. Because his loud and disruptive behavior met his need for anonymity as a non-reader, he refused to cooperate with staff and peer requests for peace and quiet in the learning center. After a couple of months, the two learning consultants working with him realized they were unable to change this young man's behavior. Since he was disrupting the program for others, they asked for my help. Due to their lack of success, they felt that Sam might need to leave Wondertree. The boy, on the other hand, was happy in our program, and his parents also wanted him to stay.

I called a family meeting to see if we could create a solution that would work for everyone. In order to meet the learning consultants' needs, I proposed that the boy needed to leave Wondertree. To meet the parents' needs, I suggested that their son stay out of the program for two months and then return, and I requested that during those two months the parents meet with me one night a week to work on shifting the family dynamics.

By this time the young boy was crying. Being asked to leave the program felt like a punishment to him. I assured him that Wondertree did not use punishment for behavior change. Instead, we believed in negotiating win-win situations to meet everyone's needs. Because his needs were as important as anyone else's, I asked him, "If you could do anything you wanted each day, what would you most like to do?"

His sobbing stopped and his answer came without hesitation. "Snowboarding!" he exclaimed. I replied, "All right, hit the slopes!" His parents agreed to let him go snowboarding every day for two months on his season pass. He was delighted at this possibility, and all thought of punishment vanished from his mind.

I believed that if Sam were doing something totally enjoyable, he would be creating what I call a "resource state," an emotional condition of feeling good that is necessary for taking on learning challenges. It was my hope that he would be able to access this resource state when we were ready to begin working on his reading.

His parents agreed to work with me each week, and we had a win-win-win situation. The consultants were hopeful a shift could happen in the next two months, the parents were happy their son could return, and the boy was delighted to have a snowboarding holiday and to anticipate coming back to Wondertree. For my part, I knew that 95 percent of my energy would go into unloading the emotional baggage the boy had accumulated from his situation and the educational experts his parents had previously consulted. It would only take 5 percent of my time to actually share strategies for reading with him.

From my work with children over the years, I have discovered that when children are unable to shift underlying negative emotional states, the state is probably not their own. For example, a deeply angry child may be modeling the anger of one of his parents. In these situations the child is able to shift only if I can help the parent move through the anger and establish a more resourceful state. In the case of Sam's family, during my weekly sessions with the parents I queried them about their underlying assumptions and emotional states. I helped them shift the language and behavioral patterns that sustained these negative conditions and inadvertently brought forth their son's so-called learning disability. Sam's biggest handicap, I showed them, was their own limiting belief about his abilities as well as their belief that his learning problems were real. I suggested that the boy was more likely fulfilling his parents' fears than dealing with an actual disability.

For two months I engaged in this kind of conversation with the parents, and I coached them to be both positive and firm with their son. We practiced using specific language techniques to shift from unresourceful states to empowered ones. For example, I encouraged the mother to change how she behaved every time the family went out to dinner. Assuming that her child had a real disability and couldn't read, she would take the menu and read it to him. This simply reinforced the boy's belief that he couldn't read and prevented him from practicing the skill. I suggested that she invite him to read the menu if he wanted anything to eat and not to respond his whining. Gradually the parents redesigned the quality of their relationship with their son, assuming he was capable and being firm about the positive actions he needed to take.

My direct work with the boy amounted to one hour during these two months. In that hour I showed him how reading worked and emphasized that reading is "quite simple, really, if you know the trick." Of course I had no idea what to do, because I didn't specifically know what he did when he tried to read. However, I offered a belief in his success and then watched closely to discover his reading strategy. Every time I saw him shift into an unresourceful state I would ask him a question about his snowboarding experience to keep him feeling resourceful.

He told me that he didn't like reading because, unlike television, there were no pictures. As I watched him read, I could see that his total absorption with struggling to sound out letters prevented him from creating pictures for each word in his imagination. When he finally sounded out a whole word, he experienced it only as the sound of the joined letters, and then he went on to struggle with the next word.

He agreed to try a different way. I asked him to stop at the end of each word and make a mental picture of that word. Talking to him about what was going on inside his head was obviously a totally new experience. We had a great time turning the meaning of each word into a picture. Then we strung the pictures together into a "movie"—the meaning of the sentence. We practiced this sentence over and over, linking the pictures and movie to the words and sentence. At the end of the hour his huge smile told me he had discovered the secret to reading.

When two months were over, the boy was in a resourceful state because he had had a wonderful time snowboarding each day. His relationship with his parents was already transforming, and he was starting to sense that he was OK and could be more responsible for himself. When he came back to Wondertree, we still had to deal with some of his old patterns, but the boy had made significant personal shifts and felt supported in his learning both in the center and at home. The family moved at the end of the year but kept contact with us. They reported that their son was doing well in school, and eventually they wrote that he had graduated from high school and was going to a university.

Through this example and many others like it, it has become clear to me why experts focusing on things like the reversal of letters are not getting significant results for kids with learning problems. So often, reading difficulties are just symptoms of complex relationships within family and school. Once a belief or label reinforced by relationships becomes an embedded belief in a child's self-perception, the challenge becomes one of peeling back layers to find the underlying cause. We must shift the conditions stemming from this original issue, and only then can we effect true and lasting change.

Schools frequently require that children take on intellectual tasks before they are developmentally and emotionally ready for them. I have yet to see children develop learning disabilities when they are truly and enthusiastically ready to learn. If we were to launch a national campaign to teach three-month-old children to learn to walk, we would have an epidemic of walking disorders. As teachers, we need to reconsider what we traditionally label as children's developmental problems. Because schooling is more efficient when all first-grade children are taught to read, those children who are not developmentally ready often experience reading problems. I encourage children to start reading when they feel ready and enthusiastically want to read. Consequently, and not surprisingly, all these learners are great readers.

The Nature of Family

The human species has a comprehensive intelligence like no other species. Scientists attribute this intelligence to an interdependence between our lengthy childhood and language development. History seems to imply that originally the smallest unit of humanity was not the individual or even the nuclear family but rather the extended family and the community. The African saying, "It takes a village to raise a child," speaks clearly to the network of relationships necessary to sustain a learning individual. The village has historically been the womb for the family.

Never before in our history has there been such an incredible opportunity for the family to support the potential of each child, partly due to our high standard of living and the educational opportunities available to us in this Information Age. However, urbanization, a consequence of industrialization, has severely impacted the integrity of the village and the sanctity of the family as we knew it. Child-rearing has gradually become the job of the nuclear family, and now far too often the single parent, sometimes with challenging consequences.

Recently a major study surveyed families across the United States and investigated the amount of time families spend in conversation in a typical day or week. The study showed that most families do not engage in conversation at all during the week. Language like "Have you taken out the garbage?" and "How many times have I told you it's time for bed?" are not examples of conversation. For the purposes of this discussion, conversation is defined as an engaging connection between people, one that opens each person to the other. It is a connection of body (rapport), heart (emotion), mind (understanding), and spirit (unity).

If we accept that human potential is affected and developed by the way we talk together, it becomes imperative that we increase our family opportunities for conversation. With the invasion of television, computer games, and the internet, and with the work and commuting demands on many families, little time is left to invest in conversation. Other studies have shown that families are less likely to eat even one meal a day together, and this is an optimum time for conversation.

The pressures of supporting the nuclear family both economically and emotionally are intense and challenging to even the most stable family. Our relational skills can take a lifetime to develop, yet we have a relatively short and specific period during which we nurture the next generation. Our children can be grown and gone before we gain the insights most helpful to their development. A key to stemming the tide of family disintegration lies in nurturing the art of family conversation. Our Wondertree program is built on the practice of conversation.

Modeling: Learning in Relationship

Our children copy our ways of thinking and of expressing ourselves. They incorporate our beliefs and attitudes, as well as our postures, gestures, and behaviors, as the basis for their essential survival strategies. Children read our underlying assumptions as well as the intentions behind our statements. For example, if we feel anxious while we are communicating something to our children, they will sense our underlying emotion as clearly as they hear the content of our communication. If we have confidence in children's abilities, we exude confidence, and our children do the same.

Because the majority of children have two parents to model themselves after, they have the unique challenge of storing information from two different sources in their own body. Buckminster Fuller stated, "The universe is minimum two and is towards one," and although he was talking about the universe as a system, he was also making an essential statement about any system. I first heard him say this in 1976, and over the years I began to see the importance of this principle for SelfDesign. His phrase aligns with NLP strategies for understanding family patterns. We are familiar with the duality of phenomena like night and day, hot and cold, good and bad, and so on. Within a biological system we have similar dualities: acid and base, stimulus and response, in-breath and out-breath, and male and female. Another insight about dualities leading to the development of SelfDesign came from my counseling and conflict-resolution work with children and families over the years. I have watched people represent inner conflicts by using their right and left hands to indicate the male and female elements of their conflicts. When I work deeply with them, I find that the source most often stems from parental conflict during their own childhood. The source issue has been integrated into the child so deeply that it lasts into adulthood. The conflict need not have been anything more than a misunderstanding or even a miscommunication, but it suffices to embed a conflicted need in the child. With this in mind we can look again at the map introduced in chapter 1, this time through the perspective of masculine/feminine dualities.

The image below illustrates Gregory Bateson's work on the bilateral symmetry existing in all animals. As whole and complete systems, we are each the integration of the chromosomes of two people combining to make one new person. When we are born, every cell in our bodies represents a unity of this duality. As infants we begin to model our mothers and our fathers, and we need some way of keeping the two sets of impressions separate and distinct as we store this information in our bodies.

My assumption is that children model their mothers and fathers onto the two symmetrical parts of their body/mind. They model or map the experiences of their mothers into the right hemisphere of their brain and correspondingly into the left half of their body. They model or map the experiences of their fathers into the left hemisphere of their brain and correspondingly into the right half of their body.

When I introduce this work in public lectures, I generally find a number of single mothers who are initially quite concerned, believing that I am suggesting their children must have a male role model in order to receive the left-hemisphere experiences of the father. However, we are each whole systems, and children of single parents tend to model the masculine and feminine characteristics of their single parent regardless of whether the body of that person is male or female. It is, of course, the most optimum situation to have two parents each demonstrating a sense of balance of the masculine and feminine aspects in their own bodies as well as demonstrating the harmony between them as a couple.

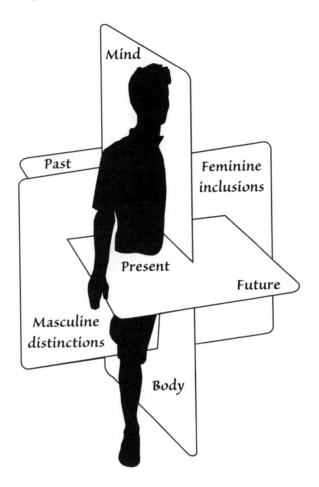

As individuals we model both our mothers and fathers and need to keep these two systems distinct in our physiology. Our directionality and volition are tied to our front and back distinctions, creating out of our present a sense of past and future. Our special distinctions of top and bottom, head and feet give us an evolutionary and universal context for growth and development.

Once again, the map above is useful only to inform us about the territory. The territory is general and is not the map of each individual, because each person carries a different balance of the masculine and feminine. Speaking universally, however, the following list below describes some of the commonly associated feminine and masculine characteristics:

FEMININE	MASCULINE
Right hemisphere	Left hemisphere
Left side of body	Right side of body
Open	Closed
Inclusive	Decisive
Chalice	Sword
Nurturing	Expecting
Holding	Action
Form	Function
Matristic	Hierarchic
Inside	Outside
Toward the center	Away from the center
Intuition	Reason
Similarities	Differences
And	But/either/or

In many families the first child models the more masculine characteristics and the second child the more feminine. Firstborn children are often high achievers, action-oriented, and using reason as their world context. Second-born children tend more toward creativity and nurturance, with intuition as their basis for experience. Through my twenty years of observing families who have chosen Wondertree for one of their children, I have seen that the first child is often doing well in traditional school, while the second child is likely having difficulty conforming to the hierarchical, rule-oriented schooling system. I believe this informal statistic reflects how schooling focuses on left-brain processing and rewards those who excel in this mode of thinking. The more right-brain-influenced second children, who tend toward creative and holistic thinking, find Wondertree's whole-mind-and-body strategies much more relevant to their learning processes.

The left hemisphere of the brain, connected to the right side of the body, tends to handle the verbal, analytic, sequential, rational, time-oriented, and specific aspects of thinking. The right hemisphere of the brain, connected to the left side of the body, tends to handle the relationship, holistic, visual-spatial, inclusive, timeless, and gestalt aspects of thinking. We live in two worlds, thanks to the left and right hemispheres in the neocortex, two worlds that are separate yet integrated to varying degrees. Because our culture focuses on and rewards the left-brain/masculine attributes more than the right, we are both individually and culturally out of balance. To move to more holistic thinking is to achieve an integrated balance of left and right by developing right-brain and whole brain/whole body learning systems.

I do not advocate the dominance of left side over right, or feminine over masculine. Rather, I encourage the discovery of both qualities in each of us and the integration of these qualities into everything that we do and think. Referring back to the "be, know, do, have" model, our gender does not determine whether we are nurturing or not; this feminine and masculine duality is in each one of us. Most men, however, are culturally trained to develop their masculine "sword-wielding" traits, while most women are encouraged to develop the nurturing "chalice" side. SelfDesign looks for ways to bring forth both the masculine and the feminine in all of us so that we develop the best qualities of both, regardless of gender.

Re-Imprinting: Deep Change Work

In my counseling work over the years, I have observed consistent relational patterns. Time and again I realize how deeply children comprehend and adopt their parents' unconscious patterns and hidden emotions. Parents with the best of intentions communicate their own unresolved historical issues to their children, and due to the design of children to unconsciously model those in significant relationships, children internally receive the information.

If you recall the circular diagram of unconscious/conscious, competence/incompetence described in the last chapter, every learning cycle spirals the mastered skill down into our unconscious. Although it is no longer conscious, the unconscious imprint is represented in our bodies, postures, gestures, and behaviors. Children model adults on these levels. As adults in roles as educators and parents, we are well-advised to work on and perfect ourselves rather than work on our children. How many families get into trouble when parents try to get their children to succeed where they have failed? When I work with parents and educators in our SelfDesign courses, we shift the emphasis from teaching to modeling and help the adults become excellent learners who then demonstrate the process for children. Sometime adults need to recover before they can discover, heal before they can learn. Healing the embedded pains of childhood so that life can be lived in more fulfilled and resourceful states is key in the SelfDesign program.

Over the years, I have seen that many of the children and adults I work with are deeply wounded from a sense of being abandoned. Few children are actually abandoned, yet many of us recount that we found our parents busy, distracted, unavailable, and distant during our infancy and childhood. I once sat in a room with thirty teenagers, many of them in tears, who had just experienced a deep, meaningful connection with each other and realized that they had not had this kind of acknowledgment or connection with their own parents. Most of us have a deep, often unmet need for human connection and engagement. We need to experience being witnessed, we need to feel acknowledged to sense that we are legitimate human beings in our own right.

Many adults and children today are experiencing a culture that emphasizes working and producing in isolation rather than connecting and relating. A significant number of mothers hold jobs and are expected to return to work soon after childbirth, despite overwhelming evidence that a mother and child are designed to bond and connect in the nursing years. Our lifelong ability to relate to others and make meaningful connections depends on the quality of our bonding experience. It might be that if our culture followed the lead of Sweden, for example, which invests in long-term infant care by both parents, we could prevent many of the social and learning problems we experience today.

In my workshops for SelfDesign, when I have invited people to look back over their lives, they often see that the close relationships they have created are more important than any of their other accomplishments. We are all lifelong learners, learning in a global learning community whether we know it or not. Our opportunity is to collaboratively and actively engage in a praxis, or intentional practice, of learning. In this way we can meaningfully create our lives within the process of SelfDesign. I invite and encourage you to invest in quality time with your children, forming and maintaining strong family bonds. Children, and the child residing within each of you, deserve the psychological nourishment provided by the "smallest unit of humanity"—the family.

CHAPTER 5

LANGUAGING

anguage significantly influences our behaviors, our thinking, and our relationships. Our words have the power to profoundly hurt or heal. Intimately linked with culture and politics, our language's nuances are deeply influenced by hierarchies of power and command, which have given us a language more about limits and controls than about opportunities and connections. Much of my work for healing and individual development has involved researching the use of language for mutual benefit. To develop a new culture that creates positive relationships, we need new language patterns that transform our relationships into enhancing and empowering ones. One of the simplest examples of this is the persistent sense of "either/or" thinking that prevails in communication rather than an underlying sense that comes with the inclusive "and" statements. Simply, if I make a statement and my friend responds with a sentence starting with "but," she is essentially saying "wrong" or "no" to my statement. However, if at the end of my statement she starts her response with "and," then she is implying that my statement is valid and her statement is also valid. This allows for the validity of different points of view and does not begin the struggle for who is right.

I use the term *languaging* in order to turn the word *language* into a verb, as this tends to shift language from a static to a dynamic process. It becomes an empowering, self-creative act, employing a wide range of verbal and behavioral strategies. We move beyond understanding grammar as a formal structure, to understanding the patterns of language as significant indicators and factors of psychological wellness. John Grinder, a linguist and the co-founder of NLP, made an interesting discovery about communication. He noted that although both successful and unsuccessful people, as generally recognized in society, use grammatically correct English, their language-pattern choices play a significant role in creating the difference that makes the distinction.

Languaging tools and strategies are fundamental to the art and science of SelfDesign. Just as a carpenter uses a hammer and saw to build a house, language patterns and strategies are the tools that shape our thoughts and relationships. Understanding the psychological patterns of language offers us the opportunity to choose words in new ways, consequently creating significantly new results.

Language: The Medium and the Message

I use *languaging* to refer to communication in the deepest sense: people in relationship sharing meaningful exchange. This includes more than language alone. Oftentimes a gesture, a touch, or a smile can communicate even more clearly than words. Through the movements of our bodies, we often say more to another person than we could with spoken language. My daughter communicated more to me in the first year of her life than did the sum of the lectures of all my university professors. Depth of meaning and quality of being can be hard to express in words, yet easy to convey with gestures, postures, glances, and touch. A felt presence between two people can resonate with clarity far more succinctly than speech. Languaging is an interpersonal communication, a conversation with or without words, and it gives us a tool for designing our lives in a whole new way.

Over the years I have witnessed that well-intentioned parents and educators sometimes communicate messages that contradict their intentions, creating the opposite result from that which is desired. For example, as parents we might say that our child could have done better at some task. In our minds this demonstrates a belief in the ability of our child, but the message is often heard as criticism. This happens because we have not learned how to check the "congruency" of our messages, or whether messages actually produce the desired effect. In my observations, many parents give mixed and incongruent messages. Tone of voice is a simple example. Because tone is more important than words, a parental message of positive words but negative tone can be very confusing. When children hear words that are supposed to be caring but concurrently suggest criticism or even attack through the parent's body posture, an inner conflict is created, as illustrated in the photo that follows.

The asymmetry in the postures of the father and son are typical of many parent-child relationships. The child's physiology is collapsed in response to the positively intended but invasive behavior of the father. Guiding our children's behavior while staying in rapport with them is the art and science of parenting in harmony.

Have you ever noticed someone saying "yes" with a smile while shaking his head from side to side, thus saying "no" with his gesture? It may sound absurd, but start watching and you will see it surprisingly often. Which message are we to believe? When I ask a child to do something and he either says, "I'll try" or "Yes, I will do it" while shaking his head, I know already that it will not happen. Once we begin to realize how we inadvertently create mixed messages, we can begin to understand and incorporate new languaging skills. If we accept that children model our intentions and emotional context as much as our messages, then it becomes important to develop our own congruency. Congruency comes when we are being true to ourselves, when we are not fooling or lying to ourselves. Part of the process involves recognizing that we may have lost our own harmony and integrity on the way to adulthood, as well as investigating whether our learned language patterns have disruptive messages embedded within them.

The following story illustrates the power of languaging and the importance of congruence, harmony, and connection.

A father approached me one day about bringing his autistic son to our learning center. By the father's description, the boy never slept in a bed and had to have bright lights on all the time. He was eight years old and did not speak. He ran from activity to activity, attending for only a moment. Some of the experts who had tested the boy had diagnosed him with autistic spectrum disorder.

A few days later the parents showed up with a bright-eyed young boy who raced past me to the first thing he saw in the room. Just as he reached up to touch it, his mother was there to take his hands off the object. The boy immediately turned and raced toward the next thing that caught his eye. His mother was one step behind him taking his hands off whatever he stopped to examine. When she tired, the father took over while I talked with the mother. This activity continued the entire length of their visit. The father spoke about his research into possible causes of his son's problems. Watching these parents interact with their son, I did not feel that identifying the cause would help them know how to help him learn appropriate behaviors. My sense from observing the dynamics of this family was that neither parent played with him, so he was missing a child's basis for rapport. Their interference with every engagement the boy made, however, was something with which I could assist. The boy's attempts to engage in activities were constantly blocked, a type of disruption called "pattern interrupt," which can negatively affect a child's development.

With a colleague of mine who was trained in a strategy called the Kaufman method, developed by two parents who discovered the importance of rapport as a means of entering their autistic child's worldview, we visited the family's home. When we arrived, the boy was playing on the floor with some blocks. We suggested that my colleague play with the boy for fifteen minutes while the parents observed her methods. The three of us watched as she sat down on the floor, just in the peripheral vision of the boy, who continued to busily play. She mirrored his exact posture and then began to move in the same patterns and rhythms he was using. If he reached for a block, she would reach in exactly the same manner for another. If he gathered three blocks together and made a pile, she would match this action exactly as he had done.

Although the boy gave no direct acknowledgment of the therapist's presence, after a few minutes he became aware that her actions were just like his. He stopped and glanced at her for a moment and then tested her by stretching to pick up a big block at some distance. As he reached, she matched his action by reaching just as far and picking up another big block. He tested her again by making a quick movement, and when she modeled him he delightedly tried once more. A look of confirmation and acknowledgment came over his face.

For the next five minutes, the two engaged in a block-moving conversation, a "languaging" in which the boy would do something and watch to see my colleague imitate him. She then changed the game by initiating an action. He paused for a moment at the interruption, but to my amazement, he quickly followed her lead.

During this meaningful interaction, the parents had both left the room, one to make tea and the other to put away dishes. When asked to return so that they could see this method for establishing rapport, their resistance to the technique made it clear that they couldn't comprehend playing in a childlike way with their son.

When my colleague had finished playing and languaging with this young boy, she came to sit beside me. The boy followed her, standing in front of her and looking directly at her. He reached out for her hands and held them. The father then interrupted, ending the interlude by taking his son and guiding him to the sink to wash his hands.

When we asked the parents to demonstrate the rapport techniques with their son, they were awkward and unable to simply mirror his actions. They constantly added blocks to his pile rather than paralleling him. When they added a block, he would grab it and throw it away. They would get frustrated and try something else, and in turn he would resist. I began to see a pattern of anxiety underlying the parents' disrupting actions. It soon became apparent that this child had not established a bonded relationship with either parent. Although they both had good intentions, their parenting style interrupted the activities and thought patterns of their son. The boy read their anxiety as an underlying condition of the world.

After my colleague and I left this family's home, she suggested that the boy was not autistic but selectively mute. This symptom can be a reaction to not feeling safe; remaining silent becomes a coping mechanism. Over the following weeks I found that the parents were unwilling to continue this work with their son. What amazed me was the astounding breakthrough achieved in just a few minutes by entering this child's world as a legitimate space and engaging in a nonverbal conversation with him on his terms. I would guess that this child never spoke because he never felt engaged, only disrupted.

Languaging: A Tool for Positive Influence

Children learning language are the ultimate scientists, investigating every nuance of tone, rhythm, and syntax. They listen, copy, and notice the results they get.

Language is about results; it is our tool for making things happen. In the process we become conscious not only of who we are but that we are participating in a significant act. When the process of naming things turns to naming ourselves and thus becoming conscious of ourselves, we emerge from the background of our own unconsciousness into self-awareness. For example, the word cat is mapped onto the actual cat. Then the image of the cat exists in our mind so that the cat can be talked about even when absent. We notice that we are *not* "cat," and our awareness of self is strengthened. We begin to construct our world in more complex ways, inventing time and imagining scenarios past and future rather than just living in the present. Language development represents an exciting, investigative time in the life of a child.

Most children master basic language and understand general language rules intuitively before they are three years old. Virtually all parents trust that their children will learn to speak, and children are in control of this task. They experiment with words and sounds. Parents respond to their children's innate need to communicate by sharing the joy of naming, emphasizing language structures through repetition. These responses, supported by hugs and smiles, help build and deepen the bond between parent and child. It is in our languaging, our conversational dance, that images, ideas, and understandings are shared back and forth. We *imagine* other people's words and we *speak* our own images as we describe the movies in our own minds. Through the creation of language and the designing of metaphors, we become conscious of our place in the world.

SelfDesign as a methodology uses dozens of languaging tools from NLP to influence learning, both within ourselves and in others. In this chapter, I would like to introduce you to five of the basic languaging patterns. In languaging terms, the SelfDesign process is largely about noticing how our inner worlds relate and how we weave them together to tell our story of experience. The *way* that we tell our story indicates our degree of integrity or self-deception, our congruence or self-distortion, our harmony or imbalance. Due to the ongoing nature of the design process, any patterns that do not work well can be changed and improved upon.

Key Languaging Patterns
Using I Instead of You

A healthy self is one that senses contentment and fulfillment within and that is also connected and in harmony with others. However, working almost counter to this, when we get caught up in our social emphasis on left-hemisphere dominance and the development of sequential, linear, time-specific, and rational distinctions in our schooling and workplace, we find ourselves seduced into seeing the world and ourselves as separate and distinct. This phenomenon has interesting implications when we consider how most individuals talk about themselves in the second person. Although we all know that the word *I* uniquely describes our "self," many people use the word *you* for self-reference during conversation. For example, a person describing their own experience might say, "When you go into the building, you are amazed at the way they have designed the lighting."

There are two strategies for remembering, one "associated"—from the inside—and the other "disassociated"—from the outside. When people use the word "you" to talk about self, they tend to be seeing themselves doing something from the disassociated position. In a therapeutic sense, the use of the word "you" for self is often a way of escaping from a discomfort in living in one's body.

In order to think "scientifically," we consciously adopt a position disassociated from the body. We pretend that we are not in or affiliated with a body, and we look objectively at situations from the outside. In my counseling and workshops I ask people to imagine a recent positive event, requesting that they notice if they are watching themselves from the outside or experiencing the event from the inside. A significant number report that they are observers to their own experience. I then ask them to imagine the experience again, this time adopting a disassociated position for one-half of the memory and an associated position for the other half. Almost everyone reports intensified feelings during the associated view and almost no feelings from the disassociated view.

My observations over the years have shown me that people who generally feel happy in life remember their positive experiences as associated and most of their negative experiences as disassociated. The use of the word *I* for self-description, despite cultural tendencies and common use to the contrary, seems essential in the quest for empowerment and integrity. SelfDesigning individuals hold their own first-person authority, "here and now," to represent how they think and feel. "This is my life, I am here now, and this is how 'I' feel, think, and remember my experiences."

A friend of mine recently offered a perfect example of avoiding discomfort through language. He came into my office and said, "It is time to stop smoking. You start to worry at some point when you see all those warnings on the cigarette packages. You want to be around to be a grandparent. The worst thing is when your kids give you that worried look." In such a case, my first job is to get this person into the room and into his body. It is amazing to watch what happens when I ask someone in my friend's situation to repeat their statements using the word *I* instead of *you*. The story is suddenly a personal one, with implications and consequences that create personal feelings. When people say, "You tell yourself," I ask them to describe, "Who is talking to whom?" Thus begins the journey into unraveling inner dialogue.

In parenting, a slightly different type of example points to a similar issue. Consider the effect of this kind of statement: "Son, it is bedtime now, and you need to get ready." This abstraction to a correct time for bed creates the impression of a real and absolute entity. It makes bedtime an external, non-negotiable event determined by some authority somewhere else. Although it might get a quick result, it takes all power of choice away from a child, while the needs and desires of both parties go unexpressed. An opportunity for the emergence of collaborative and cooperative relationship is lost in this instance.

Compare it with the following statement: "I would like you to go to bed now because I want you to get enough rest, and I would like some time to myself this evening." When children hear this kind of statement, they can respond from a sense of relationship. This model allows them to hear and respect another's needs as well as the freedom to represent their own needs. It creates a relational interaction rather than a disassociated action, and it fosters self-responsibility and relationship.

If you are not accustomed to it, I invite you to experiment with using the first person, *I*, to represent your experience. You might also wish to invite your children to use the word *I* and see what happens for them.

Our world can shift dramatically if we practice being equals who clearly represent our individual authority. Through negotiation and through truly listening to each other's needs and wants, we can begin to create a society that cooperatively strives to find ways for us all to be supported. For the family, for the classroom, and even for nations in conflict, the strategies for taking responsibility in our languaging can have far reaching effects.

Ilana in a present-tense, here-and-now state of "I." Maintaining this state lifelong is a key to the unfolding of genius.

Shifting from Exclusive to Inclusive Languaging

Our exclusive and inclusive language patterns relate back to the left-brain/right body and right-brain/left-body distinctions of chapter 4. Our right-body, masculine aspects represent exclusion in the nature of making either/or and right/wrong decisions. Interestingly, the phrase "to decide" takes its historical meaning from the word *cut*. In a metaphoric sense, the male part of us holds the sword in the right hand, using it to cut off or cut out in the truest sense of "exclude." It is this side that judges, and it is this side that says "no." Our left-side, feminine aspects tends to be inclusive, noticing patterns of connection and saying "yes." It is this side that holds the chalice, this side that holds the baby to the breast, next to the beating heart. It is important to recognize the value and to understand the appropriate use of both kinds of thinking, remembering that both men and women have a right-decisive side and a left-inclusive side.

Gregory Bateson asserted that the external world is one of quantity and the internal world is one of quality. Metaphorically, again, the left hand points inward to the internal world of quality and the right hand points outward to the external world of quantity. Accordingly, it is important to make the distinction that we can manipulate external objects, and that when it comes to the internal world we are best served by the relational thinking and emotions connected to quality.

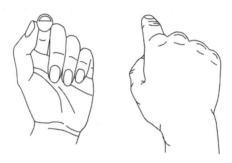

Another languaging example refers to the use of the word *but*. Most of us are aware of how it feels to be in a conversation with someone who responds to each of our statements with the word *but*. The use of *but* effectively discounts our opinions, making them wrong while making the other person right. This type of right-or-wrong thinking keeps relationships mired in an either/or competitive world. The language of exclusion inspires dominance and fear. Voices get raised because we are not sure we are being listened to or heard.

When we are responding to another person, we can introduce our own valid idea *as well as* validate the other person's statement through a simple shift from the word *but* to *and*. In this new frame, both people are right and have confirmed each other's autonomy and legitimacy. Differences of opinion can be discussed and evaluated in an inclusive and positive way as a process of negotiation.

This subtle language shift has the important effect of allowing people to feel safe, acknowledged, and equal. Children welcome conversation that allows them to express their own perspectives and discover the differences of other points of view. Experiencing confirmation through the use of *and* encourages people of all ages to expand their views of the world. Inclusion is the language of nurturing and of love. It empowers everyone involved to grow and flourish.

I wanted to keep science alive through personal discovery and discussion, so in the first year of Wondertree when we went to the beach I stuck a stick in the ground. Throughout the afternoon we revisited the stick and saw that its shadow was moving. Here we are gathered around the shadow trying to imagine how it could be moving. Someone moved the stick? No, the sun is moving in the sky. Maybe the earth is turning on its axis!

Affirming the Positive, Ignoring the Negative

According to Gregory Bateson, the unconscious mind is always in the present and always says "yes." It is the conscious mind that has invented "no." Our society focuses on conscious control and therefore consistently resorts to "no" statements: "stop smoking," "fight racism," "end war," and "say no to drugs" are all examples of conscious "no" thinking. The message may be a good one, but the message is spoken from the negative rather than the positive.

In regard to our children, we often find ourselves saying things like, "Don't forget to bring your book tomorrow." I personally have no idea how "not to forget." I can, however, learn how to remember. My most successful strategies emerge from positive messages to myself. For years I tried to quit smoking, only to find my habit become increasingly more impulsive and invasive. However, once I aligned myself with my desire to breathe clean, fresh air, I never smoked again.

One of the guiding principles of NLP is to consistently add choices rather than take choices away. The secret is to state what we want in the positive. Authority often limits our choices or takes them away altogether, and it runs counter to the development of self-responsibility and intelligence. Having more choices is a condition of greater intelligence, thereby suggesting that the limiting of options diminishes that aptitude. When we invite children to "Please play over here because it's safer," rather than demanding, "Don't run into the street or you'll be hit by a car," we help them learn how to make distinctions for themselves about choosing safety.

We shift to a new paradigm when we no longer allow our conscious, "exclusive" mind to dominate our experience. Consciousness is a valuable partner in designing strategies for survival, but it requires input from the unconscious in order to create balance. By putting the conscious mind in charge, we ignore the resources and importance of 90 percent of the rest of our brain. It is possible to create harmony using our unconscious "inclusive" and positive-thinking process for most of our strategies, saving the "no" strategies for emergencies. Let's apply this idea to the process of talking to ourselves inside.

Positive Self-Dialogue

We all tend to hear inner voices and have conversations with ourselves. With some understanding of how to manage these inner dialogues, we can significantly enhance our sense of well-being.

In becoming SelfDesigners we become aware that we generally internalize the voices of those who influence our lives, including parents, friends, or mentors. The secret is to take these voices seriously and work with them. We have probably all said to ourselves, "Well, on one hand I want to go to the movie and on the other hand I feel like staying home and relaxing." The question is, who is saying what to whom?

Studies of successful people have shown that many of them have strategies to manage their inner voices, using them to form an internal "management team" to get things accomplished. John Grinder called this phenomenon *polyphrenia*. How do we go about turning our many inner voices into a cooperative and coordinated team? I invite you to take the languaging perspectives of this chapter and blend them into the following strategies for self-dialogue, sharing them with your children so they may learn them as well:

+ Take your inner voices seriously; listen to them.
+ Use affirmative, positive language.
+ Take note of commanding or negative language, e.g., "You are stupid. You have blown it again." When you hear this language, reply with some form of "Thank you. I hear you and I'd be more willing to listen if you spoke respectfully."
+ Listen for the intent of a voice and try to discover what is behind its statement.
+ Notice the qualities of the voice (tone, volume, pitch). Does it resemble the voice or language style of anyone you know?
+ Carry on negotiations and conversations between voices that facilitate win/win solutions.
+ Use your body, and especially your hands, to represent parts and points of view.

+ Create relationships between voices with a manager guiding them to work together in different situations.
+ Remember that the unconscious/kinesthetic has no voice. It communicates feelings. A blending together of images, voices, and feelings into strategies gives us the building blocks necessary to design attitudes, beliefs, strategies, and understandings.

I am still amazed and saddened when I remember that, during my childhood, none of my teachers talked about what was going on inside of them or me. The talk was all about the conjugation of verbs, the computation of chemical reactions, and the memorizing of historical events. Now, as a learning consultant and therapist, I see how many months in Wondertree it takes some children to recover from their public school experience, and I understand the importance of focusing on the internal rather than the external reality.

Once our learners realize they are no longer under the barrage of expectations and commands (distracting voices from the outside), we can invite them to notice what is going on inside of them. In learning how to listen to their own inner voices, they can begin to design strategies for thinking. As we acknowledge the legitimacy of children's feelings and thoughts, the learners start to feel empowered. The unfolding of their infinite intelligence has begun.

Some of the Wondertree learners became very interested in making personal journals. At this time I was working on a Master's degree at the local university, and my professor was a master journalist. I asked him to share his strategies of excellence with the beginning journalists. They were fascinated, and many of them are journalists today.

Shifting from Limiting to Enhancing Languaging

In our world, time that should be spent in real conversation is usurped by the manipulating monologue of mass media. Teachers and parents more often resort to instruction and questioning than to conversation. Small wonder we grow up jostling for position in the hierarchy of controlling comments, striving for a sense of our own control through win/lose strategies. On the other hand, language that opens the possibilities for imagination and curiosity creates the space for human creativity. When children are not told what to do or think but rather hear, "I wonder what would happen if you ..." or "If it were possible, what would you ..." they feel invited to express their own volition.

Limiting language is characterized by judgments and critical comments that assume the negative. Consider an adult saying to a child, "Stop climbing that tree, or you will fall." Obviously the concerned adult is attempting to warn a child who is successfully climbing a tree. To command children to stop doing what they are doing is to initiate a condition of internal questioning. To add injury to insult, the hypnotic embedding of a command to fall—"you will fall"—sets children up for self-doubt in their ability to accomplish their goal. Children live in the present moment in a "yes" condition. Only the conscious mind says "no," and an appropriate relationship between the conscious and the unconscious is one of equality rather than domination.

How different the quality of children's lives and the nature of our relationships with them become when we frame the future like this: "Be sure to pay attention up there. I would feel more comfortable if you climb on the lower branches." We move from a frame of negative outcomes to a world of unambiguous statements and clear possibilities.

A well-known educational study placed average students in groups that were labeled as either gifted or learning-disabled. At the beginning of the school year, teachers of the groups were informed of their class's purported ability level. Not surprisingly, the expectations of the teacher shaped the outcome; the "gifted" class did much better than the "disabled" class. The old adage "Be careful what you wish for" could be restated as "Be careful what you expect."

At Wondertree, the learning consultants hold the "as if" frame. To assume that anything is possible creates a large stage for the unfolding of any outcome. Learning is sometimes a simple consolidation of what we already know, and frequently it takes us far into new territory. While traditional education seems designed to only let students learn within the limits, SelfDesign continually challenges all assumptions, both in and outside of the box.

All the should/shouldn't, can't/won't, never/always parameters set limits and expectations with respect to the possibilities of children's efforts. I have often seen learners fail at some task and then state, "I can't do ...," and suddenly the past becomes a predictor for the future. In contrast, a statement like, "The things that I tried didn't work, so I will try something different next time," establishes a set for learning and possibility. The process of languaging is a tool for designing positive outcomes in our experiences.

One of our most creative and popular mentors was Lawrence the clown. Here he coaches Anna in mime. In any given interpersonal situation a clown demonstrates creativity and choice of response, often outside the norm. As Lawrence presented unusual mind-sets, he connected with the learners' natural propensity to model newness.

Shifting from Content to Process

We name things and we name processes. We do not commonly mistake the name of a thing for the object itself; in other words, we know the difference between the word *rose* and the actual flower. However, because processes are more abstract and elusive than objects, we sometimes get confused and assume that the named process is real. For example, we name a behavior like dyslexia and then shift that label to name the person as dyslexic. We mistake the do-er for the process. Although the naming of things and events is important, it is equally important to appreciate that the name of a process actually shifts how we relate to that very process. This is like eating the menu rather than the food, or showing a picture of yourself to a friend and saying "This is me" rather than "This is a picture of me."

Teachers are trained to teach subjects. Students are told to learn coursework. The brain is seen as a muscle that must be exercised in order to develop. Although this is true in a sense, the theory does not hold when it comes to memorizing things like math and history facts. The real learning and internalizing comes from understanding processes and from seeing how these processes are relevant to living.

SelfDesign uses the reverse process; it starts with the learner and what the learner wants to learn from a place of curiosity, relevance, and enthusiam. We help learners explore what they are curious or excited about, and then we support them in how they can learn most efficiently. The "why" and the "how" are much more important than the actual content of their learning. Over the years our graduates have demonstrated time and again that being an enthusiastic, self-directed learner is at the heart of being a successful student and becoming a successful adult.

SelfDesign is about focusing our attention on our personal experience. We become aware of our own learning when we begin noticing and attending to our own experience. In a traditional classroom the teacher stands at the front of the room saying, "Pay attention to me!" In SelfDesign we sit beside learners and invite and encourage them to look inside and give attention to what is going on "here and now." They are invited to daydream, and we want to know what is going on inside their imaginations.

In the early years of Wondertree I had a parent who would go over to her daughter's journal day after day and find it empty. After weeks of this, she finally came to me in frustration, and I informed her that she was looking in the wrong place. I told her that we invested most of our day in our imaginations, and if she wanted to find out what we did today she needed either to come during the day and participate or to inquire of her daughter about her images, thoughts, and feelings.

It is out of our daydreams and our rich fantasies that the real curriculum emerges. A child's ability to share these inner landscapes is a measure of the ability of a child to access inner genius. For example, one of my long-term colleagues in SelfDesign, Kathleen Forsythe, focuses on Observing for Learning. She describes observing as a process in which the learner and the mentor allow the creative play of the learner to emerge. Observing is also a state of love, acceptance, and permission. As the mentors or consultants observe and reflect what they notice back to the learner, the child is invited to be aware of what he is doing and to explore and experiment with ideas of his own creation. In SelfDesign, by becoming aware of the learning process the learner is able to design and influence that process using a variety of strategies. This is the true measure of intelligence, and it is the place where the world of choice and possibility begins.

As a consultant, my primary work is to get out of the learner's way. However, I am always at hand to offer insights and to help learners observe their own processes and design new strategies when they are stuck. Teachers are commonly referred to as "the sage on the stage," where as SelfDesign consultants are "the guide on the side." Although both processes have their place, I believe that our children need to be learning to play their own music rather than learning to be members of the audience.

I once worked with a ten-year-old boy named Peter who was so terrified of reading and the idea that he couldn't read that he constantly cowered. His life seemed to consist of anticipating the next moment he would be expected to read, and this was the most painful, threatening thing possible.

My initial approach was to ignore the fact that he couldn't read. I established a relationship with him by being curious about all the things he liked doing and all the things he enjoyed talking about. One day when he felt pretty comfortable with me, he mentioned that he couldn't read.

I suggested that I didn't think that this was possible, that of course he could read and that reading was easy. When he insisted that he couldn't read, I set out to show him that in fact he was already a reader. I knew that his problem was not about reading; it was about fear and all the feelings of inadequacy and incompetence associated with it.

I guessed that because he liked cats that he might be familiar with the word CAT. I wrote a C on the whiteboard and asked him if he could identify this letter. He said yes, it was a C. I said good, erased it, and wrote the letter A. He said, A. I smiled, erased it and wrote the letter T, and he said T. Now I wrote the letters CAT on the board. I asked him if he had ever seen these before, and he said yes. I asked him what these letters stood for.

He said, "Cat."

I asked him, "When you look at these letters, do you see a picture of a cat in your head?"

And he said, "Yes."

I told him that this was all there was to reading, that because he could see the letters CAT and say the word *cat* and see a picture of a CAT in his head, he could already read. Reading, I offered, was nothing more that what he had just done. The only difference between him and other readers was that they knew more words. I added that they, too, had learned them one at a time through practice. Reading was only practice of the skill that he already had. I left him with an open invitation that he could learn more words anytime he wanted and that if he wanted help, I would be willing to help him.

With that simple shift in understanding, Peter was easily able to engage in reading before his family moved away and left our program. This child was more limited by his belief about himself than by his actual abilities, as is so often the case. The assumptions he held as truth had immobilized his learning, and transformation occurred through a shift in his self-perception rather than a focus on his inabilities or on the "content" work of phonics and repetition.

How we talk to ourselves and to others holds important keys to the process of human development. Our languaging either guides or blocks us, and a comprehensive understanding of how languaging affects our psychological processes is probably the most important aspect of SelfDesign.

CHAPTER 6

Learners' Rights to SelfDesign

Imagine going to any public place on a hot, sunny August day and interviewing students of various ages who are getting ready to go back to school. You would probably find two distinct groups of learners. The first would consist of children who were bored with summer and eager to get back to a classroom environment that provides them with books, ideas, and the fun of socialization. The second group would consist of a significant number who would be happy if school disappeared altogether and who have a clear sense that school does not serve their real needs. I suspect that this second group contains either bright youngsters who have seldom been allowed to follow their passion of learning under their own authority, or those who have difficulty learning in the singular way that schools teach.

In a recent conversation with a superintendent of schools, I was told of a U.S. study suggesting that 20 percent of learners are being well-served by public education while a shocking 80 percent are not. On another front, business leaders and university professors state that the vast majority of the graduates of schooling do not have the skills necessary for either the world of work or the world of academics. Given my experiences over the years, I would agree. Some learners succeed in our traditional system and some do not. Some might succeed in either but prefer one over the other—and who gets to decide where they should go? Because we are a schooled society, there is a strong bias assuming that schooling provides an educational standard and value for all. SelfDesign, based on a much more modern and comprehensive understanding and definition of wellness and success, challenges existing beliefs. A child's right to self-determined learning is a fundamental operating principle of SelfDesign. When learners are governed by their own authority and when their opinions make a difference, they can see that they are collaborative participants in designing a better world.

Unfortunately, schooling often adds injury to insult. It is an insult to individual rights when it is assumed that our children must go to school. The injury occurs when children are no longer allowed to think in terms of their own sensibilities, when they must do only what an educational authority deems worthwhile. If an educational system assumes it knows what is best for another person, it stands on a fine line between authority and coercion. That line is crossed when learners are told what, when, and how they will learn.

While we can all appreciate that certain rules help sustain a civil society, it is the understanding of and agreement to the rules that actually gives them value. In Wondertree, we have chosen to forego rules altogether, substituting the process of making agreements with learners. These verbal and written contracts are made yearly with each child, out of real needs for safety and well-being within the context of our community. Over the years, we have found that it is far easier to maintain agreements than it is to enforce rules. Young people gain the skills of creating, managing, and participating in community when they actively make and keep agreements, learning the dynamic skill of negotiation when those agreements are not kept.

It is an entirely different process to be actively included in agreements and empowered to take responsibility for our actions. In a community based on self-responsibility, we find citizens with internalized controls and a sense of their own authority.

Happiness Is a Guiding Principle

Several years ago I was in counselor training with Andrew Feldmar, a Vancouver psychologist and a protégé of R. D. Laing. One day during the training, Andrew made the following statement: "Happiness is a biological condition." After a brief but significant pause he added, ". . . and unhappiness is a political condition."

In other words, happiness comes to us naturally. We associate happiness with well-being, love, and balance. It is our fundamental condition and our indicator of essential fulfillment. Unhappiness arises when someone or something moves us out of this balance, which happens most often in relationships with others. Some relationships support and sustain our happiness while others limit us and reduce our freedom. A feeling of unhappiness, like the feeling of hunger, gives us the clue that something is missing and that a change needs to occur. In the politics of relationship, when our rights are diminished we feel frustrated and controlled. We succumb to apathy, or we fight for change.

The photograph above, taken at a textile factory in Pennsylvania in 1908, is a symbol of oppression. Compulsory work for children has been seen as a violation of children's rights since the beginning of England's Industrial Revolution. We are wise enough to recognize child labor as exploitation, and there is currently a worldwide effort to ban this practice. At the same time we have seen a worldwide push for compulsory public education. An example of this can be found in the 1989 United Nations' Convention on the Rights of the Child, where, contradictory to the title of the convention, a section of the written document centers on making schooling compulsory. Although education can indeed be a liberator by providing a larger context in children's lives, the "compulsory" part of education is fundamentally a violation of children's rights.

It is easy for adults to dislike the oppression of compulsory work but not realize that sending a child to twelve years of compulsory learning can be just as oppressive. SelfDesign goes beyond the idea of compulsory education, believing that children should have the right to learn in an environment where personal authority, or authorship, is affirmed.

Standing as a universal icon of self-determination, Gandhi's efforts to free India from the tyranny of control by the British Empire still inspire freedom movements worldwide. Yet in the following photograph we see him spinning thread for cloth, just like the little girl in the previous picture. What difference is evoked between these two similar actions? We have a young girl whose job is to spin thread, an image of oppression, and Gandhi spinning, an image of self-determination.

Our initial guess might focus on the fact that the little girl is but a child, while Gandhi is an adult. In truth, however, the difference lies in the driving force behind their respective actions. The young girl is spinning for someone else, for the owner of the company who is paying her a minimum wage at best. Gandhi is spinning cloth for an even lesser wage, yet he is spinning it for himself. He is meeting his own needs, making his own choices, and determining his own outcome.

If we substitute the idea of learning for the activity of spinning thread, we gain an interesting insight. A child in school is learning according to the dictates of a teacher, supposedly for the benefit of society as determined by a governing agency. A self-determined student, on the other hand, is learning for himself, living in integrity with his own needs versus those of others. Both are learning, yet the reason behind the action lies at the heart of the issue. One person is being told what he must do and the other is choosing what feels important and relevant. Gandhi's actions set a precedent for significant political change in India. In North America today, most people agree that our educational system, with its 80 percent student dissatisfaction and 10 to 30 percent dropout rate, is long overdue for major change. The following graph is based on results of a survey of public-school students in 1992 in British Columbia, Canada. Due to the standardization of public education throughout North America, the percentages shown are likely representative of children's opinions throughout the continent. Over 2,200 school children were asked to agree or disagree with the following three statements: (1) "What I'm learning in school is useful," (2) "I feel involved in my class," and (3) "I feel cared about at school." The graph shows the percentage of children who agreed with each of the statements.

The downward trend of agreement with the three statements between grade 4 and grade 12 presents a clear picture of growing dissatisfaction as students move through their school career. If we average the responses in grade 12, we see that less than 10 percent of learners felt served by their public-school experience. In a more recent study in British Columbia, only 40 percent of public-school graduates, surveyed at least four years after graduation, believed that their formal education had given them usable skills for the future. In contrast, the majority of our Virtual High learners felt positively engaged in their learning process. Freedom of choice within a respectful atmosphere led to empowerment for these young people. Over the years, virtually all the graduates of our program have achieved significant personal, academic, and social success as adults. Many of our graduates are excelling in their university programs despite the fact that diplomas were not issued through Virtual High. Learning with consultation and inclusion is essential to supporting both a positive experience and a belief that education is an engagement of one's whole self in the lifelong journey of learning.

Industrial Education

Today, our view of schooling is influenced by the metaphors of industrialism. Our society sees children as incomplete until they have spent twelve or more years on the assembly line. Students' dissatisfaction with the process is ignored by a cultural agenda that trains them to be obedient workers. Each year we install more information and knowledge until children come out at the end of the conveyer belt as finished products. No factory in the world would continue to manufacture a product if it gave only a 10 percent satisfaction rate, and hopefully no one would buy such a product. Why is it, then, that we continue the assembly line of dissatisfied participants in our industrialized system of education? By all rights, public education should be out of business. Yet we continue to blame learners for the failures of schooling, and we intensify the demand for accountability with new programs focused primarily on measurable results. We intimidate parents, children, and teachers with consequences for questioning the schooling process and its standards. Because we as adults have "survived" the school experience, we think our children should be able to do the same.

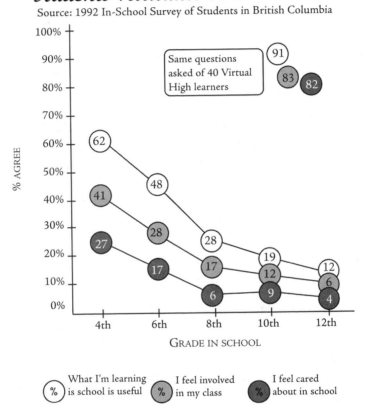

Students' Attitudes Toward School

Source: 1992 In-School Survey of Students in British Columbia

There are two possible explanations for our cultural complacency about this issue. Many children learn to feel powerless by being denied choice in their education, going on into adulthood accepting powerlessness within their jobs and societal roles. Our acceptance of this situation might be understood by making a comparison to the historical Stockholm Syndrome. In 1973, a group of Swedish social scientists researched the strange bond that developed between the captives and their captors in a hostage situation resulting from an attempted bank robbery. What started out as a defense tactic for self-protection on the part of the captives turned into an effort to win the favor of the captor in almost childlike ways. In ongoing research into this syndrome, it has been consistently found that the longer the time captives spend with a captor, the greater the tendency to identify and sympathize with the captor's point of view. Captives also attempt to cope with the situation by pretending that it is "all a dream," sleeping excessively and, when awake, daydreaming of a magical rescue. Is this a description of a hostage-taking, or does it describe a typical day for many students in schools across the country?

The second possible explanation relates to the fact that our culture has a long history of excluding certain groups from making decisions in areas that directly affect them. Women and racial minorities need not look far into the past to verify this fact. Time has shown us that our assumptions about these groups were inaccurate and prejudicial. Because our society tends to believe that children are incapable of making informed decisions due to their age, we disqualify them as participants in their own learning experience. We believe that until children are educated, they cannot make intelligent choices. This adult logic gives us the excuse to disrespect the stated desires of children in our families and schools. Our decision to marginalize children is caused by our tendency to give weight to quantity over quality. Because children have not had as many experiences as adults (quantity), we assume they are therefore uninformed and unable to make decisions about the conditions of their lives (quality).

However, children do make profound choices from the moment of birth. The human species is highly sensitive, keenly aware, and has a remarkable ontological ability to know how to grow and learn in the first few years of life. Psychologists believe that 90 percent of human learning potential is achieved before school age, and this unfolding of understanding is directed by the interest and enthusiasm inherent in virtually every child. We must remember that, although children may not have the same quantity of life experiences as do adults, they assuredly have a clear awareness of the quality of their lives. Once we make this distinction, it is imperative to question our prejudice against including children in decisions about their own learning process.

Over the years I have met many successful adults who either had no formal schooling or who left school partway through. I know others who finished school and now are lost, having no idea what to do or how to live meaningful lives. The need for formal education should not be the issue; the issue should be about choices, about options that provide satisfactory outcomes. Schooling is one option, and within schooling there are few real choices offering different ways of learning. Within traditional schooling there is really only one approach, with variations on that one theme. Beyond that there have been a few free schools and the choice of home learning, which are exciting and important alternatives. SelfDesign offers a learning experience beyond any schooling or home learning.

Captivity and Compulsory Schooling

Schooling has a captive audience because most people accept that it is required. Since it is sometimes difficult to understand issues that are close to home, let's look at the situation for a species closely related to our own.

In the past century there has been considerable study of primates in laboratories and zoos around the world. We have gathered a great deal of scientific evidence about chimpanzees' intelligence, behavioral characteristics, and ability to learn language. However, our initial understanding was skewed because we observed them only in captivity. Not until Jane Goodall studied chimpanzees in their natural environment, from the 1960s through to the present, did we begin to understand their comprehensive abilities as individuals and in community.

I am convinced that most learning disabilities are more an artifact of the classroom than an attribute of the learner. Like chimpanzees in captivity, children demonstrate these behaviors as coping strategies in a coercive environment. Many learners who come to Wondertree with the labels of learning disabilities lose the majority of their symptoms simply by leaving the environment of schooling. While some support is needed to heal the habits of the learning disability, most of the behaviors fall away when children realize they are no longer a captive audience.

In 1988, the Wondertree learners gave Jane Goodall the first Wondertree Award to honor her efforts to release and rehabilitate chimpanzees who had been living in captivity, separated from their natural communities. Her work has focused on asking the world to recognize animal rights and freedoms. Wondertree has made a parallel effort on behalf of children forced into compulsory education throughout the world. When schooling is not forced and children have the freedom to choose from a variety of ways to learn, they will have achieved the rights they deserve.

Presenting Jane Goodall with the first Wondertree Award. We have given the award ever since to honor adults who work lifelong to make the world a better place for children to grow up in, and who set an inspirational example. Jane Goodall's efforts on behalf of chimpanzees deeply moved our learners as they became keenly aware that the fairy-tale depiction of animals is not the way animals are treated in the real world.

Freedom of Thought

In his book *Escape from Childhood*, John Holt wrote about children's rights:

> Young people should have the right to control and direct their own learning, that is, to decide what they want to learn, and when, where, how, how much, how fast, and with what help they want to learn it. To be still more specific, I want them to have the right to decide if, when, how much, and by whom they want to be *taught* and the right to decide whether they want to learn in a school and if so which one and for how much of the time.

> *No human right, except for the right to life itself, is more fundamental than this. A person's freedom of learning is part of his freedom of thought, even more basic than his freedom of speech. If we take from someone his right to decide what he will be curious about, we destroy his freedom of thought.* We say, in effect, you must think not about what interests and concerns *you*, but about what interests and concerns *us*.

All children should have the opportunity to learn. The belief that all students should have access to public school is valid only if they have equal access to other learning opportunities. Traditional education is but one of many paths to acquiring life skills. By accepting the current view that schooling equates to learning, we limit the rich variety of available opportunities and we give students the message that they must fit the mold. It is time to allow the real stakeholders in education—our children—to trust their sensibilities and to experience choice on their educational paths as they create their own learning journeys.

Questioning Authority

The United Nations Convention on the Rights of the Child was, as of 2003, ratified by 191 countries, not including the U. S. and Somalia. When a group of Virtual High students and I first read the Convention on the Rights of the Child, we were optimistic. We assumed that the United Nations would respect the rights of children, families, and unique communities around the world. As we read the document, we appreciated that the convention was dealing with situations in which children were being killed in wars, driven from their homes, or forced into military service. These violations were obviously important issues to address on a worldwide level.

When we got to Article 28 on education, the learners all agreed with statements about children having the right to go to school. This represented choice, which everyone at Virtual High supported. But they disagreed with the stipulation that education should be compulsory and follow the Western-style assembly-line school model. Most of our learners had had negative experiences with traditional school and did not want this choice forced on children of any culture. Through our discussions with Canadian Native groups, we became aware that the compulsory schooling introduced by missionaries had severely eroded the cultural traditions of their people. The government had inappropriately achieved its stated goal to "kill the Indian in the child" by means of moving indigenous children away from their natural patterns of living and learning. We later met indigenous people from South America, who echoed a similar theme of disruption of their cultural integrity through enforced schooling.

Our study of the Convention of the Rights of the Child led us to author our own Declaration of Learners' Rights and Responsibilities. Our declaration consciously avoided use of the word *student*, as this role is closely associated with schooling and teachers. We did not use the word *child* either, because we did not want to create age-specific distinctions related to learning. We chose the word *learner* instead, preferring its association with the idea of learning as a lifelong process. Our twelve points covered both rights and responsibilities, supporting a belief that they go hand in hand. The declaration asserted that learners, regardless of age, have the right to determine the direction and course of their own learning. We used metaphors of growth and development to support the biological nature of human beings. The heart of the learning process was described as a mutually chosen learner/mentor relationship created through shared enthusiasm and a fascination for learning.

The declaration was read in four workshops and was given to the participants at the conference in June. That same week we also gave a copy to the minister of education in Victoria. Since then, this document has appeared in several books. It has been published by UNESCO and has been distributed in newsletters and magazines in at least ten countries around the world.

Declaration of Learners' Rights and Responsibilities

As a learner, I have the right:

1. to allow my own experience and enthusiasm to guide my learning.

2. to choose and direct the nature and conditions of my learning experience; I am responsible for the results I create.

3. to perfect the skills to be a conscious, self-confident, and resourceful individual.

4. to be held in respect; it is my responsibility to hold others in respect.

5. to a nurturing and supportive family and community; my family and community have the right and responsibility to be my primary resource.

6. to enter into relationships based on mutual choice, collaborative effort, challenge, and mutual gain.

7. to be exposed to a diverse array of ideas, experiences, environments, and possibilities; this exposure is the responsibility of myself, my parents, and my mentors.

8. to evaluate my learning according to my own sensibilities; I have the right to request and the responsibility to include the evaluations of my mentors in my learning process.

9. to co-create decisions that involve and concern me.

10. to openly consider and respect the ideas of others, whether or not I accept these ideas.

11. to enter a learning organization that offers spiritual, intellectual, emotional, and physical support, and operates in an open and inclusive manner.

12. of equal access to resources, information, and funding.

The Declaration of Learner's Rights and Responsibilities was written in May 1995 by the learners whose names are italicized: back row, left to right: *Sarah Partridge, Serena Staples*, two conference delegates, *Kaan Muncaster, ilana Cameron, Greg Dean*, and *Travis Bernhardt*; front row left to right: *Jesse Blum, Brent Cameron*, and another conference delegate.

The following story written by Devon Girard, a graduate of both the Wondertree and Virtual High programs, brings this chapter on rights to a close. Devon is an amazing young man, down-to-earth and delightful, whose very presence conveys an enjoyment of life. He recently went to Japan for a year in hopes of acquiring three skills: to learn to speak Japanese, to begin to master the complex game of Go, and to play the sakahatchi flute. Devon has a quality that I witness in all of the young people who have had the Wondertree and Virtual High experience. Because his unique abilities were consistently supported and respected, Devon believes in his ability to accomplish virtually anything.

Devon, now in his early twenties, illustrates the value of trusting learners and including them in the design of an unfolding curriculum, based on interests and individual needs.

Devon at 15, the age at which he graduated from Virtual High. The following article was written when he was 20.

Devon's Story: Belonging to a Unique Learning Community

Wondertree entered my life when I was a ten-year-old seeking refuge from the social challenges of elementary school. I wanted relief from the incessant teasing and crushing negativity of my classmates. Wondertree delivered, and then some.

What my small circle of new friends lacked in numbers was made up for in quality, and my social phobias began to dissolve as I settled in. I participated at the small Wondertree learning center for three years and then joined the newly created Virtual High, founded by the same organization for teenage students. After a further three years at Virtual High I chose to graduate and pursue life on my own.

Belonging to this unique learning community has influenced me beyond measure, giving me things I have only been able to fully appreciate in retrospect. During my time at Virtual High I was quite busy coping with my own journey through adolescence, and I rarely philosophized on the long-term merits of my alternative education. Now, after several years of independence and adventure, I have become aware of and grateful for the subtler benefits of my learning experience and the underlying, undeclared Wondertree curriculum.

As is the case with all new students of Wondertree, I was initially asked to outline my interests and suggest projects or subjects I might want to pursue. The students collectively controlled the budget, hiring mentors or purchasing equipment according to group interests. This was quite a change for a frustrated fourth-grader, yet the shift was highly agreeable. Soon I was strutting around the learning center like I ran the place.

And I did, in a communal sort of way.

One of my first engaging projects was a software program co-authored with a classmate, which we submitted to a regional science fair and for which we earned first prize in the computer science division. My enthusiasm for programming continued to grow, and with Wondertree's support I pursued software development almost exclusively for the remainder of my first year.

Before my eleventh birthday I had landed my first "job" as a programmer, along with several other Wondertree students and our computer science mentor. The local energy utility contracted us to design and develop a simulation that showed how one could save money by using electricity more efficiently.

Throughout my remaining time at Wondertree and the following years at Virtual High, I continued to improve my programming skills for both profit and pleasure. Upon graduation I had developed a respectable portfolio and smoothly entered a career as a professional software engineer. For several years I worked in various capacities for a number of firms, making good money from work I found both challenging and rewarding.

In 1999, the repetitive strain of constant typing caught up with me, manifesting as a debilitating injury. After months of seeking treatment and modifying my workstation ergonomics, while stubbornly remaining at my job, the pain throughout my wrists and elbows reached critical levels and I stopped working to prevent nerve damage.

In the three years since the onset of my injury I have spent an estimated $15,000 on both alternative and conventional therapies. I have seen close to thirty practitioners specializing in over ten distinct modalities in an effort to heal my arms. As of this writing I have experienced zero improvement in my condition despite my ongoing research, and I have slowly accepted that my career as a programmer is over.

This scale of crisis would rock anybody's boat, and perhaps me more than most given my specialized education. I had invested a huge chunk of my life in learning to be a competent programmer, and for my future in that field to be whisked away by an unexpected and poorly understood injury was heartbreaking. The stage might have been set for deep frustration and depression, yet I happened to be better prepared than I realized.

My academic interests at Virtual High were limited to programming, mathematics, and miscellaneous sciences. I also participated in a variety of other courses, ranging from family dynamics to NLP to chess, yet these subjects combined accounted for less than half of my studies. The largest fraction of my time and energy was devoted to a wide variety of pursuits that rarely resulted in any lasting interest or devotion. The tremendous value of this casual information-surfing has only struck me years later.

This unannounced and unscheduled activity was quietly popular among Virtual High students. Each one of us was consistently encouraged to pursue our own personal interests, and if we had none, to get some. This was a challenging request for some and demanded considerable self-reflection.

All of this time devoted to understanding and pursuing my own curiosities slowly shifted the manner in which I made decisions, and indeed the way I lived my life. This "looking-within" technique slowly evolved beyond superficial matters of subject preference and spawned an ongoing inquiry into the nature of who I am. Self-awareness and discovery was the unspoken foundation of every student's curriculum at Virtual High—a foundation that I continue to build upon.

It's taken a long time for me to perceive my injury and consequent life changes as anything but tragic, yet in several very real ways I am happier now than I ever was as a healthy programmer. I am more appreciative of the resources and abilities I still have, and I am beginning to recognize this involuntary change of course as encouragement to explore beyond my old horizons. It's ironic that this should result from a physical disability of such a restrictive nature.

It seems important to me that throughout this process, academic skills were of little value. What stood by me was not my knowledge of arithmetic but rather an understanding of myself. Effectively reinventing my identity is requiring a very thorough awareness of just how disappointed a part of me is—acknowledging that, and then choosing to re-embrace life's mystery with fresh enthusiasm. The knowledge that I need only to look within to find my new direction is precious indeed.

In the time since my injury I have learned to use voice-recognition software in order to continue using my computer. I've recently authored and self-published a backcountry snowshoeing guidebook for Vancouver's local mountains, an extremely satisfying project that I would never have attempted had my path not been diverted. I keep encountering new interests that I feel drawn to and enjoy pursuing—and it is this frame of mind for which I am most grateful. I see now that Wondertree and Virtual High nurtured not just a love of learning, but a confidence and a trust in my own ability to adapt.

Hundreds of years ago, when any one person could still wrap their head around the bulk of human knowledge, it may have been practical (and desirable) to start your child off in life with a foundational understanding of various fields. Today the amount of information available to any person at any time is staggering, and it is simply unfeasible to expect all students to study all subjects. It seems to me that the only solution, which is equally practical, functional, and satisfying, is for teachers to shift into the role of a knowledge navigator—guiding and supporting their pupils in their own curiosities.

The difference between a student studying math because his teacher or father wants him to, and a student who has a sincere, self-originating interest in the subject, cannot be overstated. Math, that infamous subject of disdain, perfectly demonstrates how a spoon-fed curriculum is absorbed only under extreme protest and promptly forgotten (more often than not) upon graduation.

Being a student at Virtual High was far more demanding than being in a typical high school. It was also far more engaging, interesting, and therefore enjoyable. Given the opportunity to pursue my own interests, I studied for longer hours with greater sincerity and retention at Virtual High than I would have otherwise. My studies seemed practical and relevant to my life, and I didn't go through the frustration that can accompany the comparatively abstract curriculum doled out in regular classrooms.

It seems ironic to me that we send our children to school in the hopes that a quality education will help them get ahead in life, when that very education so often smothers individual talent in the name of serving the many. The unique creativities and curiosities of each child (unless blatantly precocious) are downplayed or ignored in contrast with the all-important task of memorizing multiplication tables (or whatever the curriculum-of-the-day happens to be). As a result, after twelve years of disciplined attendance, our youth may have a decent grasp of basic academics and a honed ability to follow instructions, yet they lack any serious understanding of themselves.

It would be one thing if a high school education were of real value to today's youth and gave them some kind of edge, yet that is obviously not the case. Upon graduation most students still find themselves at the bottom of a very long ladder, staring up with heavy hearts—along with everybody else. The rat race is just getting started.

Giving our children control of their own education is certainly risky business. All guarantees that they are keeping pace with their peers are abandoned and replaced with a simple trust that they will explore life of their own initiative. Fear of the unknown provides strong counsel against such a seemingly irresponsible choice, and indeed not sending your children to school is considered shockingly neglectful in our society. I mean, how else will they learn anything?

Underneath this shift in educational ideology lies an even more fundamental question of societal philosophy. Our current schools seem to me a classic product of industrialization, and an attempt to efficiently churn out citizens of superior quality. In the coming years I believe our society will benefit not from greater homogeneity (regardless of quality) but much more from increased diversity and cultural creativity—and for me it is clear that key changes must occur in our classrooms.

Although the temptation to design a young person's life is supported by rational arguments of efficiency and popular social opinion, I firmly believe we will all benefit by simply helping our children find their own way, however much they may stumble. In the end, they are the only ones qualified to decide.

Conclusion

As Devon's essay so eloquently shows, our fundamental condition of happiness can be maintained by self-directed learning. It should be the marker by which we measure the worth and value of our human activities. From my experience over the past twenty years, I have seen that in an environment of freedom and respect, children who are permitted to SelfDesign thrive and access integrity as the greatest resource in expressing their intelligence.

CHAPTER 7

THE SELFDESIGN LIFESPIRAL

Several years ago in one of my parenting workshops, I introduced a non-linear timeline strategy as an aid to personal planning and healing work. I had spent many years experimenting with various models, and the shift away from a conventional, linear timeline felt like an important experiment. For this group, I drew a fifty-five-foot radius logarithmic spiral based on the Golden Rectangle. I marked each quadrant with the appropriate Fibonacci numbers, as introduced in chapter 1, to represent various ages from conception to death. The group could see that the quadrants which made up the spiral were coincident with important life passages. I invited members of the workshop to physically stand on the place that represented their current age on the spiral and to reflect on their past, present, and future. We went through many exercises using the spiral, and for the rest of the afternoon we explored each participant's life experiences.

The logarithmic spiral model dramatically helped these parents reflect on their lives as an unfolding pattern of significant events. They examined various life stages, and striking insights emerged. In this chapter I offer the SelfDesign LifeSpiral to you. I will show you how to use it to inform and guide your own life's journey, and I will describe the method for building one. I hope that someday people will construct LifeSpirals in parks around the world to use with their families and friends. This tool helps us better appreciate our life experiences and our various roles as we work together to create community. When children are included in the process, it gives them a sense of the unfolding of their entire lives. The process puts time in perspective especially if children experience it with elders who are important to them.

Being Present and Traveling Forward and Backward

One purpose of the SelfDesign LifeSpiral is to develop multiple perspectives, to create the experience of taking a variety of points of view based on time. The very act of standing in the present moment, at your current age, and thinking back to a significant moment in your life, can bring insight and provide new resources for living. Once you have thought of a significant event and remember at about what age you had the experience, you can remain standing at your current age position and look toward that date on the spiral. Notice how much time has passed between then and now and compare this with the entirety of your life journey.

A SelfDesign LifeSpiral drawn in chalk on a brick walkway at Antioch University in Yellow Springs, Ohio. The two people are standing at the twenty-one-year mark in a spiral that goes to eighty-nine-plus years.

Stepping off the spiral, walk back to that event. Standing at that year but remaining off the spiral, reflect on the experience by re-creating memories from a disassociated perspective, or looking at the event from a "third person" position. When you step onto the LifeSpiral, you step into the associated perspective. See through your own eyes and re-experience the event, the sounds, and the feelings. You may want to hold this state and the assumptions, carrying them into your current way of living if you so choose.

The spiral may also be used to travel forward, setting goals and imagining future events. Then in present time, you can work on strategies that might help you successfully arrive at those goals. In one of the most significant exercises, participants choose an imaginary "death date." First look ahead from your current age to the time you envision as the end of your life, choosing an arbitrary age. Look back to the beginning of the spiral, representing your conception and birth, and then to the imaginary end. This exercise gives a unique perspective on the present moment (e.g., "I am halfway through my life"). Walking along the spiral and arriving at your imagined death day, you can reflect on what you may feel when that time comes. If you sense what particular goals or achievements might still have the most meaning to you on your death day, you can put more focus and effort into these qualities or tasks as you live the rest of your life. The story below exemplifies this possibility.

I once did this exercise with a fifty-five-year-old sculptor in Ohio, who picked eighty-five as the age when he envisioned he would die. We walked to that date together, talking about the conditions of his death and the feelings he imagined he would be having. He anticipated that he would feel nearly complete, and he realized he had already accomplished many of his dreams in life. Having sculpted several important works throughout his career, he felt that each piece had brought him closer to his goal for perfection. Looking over the spiral, he thought about where his two sons would be when he died. He realized that on his deathbed, his greatest wish would be to tell them that they were his most perfect sculptures. I watched while he went into deep thought for a moment, and then he told me he was not going to wait thirty years to tell them. He vowed to share with them as soon as he returned home how important they were in his life.

The Stages of the SelfDesign LifeSpiral

The SelfDesign LifeSpiral gives perspective on life patterns as they unfold through to maturity. Looking at the drawing of the completed spiral in a slightly different way, we see that there are three "circles" of five numbers each. These three circles can be used to represent the three stages of life: an inner circle of conception, birth, and infancy; a middle circle of childhood and adolescence; and a final circle of adulthood through to elderhood. Following is a diagram representing the first circle of conception (zero), birth (one), the first year of life (one), the second year of life (two), and then the third year of life.

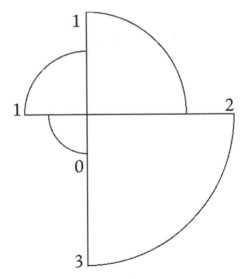

During the journey around this first circle, a cell divides and grows into a human being who can soon walk and talk. While rapidly changing and developing, the child experiences time as infinite.

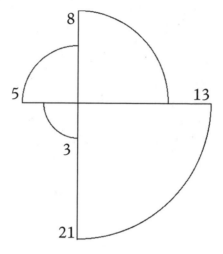

The second circle represents the time from age three to twenty-one, the years of childhood and adolescence. Children develop and transform significantly between ages five, eight, thirteen, and twenty-one. The actual amount of change and growth is not as dramatic as in the first circle, but children are now becoming aware of time and their own changes. I suggest that the area of each quadrant, though differing in size, represents equal domains of understanding as we accumulate qualitatively more complex experiences and connections in our lives. Thirteen is the age of puberty, when we begin the shift from child toward adult, but it is the period between thirteen and twenty-one when the prefrontal lobes of the brain go through their final stages of development. This is our time of preparation for participation in the adult world.

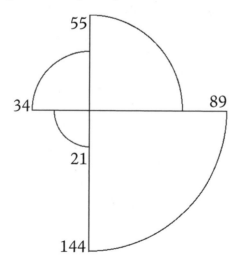

The final and outside circle is the adulthood and elderhood phase. Although our present life spans do not stretch to 144 years, we do have an increasing number of elders who live to at least eighty-nine. In the first two quadrants of this circle, the young adult is engaged in career, family, and an understanding of adult roles. As elderhood begins in the third quadrant, the focus turns to a re-evaluation of life. Retirement and service become significant, as does a deep need to connect and rediscover the child (heart) within.

As we move through the spiral stages of our lives, we feel time move more quickly and days get shorter. In this way, the time experience of quadrant eight to thirteen (five years) generally equals that of quadrant fifty-five to eighty-nine (thirty-four years). We have a huge number of new experiences during the five years between eight and thirteen, but life presents us with fewer new opportunities across the thirty-four years of fifty-five to eighty-nine. A slightly different way to grasp this concept occurs when we realize that our eighth year of life represents one-eighth of our total experience, while year fifty-five represents only one fifty-fifth.

Now picture the three circles stacked on top of one another and then viewed from the side. By connecting the end of one circle to the beginning of the next, we restore the spiral nature in three dimensions, as seen following. Beginning with conception at the bottom, this representation shows the upward nature of cyclical return.

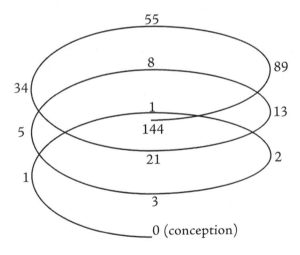

Here we have the first 12 Fibonacci numbers at each of the quadrants for three rotations of the circle. If we were looking at this spiral on end, so that the spiral faded into the distance and the center moved toward us, we would have a shape like the Nautilus shell.

Exploring the SelfDesign LifeSpiral

As we explore each stage following, keep in mind that this information applies only generally to the ages given. As individuals mature, they bring their own desires and energies to each stage and they apply their unique life-learning, all of which change the complexion of any given stage. Remember, the territory is not the map.

0-1 ↭ Conception and Nine Months in the Womb

Zero is conception and the center of the spiral. The time between zero and one takes us through the nine months in the womb. The amazing mystery of life brings together the binary aspect of life through the joining of the male and the female, the sperm and the egg, the focus and the context, the individual emerging out of the context of love.

1-1 ↭ Birth and First-Year Bonding

The first year of life brings separation and attachment. A child is unconsciously aware and present in time and space, living as the center of the universe. In this concept-less pattern of experiences, sensations and relationships begin to form into connecting patterns. A child needs to be known, needs to experience the unconscious presence of at least one significant other in order to establish a baseline for lifelong "resonance" with others.

The innermost part of the spiral represents the concentration of skill acquisition and events of the earliest years of life.

1-2 ↭ Creating Consciousness: Languaging

The second year of life is oriented to attaching words to objects, events, and relationships. It is about separating things from their backgrounds, understanding their functions, and interacting with them. It is a time for discovering others and beginning to acknowledge self as a unique and distinct system in a community of systems. Languaging begins by mimicking sounds, which initially have only emotional and rhythmic quality; meaning emerges later from ongoing interaction.

2-3 ↭ Family Mind: Discovering Self Through Imitation and Modeling

In the third year the child has developed a sophisticated understanding of relationships and language. Awareness of being part of a family awakens. Through watching and modeling others, the child experiments with different strategies and thereby discovers the nuances of perception and conception. Children begin to think about the world, organizing it into categories and relationships that influence the formation of their sentences. Children's curiosity at this stage is insatiable, and they absorb and integrate each new experience in the quest for understanding and relationship.

3-5 ᕱ *Exploring the World: The "Why?" Years*

Through role-playing and questioning, children begin to understand the complexities of the world. They are fascinated with nature and desire to understand how natural systems work. They begin to represent a worldview through art, using written symbols for objects and events. Playmates, child or adult, are sought for side-by-side or interactive play.

5-8 ᕱ *Creating Identity: Discovering Social Relationships*

Challenges of this age include discovering friendship and the dynamic of "otherness," made more difficult because of the hidden "either you or me" language patterns of our competitive society. These can affect a child's inherent attempts to cooperate. The bonded and nurtured child brings a relative ease and integrity to this process. Abstract thinking begins, as does a fascination with math and symbols. Children strive to understand inner processes and the greater relationships that govern experience.

8-13 ᕱ *Individuation: Developing Life Skills, Puberty*

Children in the early years of this stage continue to focus on acquiring academic skills such as reading and math. As they move toward adolescence, they become more absorbed with ego and self. They explore independence and expanding consciousness. The fostering of mentors optimizes this process. Many cultures offer a vision-quest type experience to mark the significant changes through puberty.

13-21 ⁊ *Adolescence: Moving into Readiness for Adulthood*

The teenager wants community and connection with peers but also desires independence. Exploration of life's meaning is marked by intensity, idealism, and opportunities for self-expression. This is a time of experimentation and questioning authority. The prefrontal lobes are maturing, preparing the teen for higher thought.

Two young women work with the SelfDesign LifeSpiral. The one on the left stands on her current age of thirteen, in an "associated" position. The other teen stands off the spiral, experiencing a "disassociated" point of view. She is looking at the beginning of her childhood and thinking about her earliest memories.

21-34 ⁊ *Entering Adulthood: Finding a Life Partner, Initiating One's Life Work*

Adulthood often begins with the delusion that learning is over because school is finished. The young adult gradually discovers that older adults have years of life experience which provide them with new domains of understanding. Young adults generally work at various jobs and begin the search for a life mate. Once they have determined a career and found a partner, they direct energy toward maintaining life work and creating a family. In this challenging but rewarding phase, the young adult balances demands of the world with the joys of family life.

34-55 ⁊ *Middle Age: Life's Realization*

In this active and productive phase of life, accomplishments are measured, and the knowledge and insight of experience begin to be contributed back to society. Career and life responsibilities are at the forefront, until toward the end of this stage the adult prepares for retirement. Family life shifts as the parent watches children move through the end of their teenage years. The adult's own parents are aging and may be becoming more dependent.

Spiral work is a powerful tool for appreciating life-stage differences. This photo shows a group of Wondertree learners experiencing the SelfDesign LifeSpiral from their parents' perspective. Standing on the place that represents the age of their mother or father, they can look back in the spiral toward their own current age. By comparing their age place to that of their parents, they each become profoundly aware of the difference in amount of life experience.

55-89 ᪣ Elderhood: Mentoring the Community

Retirement years are often devoted to hobbies, friends, and grandchildren. An elder has the maturity and wisdom of experience to give to family and community. This is often a period for reflection and the sharing of life experiences. In our technological society, we often diminish the role of the elder, missing opportunities to be mentored by our most experienced citizens. As the desire for connection and community increases for all people, the role of an elder will hopefully achieve the kind of respect it carries in other cultures.

When I am working with young people, I invite them to "map their mentors," a strategy I will share in a later chapter. I encourage them to choose a special person or mentor in each segment of the SelfDesign LifeSpiral. In our culture, which tends to segment the population by age, it is important to encourage youth to have personal connections within the full span of ages.

In my fifty-fifth year I built the first permanent SelfDesign LifeSpiral at Xenia Creative Development Center on Bowen Island, British Columbia. I hope communities throughout the world will build spirals for public use, so that people can gather and together experience the process of life's journey.

89-144 ᦷ Wisdom and the Return to Infancy

Several of my mentors, like Douglas Harding and Joseph Chilton Pearce, are going strong in their nineties. Elders like these are so significant that their beliefs tend to influence the global community. Their work and their lives become models for fully expressed humanity, allowing us to define our potential by their achievements and use their lives for inspiration.

In the very last years of life, the body's and mind's mechanics begin to fail, and many elders experience the dependence and thought processes of a young child. Again they become completely immersed in being present, experiencing each moment as eternity. This "return to infancy" brings the older person around to the end of the spiral, which is, in essence, the closing of a circle. The end and the beginning are thus joined in the circle of life.

Drawing Your Own SelfDesign LifeSpiral

In order to begin building a LifeSpiral, you can first decide whether it will be temporary or permanent. Use chalk to learn how to make the LifeSpiral and to create a temporary model, and it is helpful to practice on pavement before building a permanent spiral. Find an open cement or asphalt space larger than fifty-five feet by thirty-four feet.

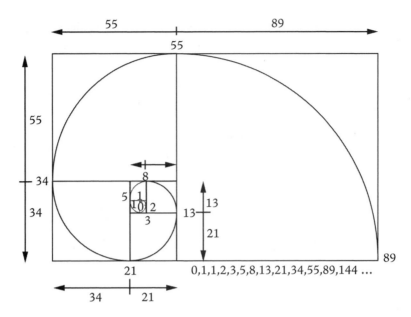

The logarithmic spiral with 11 of the first 12 numbers on it. When I build the SelfDesign LifeSpiral I usually go only to 89 with the option of going a few years beyond that, as so very few of us make it to 144 years old.

Notice the sequence that begins at the heart of the spiral:

0, 1, 1, 2, 3, 5, 8, 13, 21, 34, 55, 89, 144 . . .

This sequence of numbers is created by starting at the zero position and adding the two previous numbers to get the next number in the sequence. These numbers are the Fibonacci series, and they mark out the ratios of the Golden Rectangle, or logarithmic spiral, and its quadrant shifts.

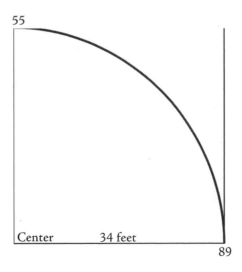

It is easiest to begin with the largest and last quadrant (fifty-five to eighty-nine, as seen on the previous page) and draw the spiral down to the zero position. Up to forty people can fit on a spiral that uses thirty-four feet for the radius of this arc, rather than eighty-nine feet. Begin by imagining a thirty-four-foot square, and draw the arc below with your chalk and the string held at the center point of the arc.

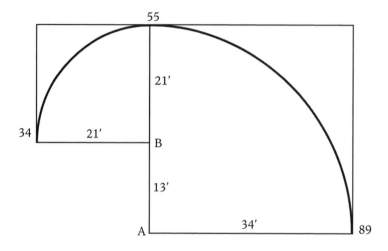

The critical measurement comes in the ninety-degree angles. If these are exact, the LifeSpiral will be accurate. Next, find a new center at B by dividing the thirty-four feet (seen as a vertical line here) into a thirteen-foot length and a twenty-one-foot length. (Note that thirteen plus twenty-one equals thirty-four and that these numbers are sequential in the Fibonacci series.) Point B will be your new center for drawing the second arc from fifty-five to thirty-four, as seen above.

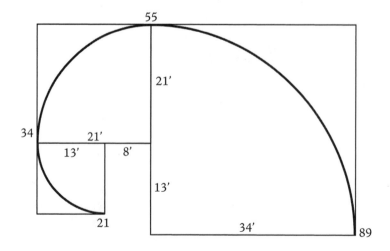

Now you can divide the distance at the thirty-four mark into the next segments of the Fibonacci series. The point between eight feet and thirteen feet is your new center, and the radius of this new arc will be thirteen feet. Draw a new arc again ending at the twenty-one point, making sure to mark the thirty-four and the twenty-one on the gradually decreasing curve.

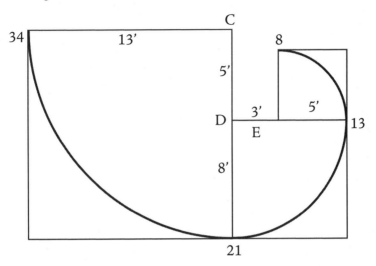

In the final stage, measure between point C and the twenty-one mark to find point D, five feet from point C. Draw the curve from twenty-one to thirteen, as shown on the drawing above. From the center at point D move up three feet to point E and draw another arc, this time with a five-foot radius. (Notice that the chalk doesn't disappear nearly as fast on these smaller arcs!)

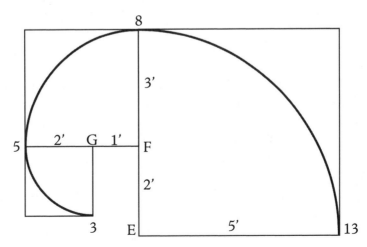

At the five-foot radius you can continue the process of following the Fibonacci series until you get to point G and draw an arc that has a radius of two feet.

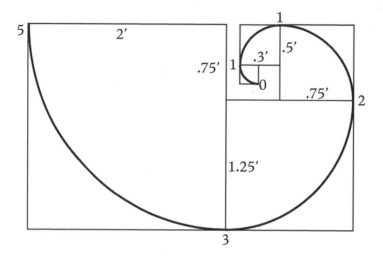

After you finish this arc, you will need to shift your measurements to the ones illustrated in the above diagram. These will give you approximate distances to reduce your spiral to the two ones and the zero. Make sure that you have all the Fibonacci numbers at the ninety-degree points on your spiral, which is now ready for use as a map of your lifelong learning journey.

Try walking the entire curve from zero to eighty-nine and back. Stand at various places and look at the spiral from different points of view. Notice the sections that are infancy, childhood and adolescence, adulthood, and elderhood. Notice the difference in scale of the varying sections, and see how they relate to the other sections.

Being and Time

The SelfDesign LifeSpiral provides us with the opportunity to experience many perspectives on our lives and the lives of others. It gives us a chance to physically create our passage through time as a lifelong journey. In this experience, our orientation to the center of the spiral never changes; at any moment on our life's journey we are "in the moment," during which there is no time. This dual experience of time as a continuum and also an "infinite now" is an important exercise that joins our brain's left and right hemispheres. The two sides inform us about our patterns of living, both in the moment and throughout our lives.

Building a spiral and sharing it with friends and family is a powerful experience as one sees children, adults, and elders spread out over the spiral. Children are amazed to see where grandparents are in comparison to their parents. Parents look back at their own childhoods and better understand their children.

When we had our twenty-year reunion for Wondertree and our ten-year reunion for Virtual High, we gathered fifty children, youth, adults, mentors, and elders on a

LifeSpiral. A community conversation developed while we played on the spiral as a group. The young adults suddenly noticed that the markers for infant and toddler years were empty, and several of them looked to their partners as we all playfully encouraged them to repopulate the zero space. I have never experienced a more profound way to discover family and community, a sense of lineage, mortality, self-knowledge, and an appreciation for the unique phases of life than the SelfDesign LifeSpiral provides.

A group of youth and young adults use the spiral to revisit child-hood at the Wondertree/Virtual High reunion. An adult has moved to the zero space to describe the recent birth of his child to a group of young adults who have not yet had children of their own.

The elders of the Wondertree community, with Michael at 47 and virtually everyone else in their fifties plus. We are looking back at the empty space between 0 and 13 where there are no children. At this point we jokingly invited the graduates from Virtual High, who were in their twenties, to get busy and create some new entries into the zero point.

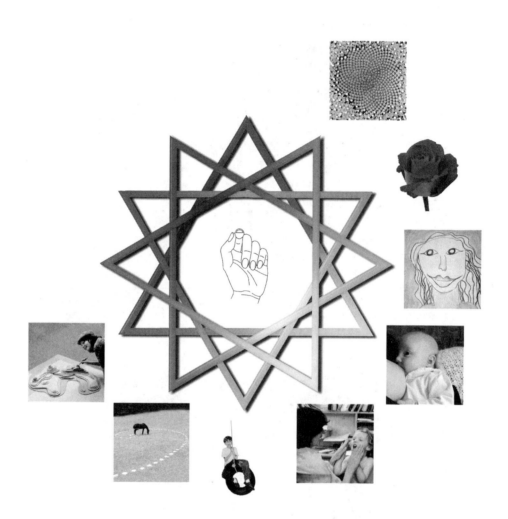

CHAPTER 8

DESIGN STRATEGIES

We are fundamentally creative beings; it is a function of our design. The ultimate creative opportunity comes when we are able to "design" ourselves. In SelfDesign programs, we watch children transform as they gradually understand that we are truly interested in what interests them. Feeling legitimized is a wonderful, self-confirming experience. Recently one of our learning consultants was helping a six-year-old boy develop a SelfDesign learning plan for the year. She visited him and his family in their home and asked the boy what he might like to do when he grew up. He thought for a moment and replied, "Well, it's not so important what I do. I think if I can keep on enjoying everything like I do now, then I'll be happy with whatever I do when I am an adult." The learning consultant, wondering how to write a plan from such a statement, called me for advice. I suggested she write down every word of the boy's comments. It seemed to me that his words were, in themselves, enough to help him design his life, let alone his learning plan! Many adults invest a lot of money in personal-development workshops hoping to rediscover what this child already knows. The fundamental role of SelfDesign is to support and acknowledge such essential qualities of natural intelligence so that learners continue unfolding their paths from a place of fulfillment.

I have been privileged to witness so many children who *want* to learn and who love learning. I have watched them make the transition from schooling, where they were under the direction of others and where they had no authority in determining their own learning. I have seen them come alive as they are acknowledged for being the authors of their own learning, realizing that what they are interested in is relevant and important. I have seen that the paradigms of schooling and of SelfDesign have distinct self-fulfilling prophecies that create and then meet their own expectations of learners.

The structure of the educational system is such that it prevents opportunities for learning that arise spontaneously or are generated and designed by learners. To my mind, one of the most damaging things about schooling is that students are taught to accept the illusion that they will find happiness in the future if they suffer through twelve years where the present moment is often boring. In this constant focus toward "later," the reality and experience of "now" is lost. Even when we are academically successful, many of us sit through our school days hoping the clock will move more quickly. We are not consulted about any of our learning, and no one ever asks us how we feel about it. We postpone present happiness for the future, when adulthood will surely bring the freedom and excitement we miss now. When our schooling is finally finished we realize that adults, too, keep looking to the future. Have you observed your parents or grandparents in retirement, still unaware that their golden window of opportunity is truly available to them now? So many of us acquire the lifelong habit of denying the present moment.

SelfDesign is the art of living in the moment and creating the future out of our present. As John Lennon said, "Life is what happens to you while you are making other plans." The most rewarding dance of life combines the art of creating a plan while simultaneously responding to spontaneity in present time. Living life as a design process allows us to continually re-evaluate how we live and the choices we make along the way. If we only perceive the future as something we are trying to reach *out there*, then we must leave our present place so that we can find it. I think it may be far more accurate to imagine the future at a distance in time, moving toward us as we stand *right here*. In this way, events come toward and through us in ways that encourage an internal, associated creation and realization of this moment. It is in expressing and guiding this response that we can determine what our next step will be. The quality of our lives in the present moment is the fundamental awareness we need to hold.

Bringing Integrity to Our Design Strategies

We have many words in our language that describe emotional and attitudinal states, and although we are aware of the states, we don't necessarily know how to create them or change them. For example, we talk about congruence, happiness, integrity, and fulfillment, but many of us seem unable to achieve these states intentionally. In SelfDesign, we call positive states like these, which form the foundation and generative quality of our experience, "resource states." SelfDesigning is about learning how to create resource states in our lives on an ongoing basis.

The "be," "know," "do," and "have" aspects of self-description, discussed in chapter 3, often contribute to our difficulty in keeping our resource states distinct. Remember, if I "do" carpentry, I tend to say, "I *am* a carpenter." The confusion between the "do" and "be" domains tends to equate an action with a quality of being. Any of us may be described as *be*-ing one of the following ways: "He *is* confused, disorganized, forgetful, apathetic, learning-disabled, slow, dull, absentminded, unfocused, distractible, impatient, anxious, or disinterested." Once labeled as such, we tend to act as if these are aspects of personality and are immutable attributes of our identity. The label diminishes our ability to change our behaviors or habits, because it has become our identity. If, on the other hand, we see these behavioral states simply as unsuccessful strategies, then we create an opportunity to affect and change the strategy itself.

These negative or limiting behaviors can best be understood and changed if we look at them as the result of an internal conflict. One part of us is trying to achieve something while another part is operating at cross-purposes, and in the struggle we lose our harmony and integrity. Our energies are no longer in alignment and our behavior is a demonstration of our inner conflict.

Procrastination is an example of a limiting state arising from inner conflict. If people want to do something and yet put it off, the conflict stems from either a belief that they can't do it or that they don't deserve success — or perhaps that the task isn't really worth doing. Such self-sabotage occurs because the idea of success challenges the deepest part of self-image. These are all strategies for failure that arise from an unecological inner state, one that is out of integrity.

There are methods for attaining goals through the resolution of inner conflicts and the achievement of a balanced state, as we see in the section below. "Ecological states" are resource states defined by qualities like balance, harmony, integrity, and congruence. Such states are fundamental for achieving positive results.

Goal-Setting Strategy

The following goal-setting strategy echoes several basic principles discussed in preceding chapters, and it has been introduced to many learners and parents with great success.

For professionals in fields such as architecture or event organization, the mapping of activities, resources, and schedules in flowcharts is a standard strategy. The rest of us, however, do not typically integrate project and goal-planning into our lifestyles. The secret to setting and reaching goals lies in the very nature of how they are planned and the way they are expressed. Several of the key ingredients are found in NLP methods.

In SelfDesign, the learning consultant supports and influences learners in the setting of their own goals, with the following guidelines:

1. When we set a goal, it should be framed in the first person. For example, "I want to climb Mount Rainier. I want to study archaeology. I want to learn to read."

This first point is key for parents and educators because we often set goals for children, when in fact and no matter how much we care as parents or as educators, it really is none of our business what another person chooses to learn. We certainly can help and support, but it is fundamentally a violation of another's rights to set goals for them. "You will learn to read this year (whether you want to or not)" is unfortunately typical of how both parents and educators often treat children.

2. The process needs to be stated in the positive. For example, the statements "I want to quit biting my fingernails" and "I don't want to have stage fright" do not describe what we actually hope to do. A well-formed goal about fingernail biting would sound more like this: "I

want to have nails that are long enough to look good when they're painted." The second goal, stated in the positive, would look like this: "I want to be confident and centered when I step onto the stage."

In the process of designing positively stated strategies, we often notice aspects of the process that stop, block, or divert us from our path. These can be dealt with as substrategies of the main goal.

3. Keep the goal in sensory-specific terms. "I want to be healthy" is vague, whereas "I want to be able to climb ten flights of stairs while still breathing easily" is sensory-specific. This helps us clearly design our objective and recognize the goal when we reach it.

4. State the goal in contextually specific terms, with special reference to place and/or time frame. For example, "I want to be in shape (climb ten flights of stairs) by the start of this summer." With specificity, we can employ simple project-management techniques to create a daily and weekly schedule. This type of design can make the practical difference between success and failure. Good intentions aside, we need a workable plan.

5. The goal needs to be ecological. In other words, it must make sense in all aspects of our life. If we have an unconscious negative self-image, then the achievement of a positive goal challenges our sense of self. We will likely block or resist achieving the goal in order to keep internal consistency. The question we need to ask is, "If I get what I want, will the changes satisfy me and will I be comfortable with them?"

Step 5 is in many ways the most important, and our unresourceful states tend to show up here. When we experience internal conflict, we are essentially stuck until we can create a shift. Therefore it is most important to check for inner agreement about our goal. Being in a resourceful, harmonious state is our greatest ally in attaining our desires.

Learning is very much about developing awareness of our lives as a design process involving the creation and management of personal strategies. Our thoughts about our patterns of living give us the opportunity to shift and change so that we can be more successful and solve problems that arise. When we are unaware of, or don't give value to, our own inner processes, we tend to think that external events create our lives. We fall into believing that circumstances and other people direct and influence the outcome of the things we experience. Statements like "He made me angry" are examples of how we give our power and responsibility away. Taking responsibility for our lives involves focusing on our own goals and strategies and putting our full energies toward attaining our desires.

The art and science of designing strategies provides us with a great number of options. It defines our intelligence as human beings. Strategies provide us with choices and opportunities to use our skills in ways that get results and sustain our natural integrity. The remainder of this chapter takes a closer look at Wondertree's history, demonstrating how the principles of these strategies actually work.

Designing Learning

During my years as the SelfDesign learning consultant at Wondertree, I would begin the fall by sitting down with a group of young people around our circular SelfDesign Mandala table. We were eager to start brainstorming our new learning year together. I began with, "I wonder what is going to happen this year? I wonder what we are going to learn? Of course, there is nothing that we 'have to' learn, nothing that we 'have to' do. I wonder what we are going to create this year on our journey of lifelong discovery?"

As a starting point, I asked each learner to describe what he or she would most like to do, explore, and learn about. In other words, I made sure that the curiosity of the children drove the program rather than my expectations or those of parents or the government. Parents and society can have a significant influence on children's learning However, I have never supported either of them dictating what children are to learn. The experiment of Wondertree has been to see what happens for children and adults when they are free to explore the world and to learn as a creative, self-expressive act. Our belief in the rights of each individual to create and design their own learning process within a supportive learning community remains the key to our program's success. It allays children's fears and personal doubts while encouraging and nurturing the seeds of self-confidence.

Imagining the Possible

The Wondertree philosophy has always explored the question of whether our life's "glass" is half-empty or half-full. Are we guided only by the expectations of others, or is living about challenging our own aspirations and discovering through exploration? Certainly a life is about both, yet if we always meet the needs of others first, we may never get around to meeting our own. By starting with our own dreams and desires and then including others within the context of our goals, we create an inclusive way of being. If we begin by exploring things that feel relevant to our own lives, we are much more likely to learn what is meaningful and possible than if topics are only imposed by others. Learning through self-authority becomes a joyful, challenging adventure.

During the Wondertree brainstorm each fall, we imagined all the things that we might like to learn about and do. We dreamed about going to Africa or to the moon; we designed potential science experiments; we decided to learn to juggle. Because the SelfDesign curriculum has always focused on opportunity and possibility, every idea has been welcomed, and consequently the children have been transformed by the experience of having their wants and desires endorsed and taken seriously.

The youngest children often created fantastic goals, beginning many projects and finishing few of them. Over the years their projects became more "do-able" yet also more comprehensive and challenging. Learners began to get a sense of personal value through their involvement with projects. They established criteria of excellence as well as standards for completion.

There is a significant difference between going on an adventure and walking through the neighborhood to a predetermined destination. One path tends to awaken the "child-on-a-treasure-hunt" part of us, while the other path may dull our senses if it feels like an assigned task. SelfDesign learners have always been encouraged to go on treasure hunts. Humans are designed for novelty because we are designed for the newness inherent in the process of continuous learning.

In conventional school, students must participate in the process of memorizing facts that may have marginal, if any, interest or relevance to them. Making mistakes equates to failure, primarily teaching children that they don't measure up to someone else's standard. Authentic learning, on the other hand, begins with a sense of adventure, with an inner sense of enthusiasm. Discovery learning through self-set goals arises from an intrinsic motivation to learn. It includes making a lot of mistakes, because real learning comes through trial and error. A SelfDesign curriculum revolves around trial and error, and learners want to correct their mistakes because the errors stand in the way of achieving their learning goals.

In this chapter I would like to share a sampling of Wondertree adventures with you. By opening the space for possibility and tapping the enthusiasm of the learner, we accomplish far more than I have seen possible in any traditional classroom. In the process, our learners manage and guide their own explorations, which helps them mature and become self-responsible individuals. Because the process is collaborative, learners feel the safety net of group experience. Ongoing, relational interaction helps them increase their communication skills and experience the exponential learning curve that grows out of group experimentation and success.

The Island Game

Earth's living systems generally develop from simple beginnings and increase in complexity over time. Trees, insects, or shells such as the chambered nautilus exemplify this process. The intellect of human beings develops in much the same way, beginning with simple awareness and response and becoming increasingly complex over time. Rudolf Steiner embraced this concept when he designed the Waldorf School curriculum to closely parallel the psychological development of children. As an example of this type of model, many young boys are fascinated with dinosaurs around the age of three to four. Their amazing ability to understand and connect with the variety of species often turns into a fascination with mammals. This gradually develops into an interest in human beings and past history, with the interest manifesting through play as cavemen, Indians, knights, and adventurers. In Wondertree, I weave the emerging interests of the children together with these developing themes, which evolve into historical or sociological research projects that continue year after year.

The Wondertree Island Game was just such a project. One year, a discussion within our group became focused on the topic of exotic islands, which seemed to fascinate everyone. We began talking and thinking about what it would be like to live on a remote island. Imagining what life would be like before the invention of boats, tools, or water systems, the learners began to write stories in the first person, pretending they were inventing these items.

We moved deeper into our island-life exploration, making believe that we each lived on an island. We were members of different tribes and we had all developed different skills. The children decided to make a giant board game, with each of them first building their own islands on a meter-wide square of cardboard. I shared with the children my understanding of topographical mapping, and the islands began to take shape.

The learners became so involved in their projects that their islands became real to them. The following picture shows my daughter, ilana, building her island. Each night as she readied herself for sleep, she would share with me her fantasies about what it was like to live on this remote island.

Enthusiasm for island-building continued to grow. Once the children finished the basic topography, they used papier-maché to build up the land and then they painted grass, trees, rivers, and rocky areas. The islands looked real, and when we put all twelve of them on the gym floor upstairs, we could imagine an ocean filling in between the small contours of land. We started planning the game that we would play among the peoples of the various islands.

We placed the islands a few feet apart with walk spaces in between, and then we populated each island with about one hundred people. To find out what particular life skills the island people had, we made up resource cards. Some groups were vegetarians and gatherers, others were hunters, and still others had farming skills or raised domestic animals. Some had flint mines and could make excellent stone tools, and some had knowledge of medicinal herbs. Several islanders were fishermen, others could build boats, and one group knew how to make sails.

The game was organized around four blocks of time that marked out the seasons. Every twenty minutes or so there was a season change, and the wind would change direction. When spring came, for example, the westerly winds would begin to blow and boats would be launched, setting sail for different islands. When one group landed on another island, resources were traded and skills were taught between the two groups. Soon all the islands had groups off sailing and trading. At various intervals during the game we would gather together to receive an event card. The event might be a volcanic eruption, a crop failure, disease, a hurricane or fire, all of which would obviously affect the well-being of the island communities. Strategies were devised to adjust to and survive these events. Sometimes the events would be positive, like the discovery of a new medicine, fire making, or the invention of the rudder. The idea of the game was to create a balanced ecology among the islands, developing skills and utilizing resources in a sustainable way. Occasionally an imported animal would upset the ecology of an entire island, and a new strategy would be needed to reinstate balance.

The Island Game was exciting. It was constantly being created, and we looked forward to playing it each week. With so many factors being introduced over the months, the game was soon hard to track, and we decided to try using our computer as an aid. In discussions with my advisors, I learned of a new software program called HyperCard that would help us with our increasingly complex variables.

That year much of my Christmas break was devoted to learning HyperCard. When the holidays were over and I showed the children what I had discovered, they immediately wanted to try it out for themselves. With thirteen of us all wanting to use Wondertree's one computer simultaneously, we had a problem that needed solving.

Using the SelfDesign model of inclusion and collaboration, the learners and I gathered the following morning for our roundtable meeting. Together we focused on the issue at hand, coming up with a number of solutions. The most profound idea provided a way for us to afford to buy six more computers.

Each semester at Wondertree the learners would look over the budget to decide how much of our money should go toward hiring mentors that we would interview and select. They would consider clowns, artists, potters, musicians, scientists, and dancers, to name a few. This semester we had allotted eight thousand dollars for mentors, and we had additional monies budgeted for other activities. But now, with our computer dilemma, we made a group decision to ask the mentors to take a sabbatical until the following September. With their full support, we headed off to the computer store to purchase six new Mac computers. Problem solved!

We worked in pairs, experimenting with HyperCard by making our own programs and writing our own HyperTalk scripts. It was the perfect learning environment because we could watch what happened with each line of computer code. The learners could try something and get immediate feedback on how that line of code worked.

Every time someone discovered a new feature, an excited shout would bring the entire group over to learn about the successful breakthrough.

Once we mastered HyperCard, we began to see amazing potential for our new-found skills. The Island Game slowly lost its attraction as we became fascinated by the possibilities for using this programming environment in another of our developing projects, the Map of Distinctions.

Map of Distinctions

Not long after our fall brainstorming session, we began a philosophical discussion about how the universe works and is organized. We wanted a map to show us how it was all connected, helping us understand it. I suggested that it might be interesting for everyone to come up with fifty questions they were interested in exploring.

Over the next several days, I looked around for models of how other people had organized large bodies of knowledge. Locating an index in the macropedia for the *Encyclopedia Britannica*, I noticed that all the material there was organized into ten categories. The categories formed a circle, stemming from the word *encyclopedia*, which suggested the idea of a circle or cycle. I reorganized and renamed the categories, adding two more: *everything/one* at the top, and *nothing/zero* at the bottom of the circle.

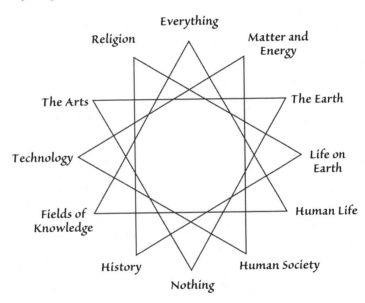

The twelve topics in a circle derived from the *Encyclopedia Britannica*. We included everything and nothing to show that there are actually no categories in human experience. We make up the categories out of nothing and divide everything into groups that make sense to us.

The children liked the idea. We got things from around the room and set them on our table as a map to represent the different categories. For example, at "matter and energy" we put samples of elements from the science area, as well as a model atom. At "earth" we put one of the globes we had built; at "history" we put a castle and a picture of a caveman; and at "technology" we put a computer disk and a portable radio. The children walked around the table, mentally photographing the contents at each location on our table map.

When we had each come up with our fifty questions, we sorted them into the same categories that made up our map. We built a graph based on how the questions fell into the categories. Interestingly, the majority of the questions for this age group were focused around life on earth and human life. Most of their questions were about animals and nature. The following graph illustrates how the questions were distributed. Notice that for this age group most of the interest is in living things and human community.

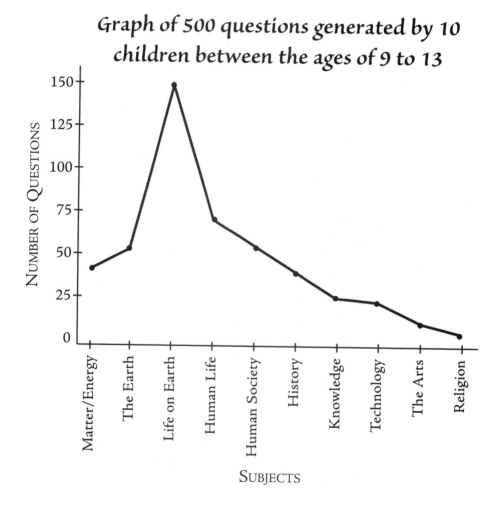

Graph of 500 questions generated by 10 children between the ages of 9 to 13

Subsequently, we created a large wall map of the twelve categories and of related topics that branched off from the twelve areas. Our final product looked like a tree—a branching system viewed from the top. A mind map. We placed ourselves in the center, as the trunk of the system, and as such we were able to turn and focus on any main area. We started a list of famous people and placed them like leaves on the branches with which they were associated. Einstein went into "matter and energy" and into the subcategory "universe"; Johann Sebastian Bach went into "the arts" and into the subcategory "music"; and Jane Goodall went into "life on earth" and into the subcategory "animal behavior."

Our excitement about this project led us next to buying a scanner as well as a microphone. We began to illustrate and add sounds to the computer program developing around our map. We wrote biographies about the famous people who most interested us. This was learning at its best, as one goal moved us to the next. During the six-month period of our work on this program, several hundred visitors to Wondertree marveled at our accomplishments. We began to realize that what we were doing was more than just an exciting learning adventure. It was a significant example of excellence as a learning project.

The computer program took on the name Map of Distinctions, and we programmed what I now call the SelfDesign Mandala table map into HyperCard as an introduction. As the project neared completion, we received notice of a national "innovative use of technology in education" contest sponsored by Northern Telecom, then the largest Canadian information-technology company. We submitted our collection of interrelated biographies to the contest. About two months later, we received notice that we had been awarded one of the top four awards for elementary education. The prize was five thousand dollars. Excited as we were about the money, we knew that our real fun and learning had come in creating the software and learning how to be programmers. As a group, we decided to invest our winnings in the purchase of our first color computer to do video animation. We made a consensus agreement that learners should be paid ten dollars for each biography they had completed. As a result of that decision, the children received between forty dollars and eighty dollars apiece for their biographical works.

Those who have viewed the Map of Distinctions have been consistently impressed by the range of the biographies, the depth of the writing, and the wealth of information. They always assume that I directed the project. When they discover that I played a minor role in its creation they are amazed that children could create such a complex and in-depth project on their own. I find this to be a testament to self-directed, SelfDesign learning.

Another unexpected gain from our project was that learners were able to emotionally identify with many of the positive mentors chosen for the map. Because they were particularly interested in the childhood events of these mentors, it didn't take long for them to discover that several, like Albert Einstein or Michael Faraday, had either done poorly in school or had not gone at all. What these leaders had in common with our learners was a fascination with understanding the world combined with an intense self-initiated learning ability.

Carmanah Valley

The following year we found our interest in the biographies drifting away as we got involved in another fascinating project. We had invited a representative from a local environmental group to come and speak to us about the group's effort to save the largest, oldest trees in Canada from being logged. Listening to him, we knew we had found our next project—the Carmanah Valley.

The children decided to build a HyperCard program that would take the user on a virtual journey through the valley to experience many of the ecological aspects of the forest. Each week we worked with the environmental activist to design an interactive environment for the program. Soon, within our group discussions, we realized we were getting only one side of the story. We decided to phone the logging company that wanted to log the old-growth trees. They were keen to get involved in our project, and they sent a representative to work with us one day a week over the next several months.

Again, we created an exciting computer program, one that led the user through the Carmanah Valley to experience the ancient and irreplaceable trees. We showed how the ecological balance had taken thousands of years to establish. Research for the project taught our learners an incredible amount about the natural world, and they felt empowered by taking positive action to share this knowledge. When the program was finished and packaged, we sent it off for viewing by organizations we thought might be interested. As a result, it was sold to schools throughout British Columbia. The federal government, impressed by the learners' efforts, paid to send our entire group to the valley, where we could see for ourselves the place we were helping to preserve.

The Wondertree software development team at the base of one of the largest trees in Canada, in the Carmanah Valley.

The PowerSmart Game

By now we were gaining a reputation as software developers, which led to another opportunity, which I discussed briefly when telling Donnie's story in chapter 3. One day we received a phone call from BC Hydro, the province's largest electric utility company. They were interested in developing a game that would help children learn how to save energy in their own homes. When a representative walked through the door at Wondertree, he was surprised to see that all the software developers in this company were between the ages of ten and thirteen!

Over the next several months he worked with us to develop the project concept for our educational game. The company agreed to provide us with $50,000 of a $75,000 budget, and we signed a contract to design and deliver the project over the next year.

We started by designing a virtual house, complete with rooms through which the computer user could walk. With a click of the mouse, the user could go to the television and turn it on, or go through the kitchen door and open the refrigerator, or walk into the bathroom to see and hear the dripping tap.

A PowerSmart graphic—which was state-of-the-art on a 1990 computer— showing the front door of the house and the beginning of the game. The user chose to tour the house with either the boy or the girl and learned how to save energy in a typical home.

The kids organized themselves into four teams. A graphics team did the house illustrations, the appliance cutaways, and the television shows. The programming team, which soon realized it would take complex skills to complete this type of program, interviewed and hired a professional programmer to assist in their effort. The financial-management team was made up of one learner, who kept track of everyone's work hours on a spreadsheet and paid each person accordingly. The final team tackled the writing and creative side of the project.

An on-screen notepad could be opened by the user, and it would show the user how to solve various problems, like changing a sink washer to stop the drip. Using an on-screen calculator, the user could discover that this action would save one hundred dollars of electrical energy in a year. Changing from a regular light bulb to a compact fluorescent bulb saved fifteen dollars per year. Overall, going through the entire house, the user could accrue up to one thousand dollars in a typical home by becoming energy efficient, or "power smart."

A year later, when the game was completed, we submitted our work to the national Northern Telecom Awards as well as to the national Marshall McLuhan Awards. We won both competitions. It had been an incredible adventure, and everyone involved had increased their knowledge a thousandfold. In the traditional classroom this amazing learning opportunity could never have been accomplished because of coursework restraints. The learners obviously learned far more than they could have by using a predetermined curriculum. It was possible only because we were open to new opportunities, because we worked together so well as a team and as a community, and because the SelfDesign model gave us the freedom to decide for ourselves what was worth doing.

32 **The Province**   Friday, April 26, 1991

Staff photo by Jon Murray

Robi Chakrabarti holds energy-saving light bulb he and his classmates will help to promote for B.C. Hydro.

Wondertree students get down to business

By Bob Ross
Staff Writer

The kids at Wondertree Learning Society

Computer whiz kids

print out and show their parents.
"Then they can ask:'Do you want to pay $1000 to Hydro or do you want to pay $800? If

These are just a few examples of our project-based, emerging learning projects. I had the time of my life and so did the learners. Our days and nights were filled with one inspiring and enthusiastic learning adventure after another. Many of these young people are now well into their twenties, and through our continued contact I know that they look back on these times with great fondness. The quality of the events and the kinds of collaborative learning they experienced has set them in creative leadership positions in all walks of life, and they are thriving.

CHAPTER 9

MENTORING

In the unfolding of our infinite potential, a variety of relationships and events accelerates, enhances, and shifts the process, deepening our understandings. These opprtunities to collaborate with others help us move toward our highest potential so that we resonate with our true identity.

Although SelfDesign is about taking responsibility for our own learning, this does not mean we are left on our own without support or assistance. Learning is ultimately a personal experience and responsibility, but learners can be profoundly influenced by transformative relationships with others. Our program uses the learning consultant as one resource to help guide and support young people. Some of the deepest actual learning, however, comes through interaction with those we call mentors—people who demonstrate both excellence and passion in their area of expertise.

This chapter is about the art and science of finding and working with mentors. We will look at the strategies of learning with a mentor as well as strategies for mentoring a learner.

Resonance

When the relationship between a mentor and a learner is mutually influential and inspiring, I call it "resonance." I initially came up with the idea when I was demonstrating to a group of Wondertree learners how our emotions and feelings affect others. I created the metaphor by playing a note on my flute while a guitar sat on a nearby table. One string of the guitar began to vibrate in response to the flute, and when I played a different note, a different guitar string vibrated. Such a mutual vibration can exist between people as well. The shared enthusiasm for some activity or area of interest amplifies the energy of both a mentor and a learner. The attention each gets from the other is a reciprocal form of acknowledgement. This echoes the recursive relationship between a mother and infant, where the affirming self-and-other loop creates bonding.

I would like to refer once more to the diagram in chapter 3 that portrays the conscious/unconscious and competent/incompetent model for SelfDesign.

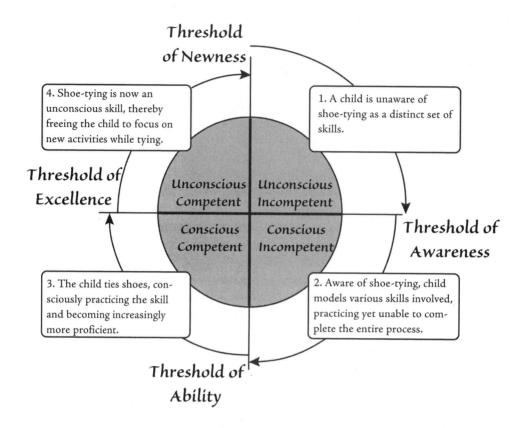

Threshold
of Newness

4. Shoe-tying is now an unconscious skill, thereby freeing the child to focus on new activities while tying.

1. A child is unaware of shoe-tying as a distinct set of skills.

Threshold of
Excellence

Unconscious
Competent

Unconscious
Incompetent

Conscious
Competent

Conscious
Incompetent

Threshold of
Awareness

3. The child ties shoes, consciously practicing the skill and becoming increasingly more proficient.

2. Aware of shoe-tying, child models various skills involved, practicing yet unable to complete the entire process.

Threshold of
Ability

In the mentor/learner relationship the learner is in the second quadrant while the mentor, in the fourth quadrant, is demonstrating excellence in a skill. When a mentor's excellence becomes so practiced that it is unconscious, it presents a challenge for the mentor to be able to communicate exactly how he does what he does. For example, it is very difficult for excellent spellers to explain exactly what it is they do when they spell correctly. The process is automatic and has become a form of unconscious excellence. Mentors must therefore first deconstruct their skills, examining what happens in each step along the way. Once the steps are delineated for and understood by learners, the transfer of information can take place, which the learners can then use for acquiring other skills. Resonance between learner and mentor strengthens the ease of this transfer.

Our online course and our workshops focus on developing the skills that help mentors, learning consultants, and learners become aware of how to deconstruct strategies of excellence and either pass them on to, or learn directly from, others. Let us look more deeply into the mentoring role and discover its function in SelfDesign.

The Mentor

Teaching and mentoring are entirely different political processes. In teaching, the instruction is the active process, while learning is the responsive and passive process.

The teacher makes the decisions and directs the process with or without the consent of the learner. Current educational curricula are based on thousands of learning outcomes for which both teachers and learners are accountable. These learning outcomes are organized by subject and grade and serve as a checklist by which students and teachers alike are judged. Many learning outcomes are introduced by the phrase, "It is expected that the student will . . ." In other words, the politics of teaching is about teacher control of student will. Within the SelfDesign model, however, the learning consultant is chosen by the learner and is also in the position of choosing to work with the learner. This mutual choosing of each other by consultant and learner sets the tone of identifying and selecting what the learner wants to learn, and the consultant can then support and help the learner enhance this process.

Mentoring, from a third position, is based on mutual fascination. The elements of interest and desire bring about a reciprocally beneficial relationship. The learner chooses the mentor, usually for a specific skill or quality of that person, and the mentor chooses to work with the learner. They create a formal or informal contract to engage in research together. The learner's enthusiasm often adds energy to the relationship, while the experience and knowledge of the mentor accelerates the learner's progress.

We are all natural learners and we are all natural modelers. Our need to explore, discover, and understand is as genetic as a baby bird's desire to leave the nest and fly. In my experience at Wondertree, young learners are initially reluctant to let mentors direct the learning process, especially if they are recovering from being controlled by teachers. It takes time and new experiences for them to trust that this relationship can be different. Before mentoring begins, the learner and mentor make a contract that includes the learner's stated willingness to have the mentor give direction to activities. In this way the mentor can encourage learners to explore challenging territory. Based on the shamanistic traditions in which elders encourage youth to go beyond their fears and personal limitations, the mentor engages the trust and respect of learners, supporting them as they try new and difficult things. From this foundation, learners' confidence soon begins to soar, leading to great rewards.

I was once shown the labyrinth as a mentoring metaphor. Fascinated with this ancient model for life's journey, I decided to use it with our Wondertree group. At the beginning of our school year, a new learning consultant, Heidi, and I drew a simple labyrinth in the parking lot outside our learning center. We introduced it to the youth as an opportunity to meet Heidi and begin a conversation around working with her over the year. Heidi entered the labyrinth first and slowly walked its curving path. As she made her internal journey to the center, I shared with the group that Heidi was obviously older than they were and had had life experiences that they had not yet had. In this way, I said, she could be their mentor as well as their learning consultant. When Heidi reached the center and stood reflecting on her journey, the youth watched her. In this place, however, she was metaphorically unavailable to them and needed to come back part of the way so the learners could reach her, if they so desired.

In the photograph that follows, Heidi is crouched in the place on the labyrinth where she could see and communicate with learners who wished to engage her as mentor.

Blair, the oldest of our group, came forward first to stand at the entrance to the labyrinth. He expressed his interest in working with Heidi. This was the opportunity for the consultant to invite the learner in as apprentice, and Heidi did so. Blair accepted her invitation, walking further into the labyrinth to begin engaging in the mutual learning relationship.

They walked side by side in the labyrinth, talking about possibilities as a first phase of their learning journey. Partway through, they met as one headed outward and the other inward, and here they needed to change places before continuing on together. In this phase of their journey the discussion focused specifically on the tasks of the learner. When they reached the section of the labyrinth where they had to part ways, Heidi finished her journey outward and Blair continued his journey to the center alone. That day, each of the learners walked the labyrinth with their new learning consultant, creating the context for their relationships for the coming year.

This was a powerful and symbolic experience for our youth, and the connection they formed with Heidi that day set the stage for her, as both their learning consultant and sometimes mentor, to introduce them to a variety of other mentors over the year. As the children deepened their understanding of participating in designing their own learning goals and desires, I watched them take increasing responsibility for achieving these goals. The process of interviewing, hiring, and then modeling these mentors of their own choosing served our learners very well through their years in our program and beyond. As our graduates have ventured out into the world, they have sustained the ethic of learning from others as one of their fundamental strategies for lifelong learning.

Modeling a Mentor

I recently had a talk with Jonathan Boese, twenty-seven, who was the first learner to join Wondertree after my daughter and I started the program. We spoke at length about the significance of the mentoring experience.

Jonathan, age seven, on the left, counts our program's money to see how much remains in the budget to hire the mentors for the learning season.

Jonathan's father, Dr. Robert Boese, fully understood what I was attempting to do throughout Wondertree's humble beginnings, and Dr. Boese's personal mentorship and commitment to our program encouraged me to start a nonprofit society. His unfortunate death not long after our incorporation led to Jonathan becoming part of our extended family. Jonathan was in Wondertree from first grade through eighth, and he enthusiastically participated in all our projects. When several of the older youth decided to try conventional high school, he decided to give it a try as well, and he finished successfully.

Jonathan's personal interest in diet and nutrition sparked his enthusiasm to become a chef. As soon as he finished high school, he secured several jobs as an apprentice cook in fancy restaurants. According to Jonathan, his Wondertree experiences with mentors gave him skills that none of the other young apprentices had.

Unlike the rest of the apprentices in the restaurants whose school experience had only taught them how to wait for instruction, Jonathan began modeling. He observed the various cooks, picking out the most competent and talented chef to copy. Unconsciously at first, Jonathan began to model their style and methods, and soon the mentors took a liking to Jonathan, informally showing him things. Gradually a formal mentor–apprentice relationship emerged in each restaurant and Jonathan became the understudy. Within four years, at age twenty-four, Jonathan was offered a head-chef position in another restaurant. Currently he is managing two very successful restaurants, creating the menus and offering mentorship to others, which is to him the most satisfying part of the job.

Spheres of Influence

SelfDesign takes subtle and often unrealized learning processes and makes them specific and comprehensive. Turning these patterns into explicit and sometimes experiential models allows for a singular awareness of how to learn a specific technique.

The process of designing models began at Wondertree when I was demonstrating to young learners how to become aware of and use a mentor's strategies. I used an NLP technique called the Circle of Excellence to introduce them to the strategies. Inviting the children to think about someone whose skills they admired, I had them imagine this mentor standing within a circle a few feet away. Once they had visualized the characteristics of their mentor in explicit detail, I asked them to physically jump into that circle and take on the look and characteristics of that person. This was a first step for them to begin looking at excellence from the inside out.

It was during such a demonstration that I suddenly envisioned the imaginary circle turning into a three-dimensional representation of a circle—the sphere.

I have often thought of people as if they were spheres of energy, traveling about in purposeful orbits and exposing others to their influence. In relationships, people's "spheres of influence" overlap and mutually influence one another as they exchange energy and information. The first time I heard Buckminster Fuller speak, he held up a sphere and asked, "How many spheres of equal size to this one can you place around it, so that they all touch the central sphere and also fill all the space available?"

The answer, which he then proceeded to demonstrate, has fascinated me for nearly thirty years. If we begin with one sphere, we discover that six spheres of equal size may be arranged around the central sphere in a flat plane.

Using this as our base, we find that we can fit three balls on top of the horizontal ring of six, all of which are touching the central ball and filling all the space above the central ball.

If we place three balls underneath the structure in the same way, we now have six spheres around the middle, three more on top, and three underneath, with no room for any more that can touch the central sphere. This makes a total of twelve spheres, with the primary and central sphere as number thirteen. Working with the Wondertree learners using the Circle of Excellence, I soon realized that they could see themselves as the central sphere surrounded by and touched by the matrix of twelve other spheres.

If we imagine ourselves in the position of the central sphere, we notice that our experience of this sphere is uniquely different from our experience of the other twelve. As we view the other spheres from within our own sphere, we see them as convex entities because we are viewing the outside of each of them. We experience our own sphere as concave. We can call this sphere our reference sphere, or zero.

If we now imagine connecting lines to the centers of each of the thirteen spheres, we see a structure like the one shown below. Buckminster Fuller, a crystallographer, called this shape the vector equilibrium, while geneticist Derald Langham called it the Genesa crystal. I was fortunate enough to meet both of these visionaries in the early 1980s, and I have integrated various aspects of their work into the learning models that I have developed.

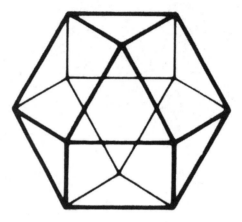

The concept of a zero point surrounded by twelve external points serves as a model for the organization of the thirteen chapters in this book, with chapter 0 being the central and fundamental chapter. The concept of an individual at the center, surrounded by twelve "spheres of influence," also acts as a basic model for SelfDesign.

Mentors as Spheres of Influence

I invite you to participate in creating your own SelfDesign Spheres of Influence by identifying the twelve most influential people in your life. Think of people who have changed your life, who have contributed to making you the person you are today. These people can be parents, grandparents, relatives, and friends. You may also have been significantly influenced by writers, painters, architects, or activists, whether they are alive or not. Your list may include choices that are not people; some of your life-shaping influences may be pets, eagles, mountains, or trees.

Once you have created your list of influential people, animals, or objects, place the names on the Spheres of Influence map that follows. Write each name in one of the boxes, and consider the significant gift each has given you. The gifts, or qualities, can be written on the list below the map, next to the corresponding numbers. In my life, for example, I have learned the power of persistence and patience from Gandhi. You may also want to think about how you wish to arrange the mentors on your circle. These maps will likely change throughout your life, although some mentors might appear in a lifelong fashion. Putting the date on your map will allow you to do a life progression as you revisit the exercise periodically. You may wish to write about what you learn from doing this map in your journal. Remember, you are the central sphere surrounded by twelve other spheres of influence.

Spheres of Influence Map

For _____ Date _____

1. _____
2. _____
3. _____
4. _____
5. _____
6. _____
7. _____
8. _____
9. _____
10. _____
11. _____
12. _____

Several years ago I did this exercise early in the school year with a group of five teenagers. To my surprise, most of their maps had no real human beings in them. All their mentors were fantasy superheroes, like Spiderman and the Terminator, and none of the teens listed family members or friends. Needless to say, these young people were all having difficulties getting along with others, especially parents and teachers. By the end of the year, when I asked them to do the exercise again, many of the mentors they listed were people they knew. Concurrently, they had all made significant gains relating to others and had shifted to more positive lifestyles. One of the people appearing on all five maps was a martial-arts instructor I had invited to the center for their consideration as a mentor. He had worked intensely with them over the months, and the shift in these teenagers was remarkable. They were now grounded in their bodies, and they were finding that being a superhero can happen in real life.

Sometimes the best way to describe what our program is really about is to ask the people who have experienced it firsthand and who, because it is based on learning, were the real creators of the program. Our results often go far beyond what is possible in the authoritarian, curriculum-driven model of conventional schooling. In the following story Kaan Muncaster, a learner who had done very well in school but who chose to attend Virtual High instead of going to high school, describes what happened to him in our program.

Kaan's Story: My Experience of Virtual High

Going to Virtual High was a major turning point in my life. I learned so much during the two years that I went to the program. Actually, it would be more accurate to speak of *creating* Virtual High, as opposed to *going* there, because that's what we all did.

My experience of Virtual High was totally unique. At Virtual High learners had their own personal curriculum, so everybody's experience was different. The fact that Virtual High was created by the students meant that there was no rigidly imposed external schedule. We were all encouraged to create learning plans and individual schedules.

In Virtual High, my life changed from being mainstream to being visionary in nature. I went from public schooling to SelfDesign, from complete ignorance about my diet to eating only vegetarian food, from financial illiteracy to some basic financial knowledge, from being employee-oriented to being entrepreneurial in mind-set, and from unawareness of the spiritual aspect of life to a daily practice of yoga and meditation. I basically went from living unconsciously to living consciously. There was a daily awakening and increasing of my awareness about my own choice making.

One of the exciting changes for me was learning some amazing study strategies. For example, I was taking a music-history course outside of Virtual High where I had to memorize pages and pages of material every week. It took me hours, and it was a constant struggle. I talked to Brent about it, and he showed me that I could memorize a list of words by associating each one with an image in my mind. We refined the technique further by visualizing different music composers and their actions as taking place in my house. At exam time, I would close my eyes and mentally walk through my house from room to room, seeing what it was that I needed to remember. Using this strategy, my memorization time was cut from five or ten hours to half an hour, and I got top marks in the class. Over the years I have refined this technique and as a result have completed several of my university courses in only three weeks.

Mentors were a whole new experience for me. I spent so much time in the small, informal classes at Virtual High that the learning consultants and mentors became like second parents and good friends. This was totally different from high school, where teachers can essentially be "the enemy." Virtual High, because of the forward-thinking principles it embodied, attracted great mentors, including scientists, artists, teachers, and businesspeople from the community. Some were even our parents!

One of the projects that really excited me was VillageQuest. I had the opportunity to work with a local architect as a mentor. I devoured books about architectural design and city planning, and I sketched a hundred colorful drawings of what I thought would make a healthy, sustainable community. I would bring my work to the VillageQuest group and we would discuss it. This project was so valuable to me because we were interacting with planners, architects, developers, and city councillors. Our work eventually influenced the City of Vancouver to rezone a whole area in the heart of Vancouver in order to plan for our sustainable community.

At Virtual High, I had the feeling that everything I learned and did was important. Every project felt like it made a difference in the world. It seems rare to find young people who have had the real-life opportunities we created at Virtual High.

The lack of enforced structure in our program felt liberating, but it was also challenging for me. I was so excited about all the choices that I "signed up" for nearly everything. In less than two years, with several different mentors, I studied physics, calculus, French, biology, sign language, creative writing, violin, jazz piano, Eastern philosophy, African drumming, acting, singing, cooking, painting, software development, and Neuro-Linguistics Programming. I did interviews on the radio, started a school magazine, published a small book of my own poems, gave piano lessons, taught a math class, and created a major personal portfolio for myself.

I admit that the situation causing my stress was unusual. How often does a student need to be encouraged to take *fewer* classes? My father tried to persuade me to do less, especially after he saw the list of all my classes and projects. He crossed out everything on my paper and wrote down the word *Focus*. What I did do was start to learn about how to deal with stress. I looked more seriously into meditation, exercise, and diet. And now, ten years later, meditation, yoga, and Eastern philosophy are still a big part of my life. I continue to keep fit and eat a healthy vegetarian diet, and stress is a manageable thing for me.

Originally, my plan was to do grade 11 and 12 through correspondence at Virtual High. However, the projects being developed there were so meaningful and so exciting that reading high-school textbooks with no relevance to my life soon dropped from my priority list. I was too busy reading the *Bhagavad Gita* and making a difference in the world.

One thing Virtual High didn't offer was a high school diploma. When I decided to go on to university, I made the choice get an Adult Basic Education provincial diploma through a local community college. I took tests in grade 12 math, English, biology, and history, scoring an A in all of them. I completed biology and history courses through the British Columbia Open University, finishing in about a week. I took grade 12 physics without the grade 11 prerequisite, and I passed.

I went on to get a B.A. in history, which took me on a learning journey from the University of Oregon in Eugene to the online Athabasca University in Alberta, then to a university in Katmandu, Nepal, and finally to Trent University in Ontario. I am currently working on a master's degree in adult education through Athabasca University via their online program. In this leading-edge program I can do my degree online from home. My classmates and I can be sitting in three different time zones across Canada and can still be working together to write an essay about research methods. Because many of the courses allow me to work at my own pace, I will be able to complete my degree in less than a year and a half.

Looking back over my learning experience at Virtual High, I can see that its atmosphere of promoting self-discovery and positive change helped me be more proactive and focused on service to society. I learned about self-discipline, which allowed me to work intensively and successfully. Virtual High was a community of learners, creating a synergy that helped each one of us realize our true, full potential. It created the seed for a multigenerational community, setting forth a model for a new kind of urban living in the rest of the world. I am grateful and honored to have been a part of this beautiful experiment in the potential of the human spirit.

CHAPTER 10

SYNERGISTIC COMMUNITY

I first heard the term synergistic community in the early 1970s, when I read a paper written by Ruth Benedict. The word synergism, meaning a combined interaction creating a result greater than the sum of the parts, had been popularized by Buckminster Fuller, and Benedict saw its use as applied to the best of community living. Psychologist Abraham Maslow made reference to Benedict's concept, discussing the need of human beings to feel the sense of belonging in a group. Twenty years later, working with the children in Wondertree and the youth in Virtual High, I felt that Benedict's term was an appropriate description of what was happening in our two learning communities.

Wondertree: Building Community Through Negotiation

As Wondertree began, I was committed to respecting every child individually, including each of their heart's desires in the design of this new learning experiment. I chose to sit with the children in a circle in the inclusive manner of the Native American, Baha'i, and Quaker communities that had influenced me over the years. Here we would speak about our coming day, designing group projects and deepening our understanding of one another through conversation. Little did I know that the discussions within this circle would create the nurturing, supportive environment necessary to create synergism. As each of our ideas built on the last, our energies multiplied and our community began to unfold.

Our discussions often led to differences of opinion about what should happen first in our day, or perhaps the best way of going about a project. Slowly we discovered that one of the primary purposes of our circle was to learn how to listen to each other, communicate respectfully, and resolve the conflicts that happen when people work together.

More by chance than by design, I did three important things during the early years of Wondertree. First, I began parent workshops in order to address my growing understanding that family patterns are often a significant factor in children's challenging behaviors and learning difficulties.

Second, I paid attention to every communication among our learners, challenging each unconscious put-down and critical comment. Over the years I have found that by the time children are six years old they have modeled not only the words but also the tones and nuances of meaning of their influential adults. In less subtle and sophisticated ways, they have also adopted the put-downs and the negative and hurtful comments that can occur in our schooling culture: "You can't touch that; it's mine." "You have to stop now; it's time to go." "You should do this before you do that." And upon seeing someone fail: "What's wrong with you? Everyone knows how to do that." In an effort to shift this type of language, I continually modeled the reframing of statements so that the children would learn another way of talking. We established Wondertree as a safe place to learn, one that used the language of respect and consideration for others. The children felt the merit of this kind of space, working hard to maintain the quality of communication they had come to value. New learners to our program were invited and encouraged to participate in this ethic of caring as they made the challenging transition from the often-cruel atmosphere of school. Because there was an underlying ethic of cooperation, the language of "winner" and "loser" soon faded from the scene. In our first years we had hundreds of visitors to the center, and their comments about the program echoed this felt sense of respect, calm, and mutual support among the children.

Third, I introduced Wondertree learners and families to an NLP tool called the Negotiation Strategy. With each emerging conflict I used this model with the learners involved, demonstrating it time and again until all were able to initiate this effective tool rather than continuing the conflict.

The Negotiation Strategy: A Win-Win Technique

The Negotiation Strategy can be used for three types of conflicts: personal inner conflict (where resolution lies in introducing the two parts in conflict to open and supportive internal conversation), conflict between self and other (where one of the parties must represent not only their own issue but must also take on the role of facilitator if resolution is to occur), and conflict observed between two parties. In the third type of conflict, an outside party can be brought in to assist the two people struggling with an issue. This situation is the most common for parents and teachers in their dealings with children. It can also arise within a business or community, and once positions are taken and two "camps" established, it takes strong mediating skills to clearly define the divisive issues and begin the process of win-win negotiation.

Conflict frequently stems from the same win/lose mentality we have discussed throughout the book. When people hold the assumption that one person getting a desired object or outcome means that they will not, then we have the makings of conflict. Each person attempts to make the other one wrong, believing that the use of either force or forceful reason demonstrates their "rightness." Both parties are in defensive positions, trying to win while defending against perceived loss. The same processes are at work in internal conflicts mentioned above, because they are simply internalizations of conflicts that have been previously modeled externally.

Using the Negotiation Strategy, from the beginning the negotiator holds and demonstrates the assumption that both parties are right from their own point of view. Being right from our own point of view is called *positive intent*. In order to build trust in the negotiator, it is imperative that both people accept that the negotiator believes they are operating from a genuine belief that their position is correct. The negotiator also establishes a context in which the people involved feel heard. Assuring both parties that they will get what they desire often creates this context, allowing them to agree to listen to one another and to put trust in the negotiator. Both parties state the situation from their point of view, subsequently seeking acknowledgment from the other that they have been heard. Agreement on each other's perceptions is not necessary. It is the spirit of hearing and being heard that matters in this stage of the process.

The essence of the negotiation strategy involves shifting the process from content to intent, moving beyond the details of the situation and getting to deeper reasons for individual positions. This is achieved by helping the parties find the true intent beneath their statements or positions. The intent most often represents a universal quality or value. It shifts a wife from saying to her husband, "I don't want you to smoke cigarettes," to "I want you around and healthy for many more years," or from a parent telling a child, "I want your plate clean before you leave the dinner table," to "I want to support your having a strong body, and eating a good dinner is one way to do that." In the case of two young children wanting to play with the same truck, the universal truth changes from, "I had it first," to "I love playing with toys in the sandbox."

Once these universal truths are established, the negotiator asks each party to suggest three things that could support the positive intent of the other person's position. This creates a fundamental shift, as now each of the parties needs to think outside the narrow range of personal desires. It is not a commitment to change but rather a view of possibilities—six possibilities, three from each party.

Because most human beings want to find agreement with one another, it is fascinating to observe the process of sorting through these six possibilities. By shifting toward support of the other person's positive intent, we introduce an entirely different process than attempting to assert a dominant position. With six suggestions or offers of support, it is often easy to see the areas of overlap in the suggestions. From children figuring out how to creatively share a truck in a sandbox, to divorce strategies, to mentor-learner agreements, to business deals, all can shift toward agreement once each person starts supporting the universal needs of the other. Creativity and collaboration become the bywords, as opposed to denial or blockage. When both people think about the well-being of the other, the relationship transforms.

I have found that children are remarkably adept at using this strategy. After they master the key elements, they move quickly from conflict to resolution, offering creative suggestions that will meet the other's needs once they believe that the other person is willing to support them as well. This model sits at the heart of collaborative play and work. Ruth Benedict's examples of synergistic community appear to be in alignment with these natural principles of living from a sense of one's own well-being in harmony with the well-being of others.

The Virtual High Community

When Virtual High was first conceived, Michael Maser and I thought that the focus would be on using computers for distance learning and on helping young people learn how to create their own businesses. We were mostly wrong about both these ideas. The focus was on people and relationships. The focus was on discovering the depths of what it is to be human and on becoming a loving community. Our young people wanted to be seen, and they wanted to be recognized on their own merit. Virtual High gave each one of them an opportunity to step out, beyond the limits society had imposed on them, to embrace life on their own terms.

In those first months we were a group in chaos. The teens brought with them every rapport-breaking strategy possible. They demonstrated sabotaging techniques that had been perfected through years of authoritative school environments. They had bonded against a commonly perceived oppressor—the adult—and their determination to undermine anything that spoke of organization was admirable, to say the least. These were individuals who were seeking a sense of power in their own lives. They could see power in superheroes, and they could feel it in the glorified worlds of rock stars and sports figures, but they had been given few opportunities to positively experience it within themselves.

The first thing we did at Virtual High was to allow the learners the space they needed in order to feel true ownership. We told them that the program was for all of us, with each of us taking responsibility for our own learning. This was a place where there was freedom to discover the true meaning of being part of a learning community.

Every week the entire learning community met to manage our own program. We did this on a consensus basis, and although it was sometimes time-consuming, it was expedient overall as it allowed us to make the most inclusive and comprehensive decisions that really worked for everyone.

The Big Group Meeting, or BGM, as it came to be called when we convened once a week, was the only activity we asked the teens to attend. Participation came slowly, but once the group realized it was a place where they could experience real power with real people, the meeting became the highlight of each week. When I realized, sometime during the second year, that Virtual High was about deep acknowledgment and acceptance of each learner, I remembered back to my encounter-group experiences during my university years. Those numerous weekend group workshops had opened me to fully expressing my vulnerability and humanity, and so I offered to facilitate a three-day intensive BGM for our teenagers.

The Virtual High three-day intensive was about as intense as I could handle. I was grateful to have my counseling and NLP skills, and all of them were called into play over this long weekend. Four adults supported the almost thirty youth in their experiences, and each one of us played key roles in facilitating the group. Life issues came forth and were resolved, truths were told, fears and joys were shared on a deep level. As we explored a full range of feelings about family and past school experiences, we acknowledged a deep sadness for the state of affairs in our society. It seemed we were on an island of sanity surrounded by a sea of meaninglessness. Many vowed to take the compassion and love created during that weekend out to friends and family. Everyone came away with a sense of the passionate possibilities of life and of meaningful relationships. We felt we had strengthened our community in immeasurable ways.

The Virtual High community during a three-week workshop.

I would like to share with you the perspectives of two learners who attended Virtual High. These are touchstone tales about the legitimacy of learning according to one's own authority. Both of these young men left conventional high school to join our learning community, and both carried the experience of Virtual High into their adult lives.

Jeff's Story

It's true enough that freedom requires responsibility, and this was one of the primary lessons that many of us learned during our time at Virtual High. We weren't required to go to classes, told what to study or what to think. We were free to make (or break) our education in any way we wanted. The self-directed nature of Virtual High was such that a student's only obligations were those that he chose. Initially, friends and family told me we would waste our time, never getting much accomplished and falling behind our contemporaries in high school.

A lot of the kids coming out of public school, including myself, "wasted" a lot of time. There were also many students who took the opportunity we had at VH by the horns and created something exciting. During my early days at VH, I remember watching people who were intelligent and perceptive, had admirable music or computer skills, were kind and patient, and always invited me to join in the fun of living a meaningful life. Meanwhile, I watched. This "cooling off" (from authoritarian high school) was necessary before I decided for myself to try something new.

Another student and friend at VH had set a particular example that interested me a lot. A source of my low self-esteem was that I was overweight, and I saw my friend overcoming this mutual affliction. With surprising ease I traded my teenage diet of Slurpees and instant noodles for one of rice and vegetables. Getting rid of stored toxins in my body, I effortlessly lost more than thirty pounds in about three months. This was the catalyst that got me to make the effort to squeeze more value out of Virtual High. I committed to doing terrifying things, getting the courage I needed when I was in the middle of them. I had no idea what I was getting into when I took a ten-day vow of silence and meditated ten hours a day at a Buddhist retreat. Another time, I remember being so nervous that I was watching myself in the third person while giving my first presentation before a hundred people at a conference on education at University of British Columbia. (They later told me I did well, but I didn't remember enough to believe them.)

During those times it was hard for me to always follow through on what I said I would do, but I had learned firsthand that the rewards for those who persevere far outweigh the pain it takes to get there. Along the way I and my fellows did a lot of growing up and internalized many values that define who I am: be kind and listen to others, pause and reflect before reacting, try new things and keep an open mind, set goals and see them through. The things that made Virtual High so wonderful and make me very grateful that I had the good fortune to be a part of it are not easily quantifiable in the terms that most people are used to. I didn't get grades or a diploma to file in a drawer or put on my résumé, but I got something else that most people can see by just meeting me: a certain *joie de vivre* visible in most unschooled young people; a foot on the path that is lifelong learning.

Stephen's Story

I had nine years of "excellent" public education. I learned everything I needed for an unsatisfying, unproductive life: destructive social tendencies, blind acceptance of authority, self-hatred, irresponsibility, and apathy. I was obese, subject to the occasional beating by a classmate, prone to apparently random fits of deep depression and uncontrollable anger. On a good week I would suffer only one crippling migraine attack. By grade nine I had marks ranging from 1 percent to 45 percent in all my classes.

But I loved learning. By the age of eight I was reading at the twelfth-grade level. In grade four, I was writing essays for myself and my family on nuclear physics, astronomy, and marine biology. In grade seven I studied classical mythology and learned the rudiments of logic from my older brother, a student of philosophy. My parents provided me with an informal education in theology and politics.

I enjoyed these learning experiences, but they lacked an important social component. Working by myself, my resources were limited. I didn't know anyone my own age with whom I could work or share ideas. My social development was significantly retarded by the lack of friendship in my life.

Five years before I entered Virtual High, I had recognized that an education worth having is self-motivated and self-directed but also requires some kind of outside support. In other words, freedom is a social condition, not just an individual one.

When I was fourteen, I left the public system on the advice of a school board representative and joined up with Virtual High two weeks later. Noam Chomsky said that "a fundamental element of human nature is the need for . . . creative inquiry, for free creation without the arbitrary limiting effects of coercive institutions." Virtual High was my first experience of an educational model that actively acknowledged this truth. In other words, it was my first experience of social freedom. The most important things I gained at Virtual High seem basic and central to a fulfilling existence and yet are neglected in the public educational system. I created many important relationships that have helped guide and support me through my continuing learning experiences. I learned about consensus, communication, cooperation, and by extension, respect, leading me to the study of political theory. I gained the courage to deliver a speech in front of hundreds of people, to put an airplane into a spiral dive, to eat a piece of broccoli, to tell someone that I love them. And do it with a smile.

Finally, Virtual High opened my mind and showed me that we all have the capacity to create our present and our future. Although my program ended some years ago, I still feel like I'm part of something larger than myself, a sort of meta-community of SelfDesigners connected through the common experience of free creation and free inquiry.

VillageQuest

A special project undertaken by the Virtual High learners is worth highlighting here, both for its social implications and because it lives on today. As our learners progressed through the program, talk turned more and more to community and to questions about the basic premises of our society. Because our youth had stepped off the conveyor belt of public education, they felt that their lives were now truly beginning. They had a sense of belonging to something greater than themselves, and they wondered what it would be like to live in a village that was designed like our learning community.

A project emerged from this discussion, and it came to be called VillageQuest. The youth realized that our modern urban environment lacks heart. I had talked with them about Bali, and they were familiar with my experience of one village on one island where millions of people lived meaningfully, sustained by politics much like those of Virtual High. Could we create an urban post-industrial community based on this type of model?

A small group of about twelve teens began meeting regularly to talk with me about VillageQuest. We wrote out fifty qualities that seemed important to experience on a daily basis if we lived in an intentional community. Searching through the newly emerging internet, we sought any information we could find about such communities. We talked to our network of friends and mentors. Soon we discovered the global eco-village movement, and we began international conversations about creating and living in sustainable community.

We talked with "green" building experts and started to imagine growing our own food on rooftops. Professionals consulted with us on how to treat raw sewage with biological systems to transform it into clean water in four days. We met with people who were using pumps to draw geothermal energy out of the earth to heat large buildings. After a year of intense research into possible sites, we located a city administrator who knew of a forty-seven-acre piece of industrial wasteland on the shores of False Creek, owned primarily by the city of Vancouver. We decided to focus on creating our eco-village on this oceanfront in the heart of Vancouver. Hiring a local architect to help us, we began to design our dream, taking our emerging ideas and putting together a model of the village.

A group of teenagers meeting with an architect that they hired to design their ideal village. We have met around this Wondertree table for over 20 years; it is the model for our mandalas and our maps for learning and self-awareness.

Around this time we were introduced to a city planner who was also thinking about development for the same site. Coincidentally, he was interested in sustainable communities and wanted to know what we had already researched and designed. Soon our group was speaking locally and internationally. Four of the youth attended the first eco-village conference in Findhorn, Scotland, and a year later another group and I presented at the Habitat II conference in Istanbul, Turkey.

Locally, we presented our VillageQuest model to over three hundred architects at an annual architectural convention. We were asked to speak to the Vancouver Planning Department, the Planning Council, and eventually to the City Council. We created a blend of our own passion for this dream of community with a high-tech multimedia presentation. Because other development groups were vying for the piece of property we had selected, it was vital for us to convince others of the merit and feasibility of VillageQuest. We succeeded, and when the proposal came before City Council for a final decision, the vote went in favor of our sustainable community. In session, several council members spoke about how the passion and creative presentations of the youth had affected their decision. Over the next few years engineers did feasibility studies into what energy efficient projects were possible in this area. Also over the next several years, architects, planners, and community advocates organized committees to present possible sustainable community plans. At the time of writing this book, a Winter Olympics village is being discussed as a possible incorporation into the development of this project.

Virtual High closed its doors that spring due to the politics of funding and the fact that we were innovative and ahead of changes to Ministry of Education rules. Now our program was even more virtual, yet all who participated in it held onto the ideals and inspiration we had created there. The years we spent together as SelfDesigners made our total experience feel much greater than the sum of the individual parts. We parted ways with a true understanding of the value of synergistic community and a deeper and more holistic sense of who each one of us was.

CHAPTER 11

SYSTEMS AND PATTERNS

In this book we have traveled a long journey together, a journey that took over twenty years to research and discover. At this point we have touched on many aspects of the SelfDesign Mandala as a tool for exploring our wholeness as individuals and for creating connection to community.

The mandala acts as a map that informs us about our territory—our experience. The map is an opportunity to deepen our reflections on these experiences. In North American Native traditions, people must travel to all four directions on the circle and must experience the whole medicine wheel in order to realize their full potential as human beings. As educators, we discover that in order to help others become SelfDesigners, we also need to embrace the diverse concepts in our own lives. As learning beings, we must also complete a circular journey in which we come to know ourselves for who we really, *really* are. The more we understand ourselves, the more sense the world makes to us. Embracing the challenges of learning and creating excellence requires that we optimize our tools for self-awareness. On this SelfDesign journey we have just about come full circle, and like the ouroborus, that medieval symbol of the snake, we are about to bite our own tail.

With the mandala as our traveling companion, let us begin to transform our circular journey into three dimensions. The flat circle becomes the sphere. The spherical mandala offers unique insights into the systems and patterns of our living so that we can understand ourselves in new ways. New paradigms emerge from these insights that confound conventional thinking, offering fresh perspectives on what we think we already know. Galileo and Columbus, among others, took us from a flat-earth model to a three-dimensional global view that forever changed the way we experience our planet. Hopefully, the SelfDesign three-dimensional model of human experience can shift our current paradigm and provide innovative insights into designing our lives with greater creativity and integrity.

The SelfDesign Matrix: Moving to Three Dimensions

We shift our circular journey on the mandala into a spherical model of the SelfDesign Matrix. The matrix is a situation or a womb-like environment within which something else originates, develops, or is contained. To begin, let us look at the tetrahedron.

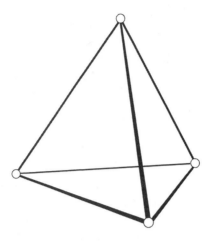

This triangular pyramid represents the minimum number (four) of unique events that define a three-dimensional space. The four points of the tetrahedron also mark out the minimum number of points necessary to create a sphere. The other four platonic solids—the cube, the octahedron, the dodecahedron, and the icosahedron—are increasingly more elaborate representations of the sphere.

Tetrahedron	Hexahedron	Octahedron	Dodecahedron	Icosahedron
(4sides)	(6 sides)	(8 sides)	(12 sides)	(20 sides)

However, I have chosen to use the vector equilibrium (or cuboctahedron) as the three-dimensional representation of the SelfDesign Matrix. This choice is based on the innovative work of Derald Langham with three-dimensional mind mapping. The twelve spheres around a central sphere form a spherical shape, as illustrated following on the left. This translates visually to the twelve points around a center point that create the vector equilibrium, so named by Buckminster Fuller.

VECTOR EQUILIBRIUM

connecting the 13 centers

All systems have patterns that are organized into common principles. The system earth, for example, has an axis of rotation as do other spherical bodies. It has an equator that marks out the spin of its rotation, as well as magnetic lines that come out of the North Pole and travel around and go into the South Pole. The illustration following graphically illustrates these patterns using points from the vector equilibrium model.

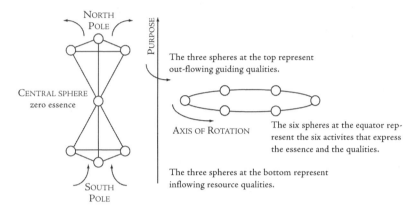

NORTH POLE

PURPOSE

CENTRAL SPHERE
zero essence

The three spheres at the top represent out-flowing guiding qualities.

AXIS OF ROTATION

The six spheres at the equator represent the six activites that express the essence and the qualities.

The three spheres at the bottom represent inflowing resource qualities.

SOUTH POLE

If we consider that human beings are systems, it follows that we, too, have common principles of organization. We think of these as patterns of behavior. The diagram of the vector equilibrium therefore gives us a template for organizing the four aspects of being human: our physical, relational, intellectual, and spiritual aspects. These equate to the four domains of body, heart, mind, and spirit. We have sphere 0—the central sphere—which represents the essence or center of our human system. At the top near the arrows we have three qualities that support and sustain us in our purpose and the achievement of our goals. We can call these three our guiding resources. The tip of the arrow is our purpose. It is the expression of our essence. The three spheres at the bottom represent sustaining resources that support our purpose and essence. At the equator we have six spheres that represent six meaningful activities in which we engage. These activities help inform and develop us in terms of our essential qualities and our goals.

Let us look again at the vector equilibrium (the twelve spheres around the central sphere) to get a three-dimensional sense of how these all fit together.

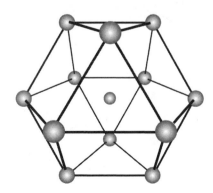

We can visualize the domains of body, heart, mind, and spirit, which represent our life experiences, in two different ways. In the two-dimensional model following, they exist as quadrants of a circle, and in our three-dimensional model the qualities correspond to the four corners of the tetrahedron (centers of spheres at the corners).

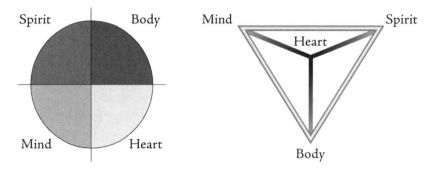

In the vector equilibrium model, each aspect of our humanness becomes a circle within the sphere. The spheres in the drawings following show equators at various angles. There are four circles within the vector equilibrium model—Buckminster Fuller called these "great circles in the earth"—and I have designated one for each of the domains of body, heart, mind, and spirit. I have chosen red for body, yellow for heart, blue for mind, and purple for spirit.

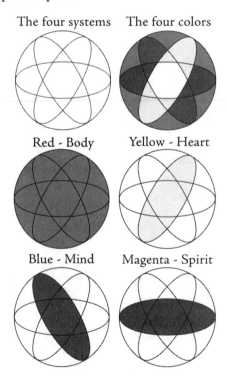

Using the purple map of "spirit" as an example, we see the essence, or center point, informed by six qualities (three guiding resources above and three sustaining resources below), with six activities around the equator that inform learners in their lifelong process. This same pattern is used for each of the four circles. When these maps are used as a basis for learning plans, they are initially empty. Learners put their own words onto the map, describing their personal learning activities. Therefore, all learners create individual paths toward the design of their own curricula.

This process of mapping our SelfDesign activities takes us on the lifelong journey toward *individuation,* a term coined by Carl Jung. Morris Berman, author of *The Reenchantment of the World,* explains the term as "a process of personal growth and integration whereby a person evolves his true center, or Self, as opposed to his ego. The ego, or persona, is seen as the center of conscious life, whereas the Self is the result of bringing the conscious mind into harmony with the unconscious." We are all unique. The only aspect we have in common is the inner nothingness that we call our essence. We manifest our differences in the details and nuances of our patterns of living, as individual expressions of the universal essential quality we share.

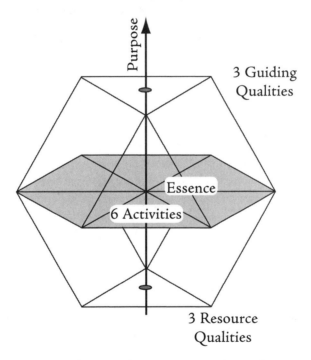

The spirit matrix, showing the six activities that influence our spiritual growth and understanding. Each individual chooses activities from their own life that inform their spirit.

The practice of SelfDesign takes on many faces, reflecting its depth and breadth. The demonstration of mapping, touched on in this chapter, is one aspect of the work, and it represents a comprehensive restructuring of how we function and who we truly are.

I am introducing the SelfDesign Matrix as a three-dimensional mind map to a group of adults and teens. Once people understand the concept of the map, they individually map their own four domains of learning as part of the SelfDesign process. We come together to share our insights from this exercise in designing ourselves.

Ilana, the Initial SelfDesigner

Enthusiasm is inherent. Figuring out how to nurture it is the interesting part. The following piece is ilana's story of what it was like to learn in a spherical and integrated way and how it has affected her life. She wrote this story in the twenty-sixth year of her lifelong learning journey, looking back over her Wondertree and Virtual High years.

Ilana's Story

Now that I am an adult, it is interesting to look back at Wondertree and think about what it meant to me. I was given the tools to understand who I was, how I learned, and ways to be excellent and successful in the areas that interested me. My father, my primary mentor, helped me to realize that I could see pictures, hear words, and integrate my feelings so that I could remember or learn things better. I remember him saying, "It's not cheating to write the answers in your head instead of on your arm or a piece of paper next time you take a test."

I loved going out into the world to find ten new words each week that were meaningful to me. I developed such a strong visual memory that now I often help my poor father, who learned to spell in public school and doesn't always use his own techniques.

Hearing stories or playing music, acting, performing, and memorizing lines gave me ongoing pleasure. I was excited every day. I was living in community, in an extended learning family. There was a cohesiveness to everything, from how we ran our center to how we planned out the days, weeks, and years. I especially remember gathering together each September for a meeting at our roundtable, discussing what we were enthusiastic about and which mentors we wanted to hire. I specifically remember our clown mentor, who helped us get through our reserved self-consciousness to become exuberant and ridiculous. We learned about subjects from people who were professionals in their fields, who gave a vibrancy and comprehensiveness to their information. I remember an anthropologist who would come to the center, taking us on "guided imagery" experiences where we dissolved into new lives in faraway lands. From the beginning, interpersonal skills were a strong undercurrent of our education. Information and facts were integrated into what we did for fun. Our happiness, relationships, and the community were the most important focus.

Eventually I became very interested in indigenous peoples from the Amazon rainforest to the Ituri Forest in Zaire. I read every book I could find and began listening to compilations of field recordings. I had the opportunity to meet people from the Amazon at one of our conferences, and I remember talking to Wade Davis, who worked to highlight the global plight of indigenous peoples. As I listened to the music of these tribes, I realized they knew things far beyond my world as a "civilized" white Canadian living in a city. I could hear qualities in their music that felt universal to our human experience.

When so-called "illiterate" cultures are made literate, they lose their oral traditions. Their ability to remember 10,000 years of history and knowledge about their forest is changed. In my recent studies in neurology and human development I have learned that the brain is actually altered when we learn to read, affecting our ability to remember certain kinds of information. While I understand the importance of helping people and cultures to function within world systems, I think it is also important to make sure this occurs with sensitivity to the knowledge and unique intelligence of the culture. Having grown up in a learning program based on respect of children, I am sensitive to the lack of respect of children and adults throughout the world.

When I was fourteen years old, a mentor and friend of mine encouraged me to volunteer at the Folk Music Festival in Vancouver. Twelve years later it is still an integral part of my life. I credit that experience for making music the passion that I pursue every day. I thought that I wanted to be a writer, an anthropologist, or a journalist until I saw the joy and beauty that musicians create and experience together, especially when their only common language is music.

Two years ago I went to India with Heather Knox and her fifteen-year-old daughter to record the music of street children. I traveled by train, moving to a new location every couple of days for two months. By the end of the trip I was emotionally and physically exhausted, but I was completely excited by the kids we had found and the recordings we had made. Today I am about to embark on a more personal musical journey, in

Europe. I hope that I will find mentors I can sit down beside, close my mouth, open my ears, open my heart, and listen—and play. I am a learner, and I will always be a learner.

ilana Cameron

Being Present as a Body-Heart-Mind-Spirit System

Standing within the physical SelfDesign Matrix is an amazing experience. As we take our fundamental place in the center, our individual world takes on the dimensionality of full, ripe potential. We work with four circles representing the spirit, mind, heart, and body. As we mark out the individual qualities of our being, we become more conscious of and begin to appreciate the patterns of our lives. Standing in the center of the matrix allows us to imagine that we are at the center of an infinite extension of concentric spheres. The spheres out to the tips of our fingers encompass all our inner dimensions, and the spheres beyond that all the realms in the outer world. We suddenly see life as an integration of significant events, a journey of endless possibility. Noticing the connections and emerging patterns that are reflected in the domains of our relational, spiritual, intellectual, and physical activities, we are provided with a unique opportunity to understand ourselves in new ways. We can create and design from our sense of ourselves as essential energies, interacting with all the events and circumstances that come toward our sphere of influence.

My daughter, ilana, learning to understand the relationships between the primary, secondary, and tertiary colors using the twelve colors of the SelfDesign Matrix.

CHAPTER 12

A GLOBAL ECOLOGY

Are we in the world or is the world in us?

I believe that both possibilities are true and that each way of seeing ourselves and the world implies a unique perspective. If we are "in the world," then we are disassociated (looking at ourselves from the outside). We become constructions of ourselves in our thoughts. We think that we are traveling along the road from here to the local cafe for a cup of coffee. In this way we become just one insignificant human being among six billion other mostly insignificant human beings. We see ourselves traveling through the world as if it is stopped, and we are busy going from here to there, trying to get the day's tasks accomplished. This is certainly our common and shared fantasy.

If "the world is in us," then we are taking an associated stance, *being* rather than *watching* ourselves. We are here, now, looking out from our still place, deep in the heart of our beings. In this moment we notice people coming toward us and people moving off into the distance. When we are driving in our cars we notice the world coming toward us so that not only are we sitting still, but the wheels of our cars are pulling the whole world under them and through us. Although this sounds absurd, it is only because we are so familiar with our more scientific ideas about our place in the world. Yet one of our scientists must have seen it this way, as it is reported that Einstein once asked a railway conductor, "Excuse me, can you tell me what time Zurich is expected to arrive at this train?" And while we commonly imagine that we move about in a seemingly stationary scene, our world is actually spiraling through the galaxy at enormous speeds. However, all this movement of rushing about a planet swirling through space is counterbalanced by a sense of stillness and calm within us. If you stop and focus on it for just a moment, can you feel that still place inside of you? It is forever the same here. Wherever we go, *here* we are. Change is illusionary, essence is constant; this is the message of mystics of every tradition. But it is also plain common sense, available in every instant to anyone who stops to notice.

Many books have been written to help us experience success in the world. This book focuses instead on a different definition of success, one where we learn how to grow and thrive from within our still place, with the world whirling through us. First of all, the map of this new worldview, which is a view of self that includes all our experiences, needs to expand from our still center out to the edge of the universe. If we stretch our fingers from our center out to about one meter, we include all our inner architecture of images, feelings, beliefs, yearnings, and expectations. At the edge of ourselves, our skin separates the inner biological/psychological/ontological world from the outer world of creatures, things, and events. Many of our intimate and familial events occur inside a two-to five-meter radius, while our community and occupational experiences exist within something like a thousand-meter radius. Our experience of the world is then inside a 12,750-kilometer radius, with the stars and planets existing beyond that.

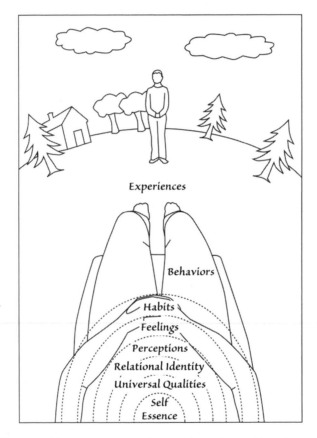

The SelfDesign Torus integrates the inside and outside of experience as concentric spheres emanating out from our center.

The preceding drawing is a model of this new, experience-centered universe. It is a blend of the Perennial Philosophy of Douglas Harding and the innovative therapy of Virginia Satir with John Banmen into a comprehensive systems model for SelfDesign. The still place is at the bottom of the picture where there is no head. It depicts how the world appears to each of us when we look out from our awareness, as we did in the experiment in chapter 0. This is called the Self, and it is our essence and universal heart or center. Moving out from this we encounter the various aspects of human experience that create the sum of how we design ourselves and our world. The first layer is that of our yearnings, or our Essential Qualities, and it includes our desires to love, to sense belonging and freedom, to feel compassion and joy, and to experience a sense of fulfillment as human beings. These constitute our fundamentally positive and harmonious selves. The next layers outward include our expectations, perceptions, conceptions, and feelings, as well as our feelings about our feelings. These aspects influence our behaviors and habits, which are the visible surface structures of our complex inner structures.

We call this systems map the SelfDesign Torus. In mathematics, a torus is a doughnut shaped geometric surface. An example of this would be the shape of the energy lines that flow out, around, back into, and through the earth. The following map illustrates the torus shape of energy currents surrounding planet Earth, much like similar lines emanating from the human heart.

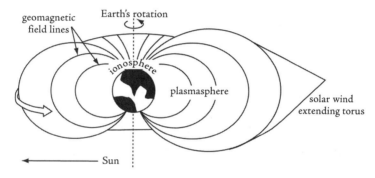

Using the SelfDesign Torus, we human beings can be characterized as living, interacting spherical systems. The inner part of the sphere demarcates "me" from the outside that is "not me." The "me" part is constantly taking in information as events of experience and then neurologically transforming those experiences outward as actions, behaviors, and responses. The continual energetic flow of information into and out from the system of self forms a kind of torus map in and through our human sphere. This inflow/outflow systems approach can be nicely illustrated with the left hand pointing toward the "Self" and the right hand pointing out toward "other," an image discussed earlier in the book.

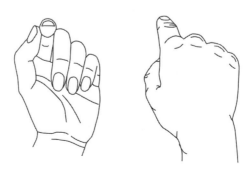

Much of SelfDesign's focus is on the awareness of our inner systems and the discovery of how the various aspects of this inner realm interact and relate. We live at the choice point, the point at which the incoming information is transformed into outgoing information. Only at this point can we make choices, can we really influence the flow of the universe. The outward expressions of this inner work—languaging, interactions, and habits of behavior and personality—act as translations of our inner work into relationship with others.

This book has been flowing into your experience with each page of ideas, blending together with your previous experiences and hopefully confirming some ideas and transforming others into new discoveries and ways of thinking. Now that the journey of this book is nearly completed, we are circling back around to the place where we may truly know ourselves for the first time. This is the torus experience, the balancing of incoming and outgoing energy as a complex pattern of energies. This book is the introduction and simple version of the story of SelfDesign. My hope is that the joining of our paths through this book will result in your interest to initiate the praxis of SelfDesign in your own life as well as in the lives of those you influence.

SelfDesign suggests a unique way to approach life learning, a comprehensive new paradigm beyond the schooling experienced by ourselves or our children. The home-school movement initiated by John Holt in the 1960s grew to a significant movement by the year 2000, though it drifted from its focus on "children's rights to learn" to a more conservative Christian agenda to resist secular education by the government. It seems that about 50 percent of home schooling is done for religious reasons and 50 percent is done for educational and methodological reasons. It is my hope that SelfDesign will become a "beyond schooling and beyond home schooling" movement that takes learning and the rights to learn back to the individual. This is a spiritual rather than a religious movement that I hope will appeal to all people interested in becoming fulfilled individuals and in raising happy children in an ecologically sustainable world.

Movements begin with one individual, and SelfDesign began out of the sensibilities of a five-year-old girl on a playground one bright sunny morning. In this present moment it is truly about *you*, about the ways in which you may wish to design your own life. It will grow as you continue to explore the dimensions of SelfDesign and join together with others who are furthering the praxis of SelfDesign. As you embrace your creativity, it is easy to imagine the spark that is passed to the next person, and the next. This visualization includes the birth of a global network of SelfDesigners, connected through enthusiasm and a sense of fulfillment. SelfDesign websites will act as a gateway to advanced information and coursework for those who wish to establish SelfDesign in learning communities around the globe. SelfDesigners will be able to share insights and discoveries, furthering the ecology of living on this planet with balance and harmony. Working together as friends and colleagues, we will unfold our own infinite intelligence in making this planet a safer, happier, and friendlier place.

Moving from the global community to the individual, from experiencing "us in the world" to "the world in us," can no better be illustrated than with the following image.

When my daughter was four years old, she used to love becoming her own canvas. She would take off her clothes and cover her body with paints of all colors. Dancing around the room, she would watch and laugh for hours as the colors swirled and blended.

It is easy to see the similarity in the swirls of ilana's paint and of the earth as both spin in their respective places in space. The individual and the earth—the microcosm and the macrocosm—are two systems in balance, connected together through community that emerges from our lifelong patterns of living.

Thinking Globally and Acting Locally

We have outlined twelve paradigm shifts in this book, and here in our final chapter we bring SelfDesigning to a global level. The following vector equilibrium model shifts us to a global perspective, placing the global citizen at the center and surrounding that individual with the twelve most significant patterns of living. This chapter points outward to the global community, suggesting twelve ways we can live more harmoniously on this planet. Each focus activity allows individuals and communities to participate in creating significant solutions to the global situation.

There are many initiatives and organizations promoting and developing these new ways of thinking. Once we develop a full awareness of the need for global balance by embracing these concepts, there arises within us a fundamental desire to join with others in an effort toward change and improvement. Through working collaboratively, we begin to express this integrity in our patterns of living. Paul Hawken, an award-winning writer and business thinker, expresses this idea in his recent book, *The Ecology of Commerce*:

Most global problems cannot be solved globally because they are global symptoms of local problems with roots in reductionist thinking that goes back to the scientific revolution and the beginnings of industrialism. We have operated our world for the past few centuries on the basis that we could manage it, if not dominate it, without respect to living systems. We have sacrificed the harmonious development of our own cultures for enormous short-term gains, and now we face the invoice for that kind of thinking: an ecological and social crisis whose origins lie deep within the assumptions of our commercial and economic systems. The compelling nature of this crisis, however, is its evolutionary nature. The array of choices and problems that face us do not call for a global triage, the further dislocation of cultures, or the division of nations. They are soluble by design, and the basis of that design rests within nature.

In line with this statement, we can design a new world by being in touch with our own design process as individual human beings. Following are some basic ideas that a SelfDesigning learning community could include in its strategies for sustainable living.

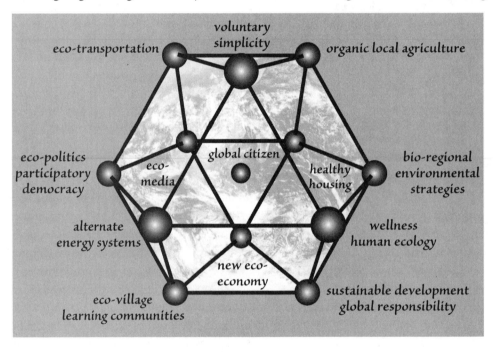

These twelve attributes of community are associated with a shift to ecological life-long learning strategies. In order to shift our traditional educational programming, we need to address the way we live in society and on this planet. We must think of ourselves as a global species, a species that needs to live more gently on the earth. These twelve topics address the range of activities that can be implemented to make a significant difference, giving us all a sense of belonging and fulfillment.

1. *Sustainable development.* How we live in each of our communities needs to be assessed to minimize our impact on the planet and its resources. Learning how to do more with less creates a call for voluntary simplicity as well as for continuing scientific breakthroughs in ways to do things more efficiently.

2. *Global media.* Since we are significantly influenced by our media, a shift toward positive and responsible journalism can allow us to understand our opportunities to participate in solutions rather than simply hear about problems.

3. *Alternative transportation.* Advances in technology to reduce our dependence on fossil fuels can allow us to live and move about without polluting our environment.

4. *Intentional community.* We can see that by living in eco-villages within urban environments as well as rural ones, we can increase densities and efficiencies of living and reduce extensive transportation needs.

5. *Energy-efficient housing.* There are many existing technologies to heat, cool, and service our homes and offices. If these technologies are integrated and included in housing developments, we can shift our energy usage and our attitudes about living sustainably.

6. *Bioregional living.* If we adjust our living styles to our bioregions, we can live more harmoniously and efficiently in our cities and villages.

7. *Natural foods.* Returning to our traditional strategies for nutrition suggests that by growing and eating organic and local foods that are seasonal, we can reduce transportation and processing costs as well as health care costs.

8. *Natural clothing and housing.* Using natural fabrics in our clothing and utilizing natural building materials can reduce environmental stresses on our bodies and minimize pollution of the environment.

9. *Wellness.* We can learn to take responsibility for our lifestyles by incorporating healthy practices and attitudes.

10. *Eco-politics.* When we extend these strategies of wellness into our societal concepts of relationship, we can change politics and law from an adversarial base to a more collaborative structure.

11. *Eco-economics.* We can shift our relationship with money so that we are investing in ecologically and socially sound development rather than exponential growth.

12. *Inclusive thinking.* This awareness includes deepening the concept of global citizenship and learning to live as if we are all "crew on spaceship earth," as Buckminster Fuller so aptly stated. Here our goals need to be aligned with the needs of all people in this global community rather than only a few.

While all twelve points speak to a return to the concept of village living, a true SelfDesign community would move the pre-industrial village toward a new, global, post-industrial design.

A Historical Perspective on Creating a Post-Industrial Community

Several years ago I had the opportunity to talk with social scientist Jane Jacobs. Her writing on city planning and the history of cities is world-famous. I shared with her my dream of creating an urban eco-village intentional community. I told her about Wondertree and Virtual High and our success working with children and youth beyond the paradigm of schooling. We both agreed that schooling is very much part of the industrialization of the world and not appropriate for the next age—the ecology age.

She shared an interesting idea with me, explaining that in the pre-industrial villages of Europe, the average child engaged with five to six adults throughout the average day. Parents, relatives, and neighbors did their necessary work close to the home and in the community. Young people observed these adults during the workday and learned various skills through modeling.

Today, however, typical urban children begin each day with little adult interaction, as parents are busy rushing off to work away from home and often away from community. Children are sent to school for most of the day to experience one significant adult, their teacher. An average teacher, however, spends little time interacting with individual children, because there are typically twenty or thirty children in the classroom. Regardless of this fact, teachers become important figures, but children change teachers each year, limiting the consistency that family and community modeling offered in the past. The only constants in children's lives are their peers, or perhaps the action figures of their television or video-game worlds.

Schooling has become the necessary childcare for working parents. After a day of compulsory learning, many children either go home to an empty house or go to daycare, where they again do not experience meaningful connection with their primary adults and must compete for attention from a limited number of caregivers. At the end of their day they are bored and discouraged, and their parents are often too exhausted to make a genuine connection with them.

The assembly-line model of schooling prepares children for life on a treadmill. It trains children toward the industrial model of the work world and of consumerism. For example, the average Canadian family of four with both parents working earns $60,000 per year (Statistics Canada, 1995). The cost of living for this family is $59,000 per year. In an attempt to get ahead, most families attempt to earn more money rather than reducing their costs. If costs could be lessened without a reduction in the standard of living, the family would truly have an advantage.

Part of our Virtual High research into eco-villages and sustainable communities looked at the cost advantages of an intentional community. We calculated that the typical family described above could reduce their cost of living to $30,000 per year in an eco-village. Lifestyle choices would then be available, one of which might be for both parents to work part time, allowing them more personal, family, and community time.

Clearly this is not a recommendation for a return to pre-industrial village life. Instead, we are looking, along with many others today, at ways to adopt the important characteristics of human-scale living situations where people work, learn, and play together. This is a strategy for a post-industrial community consciously designed by its members.

The following examples are stories of two projects that are influenced by SelfDesign, one in Colorado and one in British Columbia. These efforts to create learning communities establish an ethic for learning in the context of living in community.

The VISION Program

In 1999 I was invited to visit the small town of Paonia, near Aspen, Colorado, to give a presentation and a workshop on SelfDesign methodology. I arrived in town and met various people, talked on the local radio station, and gave a presentation. At the end of my multimedia presentation about Wondertree and Virtual High, the community was very excited about the images they had seen and the success stories of learners in our programs. That evening it was also announced that the superintendent of schools had very recently committed to supporting an innovative program in Paonia, and we agreed to work together on a SelfDesign initiative in the community.

About six months later I returned to Paonia to participate in a ten-day training for interested leaders for the new program that is now called the VISION Home and Community Program. I was accompanied by my colleague Michael Maser and learner Devon Girard (see chapter 6), who assisted in sharing some of the basic strategies of SelfDesign methodology. We showed the consultants how to create learning plans that support youth-initiated learning beyond the paradigm of curriculum and instruction. Over the next four years, consultants, parents, and learners designed the project to operate within the school district, with full state funding for each learner in the program.

Currently, I serve on the advisory board for the VISION program, and I have watched the project grow to over 700 learners districtwide. VISION works with children ages five to twenty-one who learn at home and in community, using district funds to purchase educator services and materials as well as to provide support through resource consultants for each learner and family. Paonia and its surrounding towns are now thriving learning communities, with millions of dollars being invested in the learners and in community resources to mentor the youth on their individual learning journeys.

The VISION program operates within and yet parallel to the school system, with benefits for both the traditional and the alternative programs. Learners can enroll in one program and cross over to participate in programs offered by the other system. They might go to conventional school for a specific course offered there, and they work through VISION because they want to direct their own learning. The program has a strong identity, not calling itself a SelfDesign community but rather taking pride in its independent nature and focus. This is fully in line with our intention to be a support in the creation of unique learning communities around the globe.

Everyone benefits when people have choices, and communities benefit when everyone works together to support children in ways that meet the wide variety of their learning needs.

SelfDesign Learning Community

After almost twenty years pioneering our learning model in British Columbia, we began a pilot project for a province-wide online learning program funded by the Ministry of Education. It has gained approval as a program where learners can enroll in a beyond-schooling electronic augmented program called SelfDesign Learning Community, where learners are acknowledged as the designers of their own learning programs. After the first two years as a pilot project, we grew from one hundred learners in our pilot project to nearly five hundred learners and their parents. The children are learning at home, in their immediate communities, with mentors and a variety of self-chosen resources and curricula. They are joined through an online Village of Conversations, where families can connect with one another all across British Columbia. This internet conferencing environment is used to share ideas and resources, to create courses together, to address problems that arise, and to communicate and work weekly with a learning consultant who collaborates in the design of each child's emerging curriculum. Our families choose home learning because they understand that children learn naturally and organically. Many of them are part of the original home-schooling community that arose across North America from John Holt's writings. SelfDesign helps these families move beyond schooling and beyond home learning, because it emphasizes that true learning is fundamentally a neurological, individual experience, sustained through a rich variety of relationships.

Everyone in the village, learners, parents and learning consultants, has their own office. Annual learning plans, personal mail, and collaborative weekly discussions between consultants and families are all managed from your desk and office. When your work is done you can head out the door and meet with others in the village.

Our Learning Community introduces a new element into traditional child-centered home learning by adding an educational professional to the family team. Just as any author, and especially this one, needs an editor to provide an important perspective on the work, I believe that a family is well served by including an "outside the family" perspective on the home-learning process. Our educational professionals do not teach but rather act as Learning Consultants, and in collaboration with learners and parents they create Learning Committees for each youth. This committee works much like a doctoral committee for university students. It operates in consensus to support, advise, and contribute to the learning efforts of the youth in our program. Each consultant visits the family in their home at least once a year to help create the initial SelfDesign Learning Plan. Then, using our "Village of Conversations" technology, the learner or parent records each week's learning journey, electronically sending observations to the consultant. These documents are called our Observations for Learning, and the consultant responds with suggestions for resources and ideas to support the emerging and unique curriculum of each learner. Families are able to make choices on how to spend their SelfDesign Learning Investment of $1000 per year per learner in service of the learner's plan and in consultation with the learning consultant. The technology aspect of our program offers an opportunity to extend and deepen the excellent work being done by these families, as well as bringing experiences from the home into our virtual community. The picture above illustrates the graphical and metaphorical experience of sitting down in our own virtual office, and in the picture below we step out the door and join our virtual learning community.

From the balcony of your office you can choose to go to the market, garden, exploratorium, learning center, or community center. You can also go into the home, café or the art center and participate in open conversations relevant to topics of mutual interest. The tent on the hill is for special week long discussions in a Chautauqua that happen several times a year. There are rich and meaningful conversations that allow for exchanges of ideas and information that truly build a sense of community.

It has taken us many years to demonstrate to others that teaching is not necessarily the precursor for learning. The SelfDesign Community allows learning to emerge from curiosity, and it supports the natural learning process as an effective way to achieve educational goals. Through our current efforts to design studies showing lifelong learning skills developed from the SelfDesign model, we hope to demonstrate the long-term benefits of child-centered, emergent learning, stemming from enthusiasm and curiosity.

Presently there is not a level playing field for alternative and innovative learning programs throughout North America. These programs are expected to compete in the marketplace with a school-based system that has an effective monopoly. Youth and families who choose to design their own educational experience receive little or no support from the educational system. This seems prejudicial if learners can demonstrate equivalent or better learning results, as is often the case in our program. Long-term excellent results from programs like Wondertree and Sudbury Valley School in Massachusetts prove that success in life and social well-being is not predicted only by success in conventional school.

In order to obtain the kind of results we, as educators and parents, want for our children (and for ourselves as lifelong learners), it is essential that we shift toward the inclusion of children in creating their own learning adventures. A new paradigm is born when we allow education to be an opportunity rather than an expectation. Our relationships with children are instantly enhanced to include a whole new set of possibilities. If we put our trust in a shift to an inclusive mind frame and join the child's world-view, our youth will manifest their essential positive nature. This permission to discover "who we really are" through inner expression is the essential process of SelfDesign.

The End and the Beginning

Where do we go from here? How do we begin to make important shifts in our systems, our cultural norms, and in the daily activities of our children as well as ourselves? Can we begin by staying *here*, present and positive as we begin to live our lives in new ways? If you choose to declare yourself as a SelfDesigning human being, what is the next step? The answer is: simply relax. Be present and enjoy this moment. Create an inner movie of the twelve best experiences in your life. Name the quality of each experience and write these words on the twelve-sided mandala, with yourself at the center of the circle. Be thankful in this moment, and enjoy this very breath.

Once you are in touch with the optimum quality of your being, think about those you love, those you care about the most. Create a simple ceremony, a ritual that acknowledges you and your love in the world. Starting with this act, invest the rest of the day living from your twelve most profound qualities. Notice the satisfaction that arises from your positive awareness of yourself. You are living in your essence, and you deserve the happiness you feel—now.

In this space of fulfillment, look for an opportunity to create one kind act. Shift the events of the world by expressing your love and caring in a simple situation involving another. Love is what holds humanity together. Networks of loving communities, sharing conversations that confirm openness and trust, are what allow the human garden to grow.

We can each make a silent, personal commitment to support and participate only in activities that are part of the solution rather than part of the problem. Start simply, perhaps by choosing not to go to a movie that expresses violence as a theme or that focuses on fear as the underlying context. Choose to respond to another person's insensitivity by instead putting forth a model for compassion. As Gandhi said, "An eye for an eye, and the whole world would be blind." Our praxis is either part of the solution or it is part of the problem. In each moment the choice is ours, and the choice is imperative as our lives unfold in the consequence of this choice.

Our happiness is the essential quality that exists to confirm the truth of our balance, integrity, and harmony of being. Joy arises out of shared happiness. Our children are open to engagement, and they thrive when we nourish them with love. To heal this earth we need to heal ourselves first, and it will take continuous and focused loving acts to transform our communities into loving, nurturing places.

As I sat in a United Nations Children's Caucus meeting in Istanbul, Turkey, I learned the interesting fact that the sense of happiness demonstrated by children is used as a barometer to measure the wellness of an entire community. I recommend that you visit any school playground in North America. Researchers in eastern Canada have counted a violent act every few seconds on playgrounds that they observed. The amount of violence and bullying in our schools is not something to stop but rather something to prevent. Bullying is a response to feeling bullied, and our current model of education, based on expectations, often leaves children feeling bullied. As adults we need to mitigate our own fears and expectations of externally measured success. As we learn to nurture ourselves, we can become more nurturing of our children. In collaboration with them we can begin to create opportunities driven by our love.

SelfDesign is not just one more theory about educational change. It is a simple but profound message from a small group of children, parents, and mentors who have played under the Wondertree. Long ago a little girl realized that if she got off her swing and went into her school building, she would lose control of her life. She was right. She convinced me to support her happiness and her innate sensibilities. Let us begin to trust, empower, and enfranchise our children. We must start by empowering ourselves, because ultimately we are the only ones who can.

Enfranchise yourself. Set yourself free from the limits of self-prejudice and self-sabotage. Only when we become free can we commit to joining with nature's design, participating in the love that holds this world together.

AN INVITATION

We, the SelfDesign authors, invite you to further explore SelfDesign by joining our online lifelong learning community. The mission of our community is to foster natural and emergent learning for children, families, educators, and lifelong learners, beyond the paradigm of schooling.

Visit our website—*www.selfdesign.com/globalselfdesigncommunity/bookreader*—to sign up for a user name and password. Here you will meet other readers and join in conversations with the authors, and discover the emerging work of SelfDesign. You can choose to deepen your personal skills as a SelfDesigner, hear about courses and workshops that give you the tools and practical understanding to generate your own learning community, or develop a support network to share ideas within the context of our existing communities. The website will link you to a knowledge base that is shared throughout the world.

By joining with others who are using SelfDesign methods individually and in groups, we can synergistically provide meaningful learning opportunities not only for our children, but for the lifelong learner in each of us.

CREDITS

Cover

Yellow Woman
ilana Cameron
Scanning and enhancement—ilana Cameron and Farid Badabhshan.

Preface

SelfDesign Mandala (used throughout the book)
Jenny Breukelman, Imagine That Creative Consulting,
imaginethat@gulfislands.com

Ilana and Maureen
Brent Cameron

Ilana and Jonathan
Maureen Cameron

Introduction

Ilana in Bali
Brent Cameron

"We are so focused on our security …"
From Creating Quality Communities, Peter M. Senge, Ph.D., Founding
Chair, SoL (Society for Organizational Learning), Senior Lecturer, MIT,
Sloan School of Management, *www.solonline.org/static/research/qualcom.html.*

Hand pointing in
Naomi Gibb, inspired by the work of Douglas Harding.

SelfDesign Mandala
Brent Cameron

Chapter 0

Hand in mandala
Naomi Gibb

"If you want to know—to understand—what's the matter ..."
Esalen Catalogue and *A Sacred Unity* by Gregory Bateson, ed. Rodney
Donaldson, used with permission from the Institute for Intercultural Studies.

The Four Stages of Being Human
Naomi Gibb, Enchant Media, *www.enchantmedia.com.*

Earth
Used with permission from NASA.

Hand pointing out
Naomi Gibb, from the work of Douglas Harding.

Headless drawing and people
Douglas Harding and Naomi Gibb

Chapter 1

Nautilus shell
Brent Cameron

Sunflower
Maureen Cameron

Spiral path of earth and moon
Courtesy of the Estate of R. Buckminster Fuller, redrawn by Naomi Gibb.

Butterfly
From *The Power of Limits* by Gyorgy Doczi, ©1981. Reprinted by arrangement with Shambhala Publications, Inc., Boston, *www.shambhala.com.*

Logarithmic Spiral
Naomi Gibb, Enchant Media, *www.enchantmedia.com.*

Tai chi
ilana Cameron

Haida hat
From *The Power of Limits* by Gyorgy Doczi, ©1981. Reprinted by arrangement with Shambhala Publications, Inc., Boston, *www.shambhala.com.*

Parthenon
From *The Power of Limits* by Gyorgy Doczi, ©1981. Reprinted by arrangement with Shambhala Publications, Inc., Boston, *www.shambhala.com.*

Human hand
From *The Power of Limits* by Gyorgy Doczi, ©1981. Reprinted by arrangement with Shambhala Publications, Inc., Boston, *www.shambhala.com.*

Five stages of plant growth
Naomi Gibb, Enchant Media, *www.enchantmedia.com.*

Three dimensions of Golden Rectangle
Naomi Gibb

Icosahedron
Naomi Gibb

Three planes human
Naomi Gibb

Chapter 2

Flower photo
Brent Cameron
"All children are born geniuses, but are swiftly de-geniused ..."
From *Cosmography* by Buckminster Fuller, copyright 1992, courtesy, the
Estate of R. Buckminster Fuller.
Schooling as Learning
Naomi Gibb
SelfDesign Paragon
Naomi Gibb
"Thinking, which has such a high premium in our society ..."
Excerpted from *Fire in the Crucible*, by John Briggs, with permission from
Phanes Press, imprint of Red Wheel/Weiser, Boston, MA and York Beach,
ME.
Josh and Alex, Blues Brothers
Michael Maser
Four quadrants
Naomi Gibb
Tetrahedron
Naomi Gibb
Fourfold Brain
Naomi Gibb
Bi-lateral hemispheres
Naomi Gibb

Chapter 3

Baby and father (bonding)
Brent Cameron
Baby and father (in same room together)
Brent Cameron
Headstand drawing
ilana Cameron
Breast-feeding
Brent Cameron
Conscious-Uunconscious-Competent-Incompetent
Naomi Gibb
Spiral plant growth
Naomi Gibb

Yellow Woman
Painted and photographed by ilana Cameron.
Donnie
Brent Cameron
Wondertree software development team
Maureen Cameron
Be-Know-Do-Have model
Noami Gibb

Chapter 4

Three Planes Human
Naomi Gibb

Chapter 5

Ilana and Maureen clapping
Brent Cameron
Father and son in park
Brent Cameron
Ilana with teddy
Maureen Cameron
Hands pointing in and out
Naomi Gibb
Brent on beach with children
Maureen Cameron
Dr. Maurice Gibbons with children
Brent Cameron
Lawrence and Anna
Brent Cameron

Chapter 6

Girl in factory
Used with permission from PictureHistory, *www.picturehistory.com/.*
Gandhi
Used with permission from GandhiServe Foundation, *gandhiserve.org.*
Students' Attitudes Toward School
BC Ministry of Education Report 1992, redrawn by Naomi Gibb.
Jane Goodall and Wondertree group
Maureen Cameron
"Young people should have the right to control and direct their own learning, that is, to decide what they want to learn …"
From *Escape From Childhood* by John Holt, copyright by Holt Associates Inc. 1995, used with permission.

Devon Girard
Michael Maser
Devon Girard's story
Used with permission.

Chapter 7

Horse in field with spiral
Brent Cameron
People with spiral in Ohio
Brent Cameron
Spiral drawings
Naomi Gibb
Spiral photographs
Brent Cameron
Children in park
Brent Cameron

Chapter 8

Ilana making island
Brent Cameron
Map of distinctions
Naomi Gibb
Graph of 500 questions
Naomi Gibb
Brent and Wondertree learners in Carmanah Valley
Maureen Cameron
PowerSmart drawing
Donnie Madson and Steve DeMuth, used with permission, BC Hydro Power
Smart Students Program.
Wondertree students news article
Used with permission, Vancouver Province.

Chapter 9

Michael and Robin playing music
Brent Cameron
Conscious-Uunconscious-Competent-Incompetent
Naomi Gibb
Heidi and Blair on labyrinth
Brent Cameron
Jonathan and Joshua
Maureen Cameron

Wooden ball photos
Brent Cameron
Vector equilibrium
Naomi Gibb
Spheres of Influence Map
Jenny Breukelman
Kaan Muncaster's story
Used with permission.

Chapter 10

Virtual High learners in circle
Michael Maser
Virtual High students in Big Group Meeting
Michael Maser
Virtual High learners in circle
Michael Maser
Jeff Dean's story
Used with permission.
Stephen Tweedale's story
Used with permission.
VillageQuest meeting
Brent Cameron

Chapter 11

Vector equilibrium computer graphic
Travis Bernhardt
Tetrahedron
Naomi Gibb
Platonic solids
Naomi Gibb
Vector equilibrium
Courtesy, the Estate of R. Buckminster Fuller.
SelfDesign Matrix illustration
Naomi Gibb
Vector equilibrium drawing
Naomi Gibb
Body-heart-mind-spirit circle and tetrahedron
Naomi Gibb
Four great circles
Naomi Gibb

"a process of personal growth and integration whereby a person evolves his true center..."

> Reprinted from *The Reenchantment of the World*, by Morris Berman. copyright © 1981 by Morris Berman. Used by permission of the publisher, Cornell University Press.

The spirit matrix
> Naomi Gibb

SelfDesign Institute photo
> Michael Maser

Ilana Cameron's story
> Used with permission.

Ilana Cameron photo
> Pille Brunnell

Ilana and Wondertree group in Genesa Crystal
> Brent Cameron

Chapter 12

Earth image
> Courtesy of NASA

SelfDesign Torus
> Adapted from Virginia Satir and John Banmen's iceberg and Douglas Harding's headless work, redrawn by Naomi Gibb.

Earth torus
> Naomi Gibb

Hands pointing in and out
> Naomi Gibb

Ilana dancing with earth
> Maureen Cameron and NASA

"Most global problems cannot be solved globally because ..."
> From *The Ecology of Commerce: A Declaration of Sustainability* by Paul Hawken, copyright (c) 1993 by Paul Hawken. Reprinted by permission of HarperCollins Publishers.

Vector equilibrium over Earth
> Naomi Gibb and NASA, Brent Cameron, graphics

SelfDesign Learning Community office
> Jenny Breukelman

SelfDesign Learning Community village
> Jenny Breukelman

BIBLIOGRAPHY

Chapter 0: Being Present: A Journey to Our Authentic Selves

Bateson, Gregory. *A Sacred Unity.* ed. by Rodney E. Donaldson. New York: Harper Collins Publishers, 1991.

Einstein, Albert. *Relativity: The Special and General Theory.* Trans. by Robert W. Lawson. London: Methuen, 1920.

Harding, D. E. *The Hierarchy of Heaven and Earth: A New Diagram of Man in the Universe.* Florida: University Presses of Florida, 1979.

Harding, D.E. Head *Off Stress, Beyond the BottomLline.* London, England: Arkana, 1990.

Harding, D. E. *On Having No Head: Zen and the Re-Discovery of the Obvious.* London: Arkana, 1986.

Harding, D. E. *The Science of the First Person.* Ipswich, England: Sholland Publications, 1974.

Maturana, Humberto R. and Varela, Francisco J. *The Tree of Knowledge: The Biological Roots of Human Understanding.* Boston: Shambhala, 1987.

Whorf, Benjamin. *Language, Thought, and Reality: Selected Writings of Benjamin Lee Whorf.* Ed. by John B. Carrol. Cambridge: MT. Press, 1956.

Chapter 1: Beautiful by Design

Doczi, Gyorgy. *The Power of Limits. Proportional Harmonies in Nature: Art and Architecture.* Boston: Shambhala. 1981.

Garland, Trudi Hammel. *Fascinating Fibonaccis: Mystery and Magic in Numbers.* Palo Alto, California: Dale Seymour Publications, 1987.

Chapter 2: Unfolding the Infinite Interior

Bandler, Richard and Grinder, John. *Patterns of the Hypnotic Techniques of Milton H. Erickson, M.D.* Scotts Valley, California: Grinder and Associates, 1975.

Bateson, Gregory. *Mind and Nature: A Necessary Unity.* New York: Bantam, 1979.

Bateson, Gregory. *Steps to an Ecology of Mind: A Revolutionary Approach to Man's Understanding of Himself.* New York: Ballantine Books, 1972.

Cobb, E. *The Ecology of Imagination in Childhood.* New York: Columbia University Press, 1977.

Hillman, James. *The Soul's Code: In Search of Character and Calling.* New York: Random House, 1996.

Montagu, Ashley. *Learning Non-Aggression: The Experience of Non-Literate Societies.* New York: Oxford University Press, 1978.

Piaget, Jean. *Construction of Reality in the Child.* London: Routledge and Kegan Paul, 1954.

Russel, Peter. *The Brain Book.* New York: The Penguin Group, 1979.

Eliot, T. S. *The Norton Anthology of English Literature.* Fourth ed. Vol. 2. New York: W. W. Norton and Company, 1979. M.H. Abrams Gen. Ed.

Chapter 3: Natural Learning, Holistic Learning

Buzan, Tony. *Using Both Sides of Your Brain.* New York: Plume Books, 1991.

Grof, S. *The Adventure of Self-Discovery.* Albany: SUNY Press, 1988

Halifax, Joan. *The Fruitful Darkness: Reconnecting with the Body of the Earth.* San Francisco: Harper, 1992.

Hall, James A. *Jungian Analysis: Individuation and Analysis.* Toronto: Inner City Books, 1986.

Healy, J. *Why Children Don't think*. New York: Simon & Schuster, 1990

Holt, J. *How Children Learn*. New York: Delacorte Press, 1986.

Holt, J. *Learning All The Time*. New York: Addison Wesley, 1989.

Jung, Carl G. *The Portable Jung*. trans. Hull R. F. New York: Viking Press, 1971.

Jung, Carl, G. *Man and His Symbols*. New York: Doubleday & Company, 1964.

Maslow, Abraham. *Towards a Psychology of Being*. New York: John Wiley and Sons, 1968.

Papert, Seymour. *Mindstorms, Children, Computers, and Powerful Ideas*. New York: Basic Books, 1980.

Pearce, Joseph Chilton. *The Biology of Transcendence—A Blueprint of the Human Spirit*. Rochester: Park Street Press, 2002

Pearce, Joseph Chilton. *Magical Child: Rediscovering Nature's Plan for Our Children*. New York: E.P. Dutton, 1977.

Pearson, Carol. *The Hero Within: Six Archetypes We Live By*. New York: Harper Collins Publishing, 1986.

Steiner, Rudolf. *An Autobiography*. Trans. by Rita Stebbing. New York: Rudolf Steiner Publications, 1977.

Chapter 4: The Ecology of Family

Eisler , Rianne. *The Chalice and the Blade: Our History, Our Future*. New York: Harper Collins, 1987.

Jaynes, Julian. *The Origin of Consciousness in the Break-Down of the Bicameral Mind*. Boston: Houghton Mifflin, 1976

Mead, Margaret. *Family*. New York: A Ridge Press Book, The Macmillan Company, 1965

Laing, R.D. The *Politics of Experience and The Bird of Paradise*. Harmondsworth, Middlesex, England: Penguin Books Ltd., 1967

Satir, Virginia, & Bandler, Richard, & Grinder, John. *Changing With Families: A Book About Further Education for Being Human.* Palo Alto: Science and Behavior Books, 1976.

Schore, Allan. *Affect Regulation and the Origin of the Self.* Hillsdale, NJ: Lawrence Erlbaum Associates, Inc., Publishers, 1994.

Springer, Sally P. and Deutsch, Georg. *Left Brain, Right Brain.* New York: W.H. Freeman, 1981.

Watts, A. *Nature, Man and Woman.* New York: Vintage Books, 1958.

Chapter 5: Languaging

Bandler, Richard and Grinder, John. *Frogs and Princes.* Moab, Utah: Real People Press, 1979.

Grinder, John and Bandler, Richard. *The Structure of Magic I: A Book about Language and Therapy.* Palo Alto: Science and Behavior Books, 1975.

Bandler, Richard and Grinder, John. *Reframing: Neuro-Linguistic Programming and the Transformation of Meaning.* Moab, UT: Real People Press, 1982.

Bandler, Richard and Grinder, John. *The Structure of Magic, Volume 1: A Book About Language and Therapy.* Palo Alto, Ca: Science and Behaviour Books, 1975.

Chomsky, Noam. *Language and Responsibility.* New York: Pantheon, 1979.

Dilts, Robert B. *Roots of Neuro-Linguistic Programming: A Reference Guide to the Technology of NLP.* Cupertino, CA: Meta Publications, 1983.

Dilts, Robert, Grinder, John, Bandler, Richard, and DeLozier, Judith. *Neuro-Linguistic Programming, Volume1: The Study of the Structure of Subjective Experience.* Capitola, Ca. Meta Publications, Inc., 1980.

Gordon, David and Meyers-Anderson, Maribeth. *Phoenix: Therapeutic Patterns of Milton H. Erickson.* Cupertino, CA: Meta Publications, 1981.

Grinder, John and DeLozier, Judith. *Turtles All the Way Down: Prerequisites to Personal Genius.* California: Grinder, DeLozier and Associates, 1987.

Laborde, Genie. *Fine Tune Your Brain*. Palo Alto: Syntony, 1988.

Lakoff, George and Johnson, Mark. *Metaphors We Live By*. Chicago: University of Chicago Press, 1980.

O'Connor, Joseph and Seymour, John. *Introducing Neuro-Linguistic Programming*. Hammersmith, London: Harper Collins Publishers, 1990

Chapter 6: Learners' Rights to SelfDesign

Berman, Morris. *Coming to our senses : body and spirit in the hidden history of the West*. New York : Bantam, 1990.

British Columbia Ministry of Education. (1994). Annual Report, 1993. Ministry of Education, Victoria, B.C.

Gatto, J. T. *Dumbing Us Down: The Hidden Curriculum of Compulsory Schooling*. Philadelphia: New Society, 1991.

Greenberg, Daniel. *Free at Last: The Sudbury Valley School*. Framingham, MA: Sudbury Valley School Press, 1987.

Holt, John. *Escape from Childhood*. Cambridge: Holt Associates, 1995.

Holt, John. *Instead of Education: Ways to Help People Do Things Better*. New York: Penguin, 1976.

Gandhi, Mohandas K. Gandhi. *An Autobiography, The story of my experiments with truth*. Boston: Beacon Press, 1957

Illich, Ivan D. *Deschooling Society*. Middlesex, England: Penguin, 1971.

Laing, R.D. *The Politics of Experience and The Bird of Paradise*. Middlesex, England: Penguin Books, 1967.

Neill, A. S. *Freedom — Not License!* New York: Hart Publishing Company, 1966

Neill, A. S. *Talking of Summerhill*. London: Victor Gollanz Ltd., 1967.

Rogers, C. *Freedom to Learn*. Columbus, OH: Charles E. Merrill, 1969.

Rogers, C. *A Way of Being*. Boston: Houghton Mifflin, 1980.

Samples, Bob. *Openmind Wholemind.* Rolling Hills Estates, California: Jalmar Press, 1987.

Chapter 7: The SelfDesign LifeSpiral

Doczi, Gyorgy. *The Power of Limits.* Proportional Harmonies in Nature: Art and Architecture. Boston: Shambhala, 1981.

James, Tad et al. *Time Line Therapy and the Basis of Personality.* Capitola, CA: Meta Publications, 1988.

Huntley, H.E. *The Divine Proportion, A Study in Mathematical Beauty.* New York: Dover Publications, Inc., 1970

Chapter 8: Design Strategies

Alexander, Christopher. *The Timeless Way of Building.* New York: Oxford University Press, 1979.

Briggs, John. *Fire in the Crucible.* Los Angeles: Jeremy P. Tarcher, Inc., 1990.

Czismenthalyi, M. *Flow: The Psychology of Optimal Experience.* New York: Harper and Row, 1988.

Dilts, Robert. *Albert Einstein: Neuro-Linguistic Analysis of a Genius.* Ben Lomomd, CA: Dynamic Learning Publications, 1990.

Dilts, Robert. *Beliefs.* Portland, OR: Metamorphous Press, 1990.

Volk, Tyler. *Metapatterns.* New York: Columbia University Press, 1995.

Chapter 9: Mentoring

Milliner, Charlotte Bretto. *A Framework for Excellence: A Resource Manual for NLP.* Scotts Valley, CA: Grinder and Associates, 1988.

Chapter 10: Synergistic Community

Kuhn, Thomas S. The *Structure of Scientific Revolutions.* Chicago: University of Chicago Press, 1962.

Maslow, Abraham H. *Toward a Psychology of Being.* Princeton: D. Van Nostrand Company, 1968.

Pearce, Joseph Chilton. *Evolution's End: Claiming the Potential of Our Intelligence.* California: Harper San Francisco, 1992.

Sale, Kirkpatrick. *Human Scale.* New York: Coward, McCann & Geoghegan, 1980.

Sawada, Daiyo and Caley, Michael T. "Dissipative Structures: New Metaphors for Becoming in Education". *Educational Researcher.* March, 1985.

Schmookler, Andrew Bard. *The Parable of the Tribes: The Problem of Power in Social Evolution.* Berkley: University of California Press, 1984.

Chapter 11: Systems and Patterns

Bateson, Gregory & Bateson, Mary Catherine. *Angels Fear: Towards an Epistemology of the Sacred.* New York: Macmillan Publishing Co, 1987.

Bennett, John G. *Enneagram Studies.* York Beach: Weiser, 1983.

Fuller, R. Buckminster. *Critical Path.* New York: St. Martin's Press, 1981.

Fuller, R. Buckminster. *Synergetics 1: Explorations in the Geometry of Thinking.* New York: MacMillian, 1975.

Fuller, R. Buckminster. *Synergetics 2: Further Explorations in the Geometry of Thinking.* New York: MacMillian, 1979.

Gardner, Howard. *Frames of Mind: The Theory of Multiple Inteligences.* New York: Basic Books, 1983.

Goleman, D. *Emotional Intelligence.* New York: Bantam Books, 1995.

Hampden-Turner, Charles. *Maps of the Mind.* London: Mitchel Beazley Ltd., 1981.

Senge, Peter. *The Fifth Discipline: The Art and Practice of The Learning Organization.* New York: Doubleday Currency, 1990.

Young, Arthur. *The Reflexive Universe: Evolution of consciousness.* Oregon: Robert Briggs Associates, 1976.

Chapter 12: A Global Ecology

Atlan, Henri et al. *Gaia: A Way of Knowing.* ed. by William Irwin Thompson. Great Barrington, MA: Lindisfarne Press, 1987.

de Chardin Pierre Teilhard. *The Phenomenon of Man.* New York: Harper and Row Publishers, Inc., 1959.

Fuller, Buckminster. *Cosmography.* New York: Macmillan Publishing Company, 1992.

Hawken, Paul. *The Ecology of Commerce.* New York: Harper Business, 1993.

Murchie, Guy. *The Seven Mysteries of Life: An Exploration in Science and Philosophy.* Boston: Houghton Mifflin Company, 1978.

ACKNOWLEDGMENTS

If I made a list of people to thank and acknowledge it would be longer than the book itself. If I attempted to mention just the most influential, I would certainly leave someone significant off of the list. The development of Wondertree, Virtual High, and SelfDesign has become my life's work and it could have been possible only with the support of everyone that got involved. So thank you everyone, thank you from my heart.

The process of writing this book has been a challenge for me because I think in images and patterns combined with nuances of feelings which become a torrent of words that flow without commas or periods. Translating my Buckminster Fuller type sentences into English was first attempted by Carolyn Mamchur, who shaped the writing of my Master's thesis in the late '80s. Then over the years my friend and colleague Michael Maser chopped and crafted my sentences into comprehensible sound bites. Luanne Armstrong worked with me over another year and transformed my one-thousand-plus-page book into around four hundred much more coherent pages. In the fall of 2003, while I was beginning to negotiate a contract with my publisher, I met Barbara Meyer in Colorado. Over the next year, as we created our life partnership, we also worked together on another edit of the book. Barbara's expertise at communication created the text much as it is in this book now.

ABOUT THE AUTHORS

Brent Cameron, M.A., is the founder of Wondertree Foundation for Natural Learning in Vancouver, B.C., and co-creator of the SelfDesign Learning Community (SDLC), an online learning village. Over the past 23 years, the programs and projects he has created with learners and colleagues have won numerous Canadian awards and international acclaim.

Barbara Meyer, M.A., has worked with children and families for 30 years in a variety of capacities. She has worked in family support services for special needs infants/toddlers, alternative learning programs, counseling and mediation, as a Guardian ad Litem for minors, and currently, as a family advocate for SDLC.

The couple lives in both British Columbia and Colorado. For more information about their work, please see *www.selfdesign.com*.

Sentient Publications, LLC publishes books on cultural creativity, experimental education, transformative spirituality, holistic health, new science, and ecology, approached from an integral viewpoint. Our authors are intensely interested in exploring the nature of life from fresh perspectives, addressing life's great questions, and fostering the full expression of the human potential. Sentient Publications' books arise from the spirit of inquiry and the richness of the inherent dialogue between writer and reader.

We are very interested in hearing from our readers. To direct suggestions or comments to us, or to be added to our mailing list, please contact:

SENTIENT PUBLICATIONS, LLC
1113 Spruce Street
Boulder, CO 80302
303.443.2188
contact@sentientpublications.com
www.sentientpublications.com